BEFORE THE RAIN

BOOKS BY JACK GETZE

The Austin Carr Series
Big Numbers
Big Money
Big Mojo
Big Shoes

The Hicks and Hauser Crime Thrillers
Before the Rain

Stand-Alone Novels
The Black Kachina
Making Hearts

JACK GETZE

BEFORE THE RAIN

A Hicks and Hauser Crime Thriller

Copyright © 2024 by Jack Getze

All rights reserved. No part of the book may be reproduced in any form or by any electronic or mechanical means, including information storage and retrieval systems, without permission in writing from the publisher, except by a reviewer who may quote brief passages in a review. Without in any way limiting the author's [and publisher's] exclusive rights under copyright, any use of this publication to "train" generative artificial intelligence (AI) technologies to generate text is expressly prohibited. The author reserves all rights to license uses of this work for generative AI training and development of machine learning language models.

Down & Out Books
3959 Van Dyke Road, Suite 265
Lutz, FL 33558
DownAndOutBooks.com

The characters and events in this book are fictitious. Any similarity to real persons, living or dead, is coincidental and not intended by the author.

Cover design by JT Lindroos

ISBN: 1-64396-359-7
ISBN-13: 978-1-64396-359-4

For Les Edgerton

1

Ray Hauser crawled to the wide stream, a mountain plateau section of Mexico's Rio Cuale. The rock-filled brook's splashing covered the scrape of his chest. The sandy color of the waterside pebbles matched his desert camo. But the river's best feature was how the water carried memories of his wife. She'd loved picnics and swimming at the lake. Even fishing. Ray's uphill, three-hundred-yard scrabble had been grueling and hot. Sweat soaked his clothes. His knees and elbows throbbed. But recollections of Alissa helped him easily master the punishing journey.

And now he was over target.

Fifty yards upstream, men talked in Spanish.

Atop the mountain wilderness overlooking Banderas Bay and the resort city of Puerto Vallarta, birds called whenever a breeze moved the hot August air. Their treetop sighs and squawks blurred or blocked many of the guards' words, the sentences impossible to understand.

Ray understood Spanish like he did quantum physics. *Poquito.* A little bit.

He peered around a boulder to see the isolated, hillside restaurant where the young woman's smart watch had brought him. The kidnappers had turned off or ruined the device's Global Positioning System, but the watch's health features—

temperature and pulse—still emitted signals. At least one US satellite-based system was collecting and relaying that data to him via his encrypted cell phone. The kidnapped woman rested against the back wall on the second floor, which, because of the sharply sloped knoll, was at ground level.

He sometimes wondered what other information his government collected.

What stuff he *didn't* know about.

The man who'd called the poor woman's father and put a dollar number on a daughter's life claimed to be with the Mexican Federal Police. Doing the father a favor to act as broker. Might be true, but Ray's information said the Morales family had been driven out or murdered, their property and restaurant taken over by the Jalisco New Generation drug cartel. And here is where the kidnappers held their captive.

A longer look confirmed his suspicions. The establishment included two dining rooms on two stories, plus brook-side seating. On a large, L-shaped patio above the riverside tables were eight young men, a few of them teenagers. Nobody wore any uniforms.

All cradled or wore automatic assault rifles.

He checked the time. Ten minutes behind. The rough, rocky terrain had done damage to his schedule, as well as his thirty-six-year-old knees and elbows. He needed to hustle, to reach his planned overlook position before dark.

He stuffed his phone and two fake ballpoint pens inside sealable plastic bags before rolling himself slowly across the shallow stream. He wasn't sure the water would damage the clip-on "pens," but he couldn't take the chance. Bringing a real weapon into Mexico was too dangerous for his employer, the US Department of Homeland Security. There wasn't enough time to be detained. No one on his team back home expected the kidnapped woman to live through the weekend. Tonight was his one chance to get her.

Saturday night.

***

Behind another boulder, enjoying the coolness of wet clothes in 90-degree heat, he removed the pens from their plastic and clipped them to his shirt collar, behind his neck. The devices were really fifteen-shot containers of Sabre Red pepper spray, an incapacitating brew of capsaicin, the heat in hot peppers. On human skin, the stuff was molten lava. Any facial contact, victims couldn't open their eyes. The production of respiratory mucus hampered breathing. In most cases, pepper spray was the most painful thing the victim ever experienced.

Pepper spray was all he had. But also all he should need.

As long as the trucks came.

Watching from inside a tree-shaded clump of dry brown grass, thirty yards above the old restaurant and creek, he wondered why Eric had picked him for this particular mission. Thought of him first thing he'd said. Asked him before considering anyone else. Did he want to rescue a kidnapped young woman in Mexico? A schoolteacher who'd been stupid on vacation, smoked killer weed at a private party, and asked about taking some home. Maybe in size because she had her dad's private plane.

Ray shook his head. Not many dumber things to do in a foreign country than buy illicit drugs while announcing your wealth. The combination can be lethal. The local police won't investigate robbery or even your murder, at least not further than the dead foreigner was buying illegal substances.

But stupid was one thing. Getting kidnapped was criminal, the kind of punishment a drug cartel might hand out. And this American citizen happened to be the daughter of a very important person connected to the US Senate Intelligence Committee. Extended family, a close friend, maybe a major political donor.

Daddy wanted his daughter back.

Ray didn't know who the woman was, only the name Mia. And not why Eric thought of him first. He hadn't been given him the woman's surname, so maybe secrecy was the reason his boss asked him. His loyalty to Eric would be especially valuable to the mission if politics were involved. Ray could keep a secret.

But he had a personal issue which might come in handy for the mission, too. He was sick about his missing and presumed-dead wife. Two years she'd been gone. Six months he'd boozed too much. And though he no longer drank, used his sponsor, and still attended Alcohol Anonymous meetings, he didn't sleep well. Lying in the dark, he sometimes obsessed. His hurt and regret over her loss attacked muscles near his center. Scar tissue being retested.

And his boss, Eric, knew all about it. The dreams. The pain. The doctors.

For Ray, saving women could be therapy.

Did the boss choose him for this mission because the intel might be wrong? Maybe the trucks didn't come *every* Saturday night. Eric knew Ray might be the only Homeland asset who would still consider a rescue if all twelve-to-fifteen cartel soldiers stayed home tonight. One unarmed man against a dozen automatic rifles was suicide, not salvage. But his boss might figure Ray would find a way.

No. Eric wouldn't do *that* to him.

Hours later, tire and engine sounds eased the tension in his neck. He watched two, dirty white Japanese pickup trucks pull into the restaurant's gravel parking lot between the river and the L-shaped patio. There was back and forth happy talk between two men with rifles and the truck drivers. Most of the men had disappeared inside minutes earlier.

Now they came outside again, in groups of two and three, eleven of the fifteen men. No rifles. Each wore khakis or blue jeans and freshly ironed shirts. About half wore straw ranch hats. If they carried weapons, the pistols were concealed. One by one, seven men seated themselves in the truck beds, with four taking the vehicles' driver and shotgun seats.

Ray whiffed a new smell on the breeze. Cologne.

He smiled. He'd been briefed how the cartel's safehouse above Puerto Vallarta almost emptied on Saturday night, pickups hauling most of the men to different spots. A dance hall in the Buenos Aires section and a crowded, outside restaurant-bar in the Benito Juarez district were two favorites. They wouldn't return for hours.

That meant the men left behind would soon do shots of tequila, mescal, or *something*, too, throwing a party of their own.

Give them an hour or two.

Then go for the woman.

The sun dropped quickly in Puerto Vallarta. In the darkness beneath that wrap-around patio, Ray could only hear the men laughing above him, four men sitting at two tables, making plans and telling jokes while they drank. They'd been slugging back the booze for less than an hour, but the sound of their guffaws suggested drunkenness.

One drinker emitted high-pitched giggles, a sound which made Ray grin—until he realized the guy's profanity-filled speech involved the captured woman. Mia.

Time to move.

Ray used a blue BIC to light the loose stack of scattered papers and dry grass he'd collected and hidden between some cardboard boxes and the building's exterior wood. He made sure the bonfire flared, then hurried outside and moved quickly up the hillside.

Now a deck below him, the guards' voices climbed.

He recognized the word *fuego*. Fire.

A herd of boots thundered down the outside stairs.

His satellite-based phone device showed the woman's heart rate and temperature still emanated from the rear corner where he stood. He explored the wall's painted, wooden slat boards, yanked one off and found plywood, and beneath that, drywall. The men had been sitting cater-corner to the woman, at first one floor down, now two floors as they tried to douse the stream-level fire. He needed to move fast, get Mia out before they discovered she'd left.

He gripped and ripped five more painted wooden slats, then pulled off a four-by-eight-foot section of underlying plywood. Even with tactical gloves on, his fingers tips complained. But the steel gave way. When he'd exposed enough drywall, he kicked out a hole, and used his hands to enlarge the passage. He needed a new pair every few missions because the finger pads wore quickly, but the new PIG gloves both protected and allowed use of touchscreen devices.

He slipped his head and shoulders inside. "Your dad sent me, Mia. Let's get out of here."

The woman, mid-twenties, was frightened and bound. On her haunches, short blond hair wet and tangled. Her clothes were ripped. Torn white shorts, now with bloodstains, and a tank top hanging from her neck in two pieces.

In Mia's eyes was the suffering and disbelief Ray had been exposed to throughout his time in Iraq. But for Mia, he knew the violent, gruesome things humans do to one another had been a frightening revelation. Each torture inflicted on her a soul-wounding discovery.

His teeth rubbed together as he came inside, removed his camo top, and slipped it over her head. Untying her hands and feet, he could see what the kidnappers had done. What they would do again and again until they'd killed her. They didn't care if the money arrived or not. Mia was scheduled to die.

He helped her stand and to slip her freed arms into his shirt. The garment covered her to the knees. A piece of him wanted to stay and take out these four men. Maybe leave the other bastards a present, something nasty waiting for them when they came home tonight.

But that wasn't his mission. Nor was any delay safe for Mia.

She latched on to his outreached hand, ducked, and joined him on the other side of the broken wall. Standing together in the dark, he handed her one of the pepper spray pens, showed her how the top came off, exposing the nozzle.

"If anybody catches us, aim for his face," he said.

Mia nodded. Her eyes were blank as marbles. He shouldn't count on her for help. He gently firmed his grip on her forearm. "Stay close to me."

He towed her straight for his shaded watching spot, then guided her down river. He'd found a narrow animal trail along the slope, above the tumbling water but well below the ridgeline. They used palm trees, boulders, and brush for cover. Scooting and stopping like rabbits. He forced her to travel faster than she wanted, but Mia was no complainer.

She knew the stakes exactly.

He steered them through thick brush and shade along the water, keeping them well away from the two-lane pavement, a mountain road which followed the river. He'd parked his vehicle well off-road, and partially covered three sides with branches.

Mia tripped and fell twice before her legs gave out. The distraught woman was weak and sick. Halfway back, he lifted her off the ground and carried her in his arms.

After their wedding, he'd tried to carry Alissa this way across the threshold of their new apartment. But she'd refused, said she'd make her own entrances, and on her own two feet. The pretty redhead said the words with a wide smile.

But they were no joke.

Back across the river, less than thirty yards from his rented

Volkswagen, Mia gasped. Her neck was cradled in the crook of his elbow, her gaze focused behind them. His pulse jumped, his body tense because they were so close to the car.

He turned to glance back.

A blur came at him from the front. From behind a bush, he'd been about to carry Mia past. His peripheral vision caught the movement, but threat recognition was late. He relaxed his knees, letting Mia's weight pull them down. Trying to duck.

A wooden baseball bat glanced off his scalp line.

The world exploded. Stunning pain wracked his head and spine.

Because he and Mia had been moving lower a split second before the blow struck, the club bashed his head's rounded top, not his flatter forehead, a one-inch difference that probably saved his life. And the young woman's, unless she was better than he expected with the pepper spray.

His vision flamed with flashing stars. He couldn't roll when he landed because of carrying Mia, so he dropped her onto the grass as gently as he could before reaching the turf himself. He landed hard on his left shoulder. Bounced his head, too. But he was fortunate to be alive. Charmed to be conscious.

Lucky, but maybe not lucky enough. Flat on his back, he couldn't find his own pepper spray and couldn't see much but flashing lights and gray shapes. He focused on a motion, saw Mia rising to her knees on his left. He glanced right when a large man stood over him and straddled his ankles. The baseball bat hung by his side.

A *swishing* noise.

Mia fired her pepper spray as the Batman raised the club above his head.

She was a terrible aim. Her stream of hot pepper juice strayed to the left, then zeroed in on Batman's leg. But she was a great distraction. He cursed and swung backhanded at her with the bat. An impressive motion, the guy maybe a veteran of *Liga Mexicana de Beisbol*.

Mia jumped out of his reach as Ray dug in his hands and heels, pulled himself along the ground to his attacker. Before Batman saw him again, Ray punched his crotch from underneath. He drove the first two knuckles of his right hand into the guy's package as hard as he could.

The Batman screamed, then groaned, bent over at the waist, holding himself. Ray pushed all the way through the guy's open legs and scrambled to his feet. From behind, he circled an elbow around Batman's thick neck, Ray's other arm reaching beneath the man's opposite shoulder to press a hand against Batman's head, forcing him into Ray's elbow.

The man struggled, but Ray was six inches and fifty pounds bigger. When he bent the guy's head and squeezed his elbow—shutting off circulation to the brain—Batman went limp in seconds. Dangerous cutting off a man's oxygen. But the chance of death or injury had to be taken. At stake was the mission and Mia's innocent life.

Plus the Batman tried to kill him.

Even so, Ray checked his pulse. He'd wake up.

He kept Mia stretched out in the back seat and Batman bound and gagged in the trunk until five minutes before they reached Puerto Vallarta International Airport. Batman he let go by untying his feet two miles from the nearest phone. Then brought Mia up front to ride up with him and drink another bottle of water.

The airport's private-plane entrance had Mexican Federales at the street checkpoint. Four of them in dark blue uniforms and assault rifles. They'd been briefed, paid, or both. Their captain greeted him at the driver's window by saying *buenos noches* and checking their faces against his own pictures of him and Mia.

The young woman cried as she climbed the ramp to her father's jet.

Behind her, Ray felt like weeping, too. Not from the physical pain, although the lump on his head grew bigger and sorer each minute. Nor did he feel guilty about being tricked into turning his head and nearly getting killed. No, his eyes nearly spilled watching Mia fall into the arms of her father at the top of the gangway.

Dad had gotten back *his* missing woman.

Alissa was *never* coming home to Ray.

2

Vincenzo already sat at his favorite table when Ray arrived ten minutes early. He eyeballed the older man behind the Chinese restaurant's plate-glass window while he parked his black government Suburban. The older man sipped his iced coffee, asked the waitress Diane to bring him something. Probably more milk and sugar.

Vincenzo liked iced tea milkshakes.

Ray didn't go to many Alcoholics Anonymous meetings anymore, one or two a month in Oceanside because the church was close to base. But he liked having lunch with his sponsor once a week in Solano Beach. Vincenzo had lived in Southern California all of his sixty years. A funny and thoughtful man, and a much better stay-sober experience than most AA meetings. The two men usually met on Sunday afternoons when Vincenzo didn't work and Ray only taught a single morning class.

The accountant and avocado farmer wore blue jeans, which meant he had something for Ray to lift, pull, or carry after they ate. That was okay. That's what Vincenzo did to all the men he sponsored. Alcoholics had to *earn* instruction from a man who'd been sober twenty-five years. Vincenzo often used Ray's unusual size and strength like he would a farm animal.

"That's some lump on your head," Vincenzo said.

"Biggest mosquito I ever saw. You're wearing jeans. Should I eat light?"

"Remember those shingles we unloaded last week?"

"Uh, oh. You said you'd have professionals re-roof your house."

"I am. Well, semi-professional. He's done some roofing. I'm not asking you to install the new roof."

"Good. What do you want me to do?"

"A little lifting."

Ray examined the restaurant's computer-printed list of daily specials. He liked the dishes with red hot chilies printed beside them. "You mean you want me to carry those bundles of composite shingles up a ladder, stash them on the roof?"

Vincenzo nodded.

"Did you ask the roofer for a discount if you put the shingles up there?"

"Seventy bucks."

Grinning, Ray shook his head. He'd been back from his Puerto Vallarta rescue mission two days. Exercise would be good for sore muscles. His head and shoulder still aggravated him, and a new, possibly major assignment loomed. The boss was being secretive.

"I'll buy lunch," his sponsor said.

Ray lifted his eyebrows, glanced once again at the specials list, then waved at the waitress Diane.

"It's a deal," he said.

Three hours later, Vincenzo strolled with him to the SUV. Ray had discovered ropes and two pullies in his friend's barn, so the lifting had been easy. They'd spent the last thirty minutes walking through Vincenzo's avocado trees, discussing water shortages, guacamole, and Oceanside's historic San Luis Rey Valley.

Being born and raised in Jersey, Ray had never heard of

Father Junipero Serra and his California missions. Vincenzo was happy to explain California's role in Spanish and Catholic ambitions, the Southern California's native population before and after, plus the mass migration of English in the mid-nineteenth century.

"Thanks for your help today," Vincenzo said. "The new roof is costing me a fortune. Every little bit helps."

Ray felt a pang of guilt opening the door of his SUV. He'd eaten too much. "My pleasure. And thanks for the lunch."

His sponsor squinted like he'd forgotten something. Standing at Ray's driver window. "We didn't talk at all today about your recovery. You don't come to many meetings these days. Everything okay? You're on track?"

"I'm doing fine. Clean and sober, thanks to you and my sister. A year next week."

Vincenzo reached up to touch his shoulder. "Good to hear, Ray. Thanks again for your help."

Ray hustled the narrow trail down Camp Pendleton's ocean cliffs, curiosity and anticipation propelling his size-16, steel-toe Belleville military boots. His assignments routinely came via encrypted telephone calls from Quantico, Virginia, but this time his close friend and Commanding Officer at Homeland Security had arranged a one-on-one.

Eric traveled coast-to-coast to speak with him privately.

On a guarded and lonely Southern California beach.

At the bottom of the trail, a canvas-topped, two-seat Jeep waited on the wet sand. A major US Marine Corps expeditionary training facility, Camp Pendleton covered over a hundred thousand acres, and included twenty-plus miles of virgin, San Diego County coastline. Best weather in the world, Ray had decided after a year stationed there. America's national debt probably could be cut in half by selling the Marines' beachfront property.

Inside the green Jeep waited Homeland Security's Principal Deputy Under Secretary for Intelligence and Analysis, Marine Corps General Eric Johannsen. He lit a cigarette when he saw Ray. The fire illuminated his familiar, round face. The two men had known each other twenty years, meeting inside a Jersey recruiting office within a week of the September 11, 2001 terrorist attacks. He was probably the only man alive Eric trusted to witness his smoking. A two-star general, Eric was still ambitious.

He landed hard in the passenger seat. Perhaps with too much enthusiasm. The vehicle rocked on four wheels. He couldn't wait to find out why Eric wanted so much privacy.

"Careful, Ace," Eric said. "Don't hurt yourself."

His rear-end fit okay in the narrow bucket seat, but not so much his shoulders or head. In fact, any vehicle but a truck was uncomfortable.

Eric's cell phone blurted an older Rolling Stones tune.

One of twenty Principal Deputy Under Secretaries inside the Department of Homeland Security, Eric ignored his electronic summons. He slapped Ray's shoulder and plopped a two-inch-thick Manila folder on his lap. "Good to see you, buddy. Look these over while I get rid of Congressman Jaggerfield."

Eric scrambled outside to take his call. He was older than Ray, already a college graduate when they'd joined the Marines. The two men's careers had gone in separate directions for more than a decade, converged again after Ray's Marine unit helped rescue Eric and his trapped intelligence staff near Fallujah.

Ray flipped open the bulging file of reports, documents, drawings, and photographs. The top, black-and-white shot showed a GAU-8 autocannon—labeled so in the caption—stacked behind a Volkswagen Beetle. The Gatling-like, seven-barrel, rotary cannon was as thick as the famous small car and twice as long. The caption said a loaded cannon weighed over four-thousand pounds.

Eric clambered back inside the Jeep, phone in his pocket.

"You know what an Avenger is?"

"Sure. We saw them in Iraq. The autocannons inside the Air Force A-10. Hissing, flying dragons, spitting fire and smoke. The bad guys ran when they heard a Warthog coming."

Eric reached over and pulled a different photo from the stack, an image of total devastation. A junkyard-like, burned-wreckage trail of destroyed humans and vehicles alike. Death, stretching toward a desert horizon. Ninety percent of the work of Warthogs.

"I was only a kid," Eric said, "but I remember this picture. Highway of Death, the TV talking heads called it."

Ray was six when America went to war over Kuwait. But as a Marine in 2003, in Iraq, he'd seen a single Warthog take out a line of five military vehicles in one pass. He'd asked around, found out the Warthog's cannon fired at the rate of seventy shells per second, four-thousand rounds a minute. Each two-pound, eleven-inch cartridge threw a bomb equal to a stick of dynamite.

"Did you see the executive summary of potential terrorist uses?" Eric asked.

Ray pulled the stapled six-page report from underneath the photos. "Not yet."

"Check item number seven. I think they buried that one on purpose."

He glanced at his friend. "Somebody lost one of these autocannons?"

"Read number seven."

He figured he'd soon be tasked with finding a lost cannon, or rather fixing a broken investigation somewhere which hadn't reclaimed the autocannon fast enough. That's a job he often took on for Eric. Drag some stubborn-ass colonel to the 'splaining department. Find a new leader for the investigation or other group task. Maybe take the job himself. But above all, restore order and fix the problem. What he couldn't figure this time, why Eric wanted to meet on the beach. He'd gone to work for him when Eric moved to Homeland's Intelligence and Analysis unit, and in all the assignments Eric had offered him over the years, not one had been extended so privately.

"Shit." Ray rarely cursed, but "number seven" involved a rush-hour traffic scenario, the cannon mounted on a swivel and parked on a hillside near a Los Angeles freeway interchange. FBI analysts predicted two-to-three-thousand casualties within eight minutes, the shortest possible response time.

"Yes, Ray, brother, this is serious. If the Air Force can put one of these monsters in a Warthog aircraft, anyone mechanical could attach the cannon to a flatbed trailer, link the hydraulics and a generator, haul that weapon under supermarket or shipping company camouflage anywhere in the US."

"We need to find it," Ray said.

He liked his job, thought it his very nature to straighten the twisted and fix the broken. His father teaching him how to pound out automobile dents felt like torture as a child, but watching bent steel reshape itself under his guidance eventually became a gratification. Sure, his muscles pounded out each flaw with a two-pound, ball-peen hammer, but once his hands, wrists, and arms mastered the weight of his tools, their summertime, all-day use, his imagination seemed to make the surfaces smooth again.

It was his *will* which restored a thing's proper function.

He repeated his question. "So, someone lost one of these autocannons?"

"Yes." Eric said, "and you'll want to be part of finding the people who stole it, though your involvement creates an additional problem. I don't want to send anybody else, but like always, it's up to you."

He frowned. Eric sometimes tossed extra mustard on certain, baloney-sandwich kind of assignments. But his pal normally *minimized* the mess, not supercharged the mission with problems. What was going on? Unless...

"Two years you've been waiting for *this* call," Eric said.

He held his breath. "Alissa?"

Eric nodded. "The Air Force lost one of these cannons a week ago. The jerk in charge of the investigation sat on a smart theory, too busy chasing the agent who'd figured out the theft."

"What agent? What theory? What does this have to do with Alissa?"

"Special Agent Sunny Hicks is the agent. She works for the Air Force's Office of Special Investigations. She believes the autocannon was stolen off its flatbed railroad car."

His throat went dry. "While the train was moving?"

"Yup. The same way Alissa thought her generator was taken, her generator within a hundred pounds of the same weight. Plus, get this. Agent Hicks thinks an organized gang grabbed it between Tucson and Gila Bend."

"Alissa was searching the same stretch when…"

The word *murdered* had gotten stuck between his head and his mouth. There was no doubt his wife was dead. The blood evidence on her shredded clothes had been convincing. But he didn't like saying that word out loud.

Eric grunted. "That's why I said this is big."

Ray scrambled out of the confining Jeep. His fingers had curled into fists, so the door opening and the steel-framed canvas top tried to block his exit. Like wartime tangos grabbing at his arms and legs to keep him from breaking loose.

Fresh air helped. Standing free, finally, he walked on the sand in a tight circle, his mind creating photo after photo of his dead wife. Alissa's dark red hair and soft green eyes danced into his arms. The old, ripped muscle in his heart pinched him again.

"Ray!"

He recognized his anger and relaxed his hands. A deep breath and he could stick his head back near the Jeep's window, talk to Eric. "So, *this* is why we're meeting face-to-face? I couldn't figure."

Eric nodded. "If I suspect there's a connection to Alissa's case, you know regulations require me to recuse myself, then report—"

"Of course there's a connection, Eric. A theft from a moving train? On the same stretch of track where Alissa disappeared?"

"But you understand if I assign you, we can't let anyone know *we* know about a connection to Alissa. Right?"

"Because Alissa is my missing wife?" he said.

"Right. And because Alissa was my *sister*. The regulations apply to both of us."

Eric opened the Jeep door, forcing Ray to step back. Eric joined him and a dozen white and gray seagulls lined up diagonally in front of the Jeep. Everybody aimed their beaks and feathers into the cool morning breeze. A gray cloud bank blocked the horizon.

"We could both be court-martialed, huh," Ray said.

Eric shrugged. "Most likely only if the job goes south. Like we don't get the autocannon back before people get killed. Then somebody else would investigate that."

Ray envied the cigarette between Eric's fingers. He wasn't sure why. He'd never smoked one in his life, even at AA meetings when the whole place puffed away. "But that won't happen if you use the premier horse in your stable, right, boss?"

Eric laughed. "Yeah, that's the real problem, isn't it? You're the best. If you're *not* the man sent to Arizona, maybe bad guys get hold of this autocannon, kill hundreds or thousands of innocent people. And Alissa's killers go free."

"Let me handle it," Ray said. "I'll complete the assignment successfully. Like I always do."

"You forgetting Colonel Lyon at McGuire?"

"He left the task force, didn't he?"

"On a stretcher. He resigned and sued us."

Ray stared at his friend. "That was a crazy situation. Incredible coincidence, me running into the same Adam Henry I fought with in high school."

The wind whistled against his ears while the seagulls walked farther away, maybe wanting more distance from the humans or the Jeep. He figured the silence meant Eric wanted more reassurance.

"The missing cannon will be my sole focus," he said. "Alissa's case stays in the bottom drawer. If a direct connection does get made, I call you with it right away. We decide then what, if anything, we do about it."

"You can't bring her back, Ray. The autocannon, you can."

"I understand. Who did you say is in charge of the investigation now?"

"The Air Force. Their Office of Special Investigations in Virginia. It's a good, systems-based outfit, but this guy Colonel William Seager sounds like a misogynist. He's definitely a meatball, sitting on Hicks' theory for two days."

Ray growled. "Now *there's* a guy should be court-martialed."

"You'll have his job by this afternoon," Eric said, "but the problem is bigger than Colonel Seager. I might come myself. The Navy SEALs are investigating because the weapon was on its way to them, some kind of boat installation they wanted to test, plus the FBI and NSA are conducting inquiries. There's been internet chatter about terrorists."

The assignment would be life-changing. His instincts lit him up with that knowledge the moment Eric said, "two years you've been waiting." Over those ugly twenty-four months, they'd never discovered Alissa's body. He'd searched himself for over ten weeks, Eric allowing him the time off and helping support the cost. Private investigators had done no better.

"If I do come out, it'll be to handle the alphabet soup coordination," Eric said. "I'd want you to run the investigation like you always do, the way you want, the people you pick for our staff."

Even after two years, Alissa's disappearance was still difficult. He'd conquered the four-month bout with booze and depression, but occasionally he couldn't sleep, unable to force the images of his wife's blood-stained blouse and jeans from his mind. Even with meditation techniques he'd learned through martial arts, insomnia was a recurring disruption. Night-long ruminations made him sick with anger and thoughts of revenge.

"All right, Ray. Go get'm. I'm counting on you."

3

He kept a go-bag in his apartment, so when Eric called back with final approval hours later, he was already traveling east toward Phoenix on US Highway 8. Forty minutes east of San Diego, he enjoyed Southern California's five-thousand-foot mountain scenery and looked forward to the below-sea-level Yuha Desert to come.

His vehicle was a special SUV he took on assignments when possible, a black Chevy Suburban with a one-man jail in back. More precisely, a steel-tube chair, bolted to the truck frame. One that locked down a perp with an overhead bar, like a rollercoaster seat, but also with side restraints, locks, and open space in back for handcuffs.

The intelligence and analysis Eric passed on during their second encrypted call that day had included both Colonel Seager's office and private phone numbers. Being in the same room with an outgoing, out-of-favor colonel usually made the dismissal job easier. Showing offenders how big he was made most guys less confrontational. But he didn't give a rat's ass about this jerk. Dumping Romeo flyboys could be handled by phone.

"This is Colonel Bill Seager," the man said. "What can I do for you, General Hauser?"

He still wasn't used to his newest promotion. Seemed like

Eric had gotten carried away this time, naming Ray a brigadier, or one-star, general. "Like you, Bill, I'm looking for that missing autocannon. Any luck?"

"Not yet, sir, no. But—"

"How come?"

The long silence told him much about Bill Seager. Unprepared, mostly.

"It's hard to say, general," Seager said. "We can't...uh, pinpoint the crime scene. There aren't any real clues or witnesses."

He did have a point. "Not *yet*, you mean."

"Yes, sir, That's right. Not yet."

"Tell me about Special Agent Sunny Hicks."

"Hicks?"

"Yes, the Air Force Special Agent who came up with the moving-train theory."

"Well, she's tall," Seager said. "Tall and blond."

Incredible. Was he really that big a dope? Maybe he was joking. "Are you serious? I want to know what you think about her theory, Bill, not her looks."

"Sorry, general. Her idea has potential, but the center pivot point she describes would have to be impossibly strong—a tough set-up to build in the middle of the Sonoran Desert, especially at the center of a horseshoe turn. They usually encircle some natural obstacle."

"Pivot point?"

"Her theory is centrifugal force was used."

"I don't get it."

"She found a horseshoe turn—they're not uncommon—where the tracks form a perfect half-circle. If strong chains were attached to cargo near the beginning of the half-circle, centrifugal force could take the cargo right off the train at the end. When the tracks changed course."

"Oh." Ray considered three beats. "Okay, the pivot wouldn't be hard to set up, not if there's an access road to bring in equipment. Thick chains anchored by say a bulldozer, blade down, would make centrifugal force do the heavy work. I see what she's saying."

"Even with a pivot, the thieves would have to board the train, detach at least some of the autocannon's packaging, hook up the chains, make adjustments before the half circle was gone. Not easy."

"There's a way. A practiced crew, no doubt at night, dressed in black so the engineer and conductor couldn't see them."

"We'll know soon if she's right," Seager said. "Special Agent Hicks flew to Phoenix yesterday. She's hooking up with an experienced Air Force agent named Walker today, checking out the site. They should be there right now."

"Special Agent Hicks is new?"

"This is her first field assignment. She talked me into it because it was her theory."

Ray wasn't thrilled but wouldn't say anything. He didn't like criticizing agents, women especially because of his sisters. He'd been brand new once, too.

"When do you expect to hear?"

"Whenever they find something. End of today if they don't."

The conversation had reached a point where silence worked in his favor. Let Seager worry why he had called, maybe who he was, exactly. He kept his eyes on the wide mountain road and wondered if he should stop for lunch. The gas tank was low. He tried to remember if there had been a town up in these mountains the last time he'd driven through.

"So, my commanding officer called an hour ago," Seager said. "He told me Homeland was sending special help. Would that be you, general?"

"Yes, it would. I'm on my way to Phoenix now because I have a hunch this railroad theory is a good one."

"We can use all the help we can get, sir."

"I'm more than help, Bill. It's been a week, and considering the dangerous nature of that autocannon, Homeland Security thinks your investigation is broken. I'm the fixer."

"Fixer? I never heard of that. I mean, not in the Air Force."

"Where *have* you heard it?"

"Boxing, bookies, horseracing. You know. Breaking legs because a guy didn't pay."

"That's pretty close," Ray said, "but I swear I haven't broken any bones *recently*. Pretty sure that's why I earned my first star."

Seager went silent. Maybe his situation had clarified. Or not.

"Here's the story," Ray said. "I'm replacing you as head of the investigation."

"That's ridiculous. Homeland Security can't just take over an Air Force investigation. That cannon belongs to the Air Force. We lost it, and we're—"

"You're out, Bill. Call your CO again if you don't believe me. He should have explained the first time."

Seager made a sound, but it wasn't speech. A gurgle. Or a swallow.

"I'll be in the Phoenix DHS office three or four hours from now," Ray said. "Know where it is?"

"I can look it up."

"I need copies of your files there waiting for me."

"You can't give me orders," Seager said. "I don't work for Homeland."

Ray shook his head. "You're an asswipe, Bill. You want, I can have strange men in black suits come arrest you. Might take a day. But they'll come for you. You know why?"

"No, tell me."

"Because that's an extremely dangerous piece of weaponry you flyboys lost and can't find. The whole Pentagon is worried your investigation is stalled."

"You wouldn't call me an *asswipe* to my face," Seager said.

That's all he heard? Maybe this Seager guy was even a bigger loser than he thought. "Why wouldn't I? You some kind of tough guy?"

"I played football for Michigan State, first string defensive end. But my daughter is probably tough enough to kick *your* ass. Some parachute-in overseer and organization planner. Probably an accountant with team-building training."

Ray smiled. "That's me, Bill. You nailed it. Why don't you fly out to Phoenix and join us?"

"I just might."

"We'd love to keep you on the team. Agent Hicks in particular."

"You're an asshole, Hauser."

"I understand your feelings," he said. "And you are metaphorically correct. I did indeed dump a large piece of crap."

Ray turned off US Highway 8 inside a pine forest to eat and fuel his gas-guzzling Suburban. In Alpine, California, the first friendly-looking restaurant had a long counter for single travelers like him, and the kitchen emitted enticing, home-cooked smells. He ordered the day's special, roast chicken with mashed potatoes and peas.

One of the few meals Alissa had enjoyed cooking. She said the dish was easy and tasty. How apropo to find it on the specials menu. A hunch about Alissa's case getting solved on this trip blossomed again in his gut.

After lunch, Ray filled the car with gas and let his mind wander. How Alissa had pushed his life into a different gear, Ray falling in love for the first time. The physical sensation had struck him so hard, he looked for explanations on Google. Discovered some changes were his own organs releasing hormones. Chemicals to make you feel wonderful.

Nature's way to encourage mating.

They had eighteen months together.

Returning to the freeway, eastbound traffic was heavier than before. He slowed, moved to the right lane, and placed his private iPhone on speaker to make a call. Ray had three older sisters, Aretha, Dinah, and Etta, all four Hauser kids named after rhythm and blues recording artists. Each sister had been important in the building of Ray into a better man than their alcoholic and violent father. But Etta, the oldest, was one of his best friends.

She'd loved Alissa, too.

After their usual, family-based Q-and-A session, Etta loudly chopping vegetables with her grandchild, Brianna, watching Elmo's World in the background, Ray ended a lull in the chit-chat. "I might find out something about Alissa on this assignment."

The chopping stopped. "Really? How so?"

"I'm investigating the theft of equipment, like she was."

He heard Etta put down her knife. Of course, his sister was interested.

"What else can you tell me?" she said.

"I've already said too much. You know I'm not supposed to talk about what I do."

"But you just did, Ray. You volunteered information about your missing wife, a woman I loved dearly. Now, what else?"

After Etta's breast-cancer surgery three years ago, it was Alissa who'd taken off work to help with Etta's chemotherapy and doctors' visits. Not Etta's busy two sisters or Ray. His wife had spent the whole month with Etta, driving her, managing the house, her two single teenagers, one with a baby named Brianna.

"I'll know more in a few days," he said. "I'll call you then."

"Listen, Ray. You're the one who brought her up. But forget that. Let me point out the gorilla in the room. Shouldn't somebody *else* be handling a case which could involve your missing wife? Nothing personal for investigators?"

"I'm focused on an important, current case. If anything turns up directly about Alissa and her missing generator, I probably *would* turn over that part of the investigation."

"I don't think so. And finding her killer could set you off, Ray. It's an emotional sore spot. You know I'm right."

He blinked when Alissa's freckled face superimposed on a car's rear window. Almost forgot he was driving. "I'm a level-headed guy, Etta. Good at keeping things cool."

"Yeah? Tell that to your father."

"You're being silly. Getting emotional is not an option."

"It wasn't an option until you put your father in the hospital for three months. What would make you angrier than coming face-to-face with Alissa's killer?"

"Eric wouldn't send me if he thought my emotions were a problem."

"Eric's not logical about Alissa either."

"You're wrong."

"You want to find the guy who took her and choke him with your own hands."

"Nonsense."

"You *know* I'm right."

Ray considered two beats. His sister's ideas were worth consideration. He should always pay attention. And though his brain wanted to arrest the men who'd taken Alissa, bring them all to justice, even now his hands wanted to rip their heads off.

If Special Agent Hicks' theory proved accurate, and Ray's own investigation successfully tied the cases together, he actually *might* get his hands on them.

Then maybe he'd have to be careful.

Before he'd finished saying goodbye to his sister, he wondered if Special Agent Hicks had found anything yet on those train tracks.

4

At a slow but dependable crawl, US Air Force Special Agent Sunny Hicks guided her rented Jeep Wrangler alongside an isolated stretch of Southern Pacific Railroad track. Twenty miles east of Gila Bend, Arizona, hunting for what amounted to busted junk, she poked her head out the window to better search the rail bed's crushed gray rock.

A blue Dodger baseball hat and aviator sunglasses protected her eyes from the dazzling Sonoran Desert sun, but nothing screened her from the withering, convection-oven gusts of searing, dry air. At twelve-thirty that afternoon, the first week in August, the temperature topped one hundred and nineteen degrees.

The expected high was one-twenty-one.

Sunny's seconds-ago mental joke about 'broken junk' pushed a smile across her lips. True, her search list featured severed bolts, snapped links of steel chain, fragments of elastic tie-downs, and torn pieces of a particular kind of waterproof tarpaulin. But these damaged goods hardly qualified as worthless.

On this search, her first field assignment, even one item found beside these train tracks would constitute precious treasure. The discovery would prove her theory and likely get her the full-time, field status she sought. Working behind her

OSI desk, she'd figured how thieves might have stolen the four-thousand-pound weapon from a moving train.

But she needed proof, and busted junk was evidence.

For comparison purposes, she carried unbroken samples of each searched-for item in an athletic bag on the Jeep's passenger seat. Also inside the Reebok sack were four bottles of water, a special satellite telephone in case her cell phone lost signal, which it already had, and her Air Force-issue nine-millimeter, a Sig Sauer P320.

She braked the Wrangler and stared through her windshield at the train tracks. Twin steel lines crossed an expanse of desert, a light brown landscape dotted with darker-colored creosote and saltbush. A mile or so distant, the rail lines turned right and swooped behind rock outcroppings, an offshoot of the South Maricopa Mountains. Several black ridges sank into the dirt, descending lines of ever-smaller rocks, like the buried spine of a dinosaur.

A bright flash in the foreground of her vision clutched her focus, a sparkle on the sloped, gray rocks not far ahead. Something next to the tracks was throwing sunlight at her. Glaring through the glass. Her pulse rose as she marked the bright flash to the left of a particular creosote bush and scrambled from the cool Jeep. She'd only been searching ten minutes.

Dare she hope?

Halfway up the steep bed, the desert's intensity wrapping her like an electric blanket, she squatted to examine a shiny metal object among the gray rock. Her mouth fell open. A broken bolt. She gasped with pleasure. The stainless steel connector was among the items she sought, identical to the sample in her bag.

Oh, lucky me. She slipped on a protective glove from her pocket and pinched her proof of success. Thieves had taken advantage of the railroad's perfect, half-circle shape at this spot. A first piece of the missing-cannon puzzle. Now the Air Force knew *exactly* where the bad guys committed the theft.

And how. Why else would a horseshoe turn be involved?

She had an urge to kick her feet. How sweet was she going to feel calling up that butt-head Seager, telling him she'd been right. She couldn't cha-cha to the Jeep for fear of tripping and falling, but she could waggle her extended elbows like a bird as she hurried back. No time for anything more of a celebration. She wanted back inside the air-conditioned Jeep, get her hands on that satellite phone.

The military phone was ringing. Her headquarters.

"Special Agent Hicks," she said.

"Have you found anything?"

"Excuse me. Who is this?"

"Sorry. I thought the call-patch lady would have introduced me. This is General Hauser with Homeland Security. Have you talked to Colonel Seager?"

"Not today."

"Oh. Well, Homeland Security is seriously worried about that missing cannon. I've been sent to take over Colonel Seager's investigation. I was checking in to introduce myself and see if you'd found anything yet."

She grabbed a breath. "Wow."

"Yeah, I know. Surprise, surprise. By the way, I think your theory is right on target."

Her pulse ramped again, Sunny undecided on which development was more exciting—finding the evidence or Seager being gone. Best tell Hauser the good news.

"Both of us are right, general. Between my rubber-gloved finger and thumb, I hold a newly discovered, sawed-off hunk of stainless steel bolt, a match for my sample. I just found it this minute. This horseshoe turn is where they took our autocannon."

"Fan-*tas*-tic," Hauser said. "Congratulations, Special Agent."

"Thank you. I just started looking. It's amazing. Walker said he was five-minutes behind me, and I've found the bolt before he got here."

"You're there alone?" Hauser asked.

"For a minute or two. Walker lost a crown at dinner last night, stopped this morning to see a dentist. That's why we're starting so late. He was on time when we talked minutes ago. Wait. This is him now. I see his dust coming."

A rising column of dirt sped toward her on the same railroad access road. The vehicle had raced out from behind the remote, jagged ridge of mountain rocks where the train tracks passed from sight.

"Let's hope so," Hauser said.

"What's the matter?"

"These people stole a deadly weapon worth millions of dollars. They're smart and organized. They're going to watch the place where they grabbed it, see if and when law enforcement finds their trail."

What if this wasn't Walker coming? What if this was one of the guys who'd stolen the Air Force's weapon? Her stomach turned sour over the possibility of a gunfight. Twice a week she fired seventy-five rounds at the range's paper targets. She'd barely qualified with her Sig Sauer nine-millimeter at special agent training school in Glynco, Georgia the previous winter. That was reason enough to perfect her technique and prepare for the next test. But a bigger reason for her dedication to the range was the way she felt when she held any pistol.

The coldness of death chilled her.

"Sunny. I called Walker on another line. He's fifteen minutes away, at best. He's calling for help, but no one can reach you in time. Are you armed?"

She swallowed. "My Air Force-issue Sig Sauer is on the front seat."

"Better go get it, check if it's loaded."

As the vehicle and the dust cloud drew closer, sunlight reflected off a shiny square grill and windshield. She recognized an extended-cab pickup truck. Multiple unknown visitors. It would be a minute before she could read the plates.

Her heart thumped. She breathed through her mouth. Good thing Hauser couldn't see her face. She hadn't been frightened for her life since that C-17 landing at Ramstein Air Base on a rainy night. Bouncing on the runway, blowing out every tire on the plane. Going sideways.

She glanced quickly around her, all three hundred and sixty degrees. Not another human or vehicle in sight. Just her Jeep and the truck.

"Sunny?" Hauser said. "Did you get your weapon?"

The truck drew within a hundred yards. She ducked back inside the Jeep, extracted the holstered Sig Sauer from her athletic bag. The advancing truck could be anybody, a railroad employee, a tourist looking for psychedelic cactus, or a cop curious about her activities near the tracks. A few days ago, Homeland Security had issued a memo to law enforcement along the four-state, Southern Pacific route.

"Answer me, Sunny."

"Yes. Give me a second."

She needed both hands to clip the holster to her belt, so she switched the satellite phone to speaker and placed it on the Jeep's roof. What had she done? Pushing herself into her first assignment, too eager to wait for Walker. Maybe she'd lined herself up for an Air Force Office of Special Investigations record—shot dead on her first day in the field.

"If I were you, and considering the evidence you've found," Hauser said, "I'd draw my weapon and take a low ready behind the driver's door. How does that sound to you?"

She drew the Sig Sauer and checked the slide and magazine. She'd done both before placing the semiautomatic in her bag that morning but double-checks were standard. Her successes in life had always resulted from preparation and precaution. Her failures came as the result of impulse and eagerness.

"Sunny? You okay?"

Watching the truck close in, she reminded herself again most local cops and federal agents never fired a weapon on the job in their entire career.

"I'm fine, General. Ready for anything."

Less than fifty yards away and throwing dust like a mini tornado, the black truck shifted direction, re-aiming directly at Sunny and her comparatively pint-size, Jeep Wrangler. All the extended cab's windows were darkened. The truck's intimidating speed and direction had to be deliberate.

"Looks like a Chevy," she said. "State government's. That big S inside the Arizona border outline. Three-four-three-nine."

"Got it. Sounds like law enforcement."

Her weapons instructor at special agent school told her she needed to think of pistols as tools. "You want to tighten a nut onto a bolt, a wrench is your tool," he'd said. "You want to protect your life or the public from a dangerous bad guy, you need a pistol."

"Talk to me, Sunny. Describe the vehicle."

"If these are bad guys, they're going to kill me while I'm stuck on the phone with you. How about letting me deal with this?"

She shifted a step, so the Wrangler's door post provided better cover. The hot dirt road warmed the soles of her hiking sneakers. Another gust of wind chopped at the rolling dust cloud following the black truck.

"Got a search on that plate working."

"Shut up, sir." Her chest was ready to burst.

The black pickup braked hard at the last second. Rocks popped from under its wide tires as the Chevy Silverado skidded to a stop near her Jeep. The long-watched, billowing dust cloud engulfed her.

Sunny tugged the brim of her blue baseball cap and squinted into the whirling dirt. She detected nothing of the truck, only flowing sand which bit her cheeks and soiled her US Air Force T-shirt and jeans. There had been no collision, no contact. But the noisy truck engine growled only a few feet away.

She tapped her leather holster and remembered to trust her training.

All six months.

Any tool can be used for good or for evil. But she couldn't think of anything good when holding a pistol. She'd experienced a devastating gunshot death early in life and would always know well the effect on family and friends of a loved one's shooting death.

The giant dust cloud turned filmy. Her mouth was dry as sand.

She removed her sunglasses and blew chunks of soil off the lenses, once again reminding herself the idea to switch from inside analyst work to field investigations had been her bright idea. She'd always worried her apathy toward weapons might be a problem, but maybe she hadn't worried enough.

An outline of the truck's roof appeared against the blue sky.

A breeze gusted and the air cleared. The black Chevy truck had finished nose-to-nose with her rented Jeep. Two feet. The Silverado looked big enough to chew and swallow her Wrangler.

The truck's engine quit, the driver's door flipped open, and a cowboy-hatted man hopped down onto the railroad access road. Like her, he remained behind his open door, the two strangers staring at each other diagonally across their respective hoods. Face-to-face through the V-shaped space between door and frame. Eight to ten feet apart.

Her first reaction wasn't fear. The opposite.

Under six feet tall but thick across the chest, the cowboy smiled and lifted his hat with his left hand, the gentlemanly display only somewhat undercut by his right hand, which stayed hidden. His hair was black and buzzed short.

"My name is Garcia," he said. "I am with the Pinacosta County Sheriff's Office. May I ask what you are doing here by the train tracks?"

His light brown, collared shirt fashionably matched his milk chocolate-colored hat, and his dark brown trousers sported tan stripes. A uniform. But he wore no star or badge on his chest.

No visible emblems, only an unreadable stitched patch on his shoulder. His voice soothed her, though. A well-worn bass.

She holstered her weapon and closed the Jeep door, exposing herself. "I'm a federal agent. On the job. Is there a problem?"

His gaze fell. "I see you are wearing a weapon."

"Air Force-issue. I'm Special Agent S. Hicks, here on official Air Force business. I thought Arizona was open carry?"

Garcia shut his truck's door, returning Sunny's gesture of exposure. He tipped his hat. "Yes, señora, that is correct." On his hip, he wore a revolver fancy enough for a western gunfighters museum. An engraved silver weapon so long, the turquoise and silver-studded holster required a leg strap at the bottom.

Garcia slipped through the narrow gap between the bumpers. His movements were easy and confident, as was the straight-forward smile, a man trained to be friendly while giving orders or getting information. Good chance he wasn't faking his law enforcement status.

She bet he grew up watching old cowboy movies.

A passing roadrunner stopped to stare at them, or maybe it was Garcia's shiny, turquoise and silver-studded holster which caught the bird's sharp eye. The animal's feathers and blotched coloring were nearly invisible against the desert path she and Garcia stood on to talk.

"May I see your identification, please?" he asked.

Hauser squawked from the roof of the Jeep. "Ask him for *his* ID." She'd forgotten about the general. The poor guy. She'd told him to shut up and let her deal, and that's what he'd done.

She slipped a folder from her back pocket, held her identification so the hinged leather dropped open. Her right hand stayed close to her unbuttoned holster, even as Garcia's hand moved away from his holster.

He showed her a few white teeth while he read. "Sunny? That is your true name?"

She nodded. "How about *your* official ID?"

"Mine is in the truck." He widened his smile and pointed to

the patch on his shoulder. "But I'm just a volunteer, a member of the Sheriff's Posse. All sheriff offices near these tracks received a memo from Homeland Security. I was detailed for this section of tracks and told to be on the lookout."

The phone squawked. "There are nine Garcias on Pinacosta County Sheriff's website," Hauser said. "What's your first name?"

"I don't work there. I'm a volunteer. Sheriff's Posse."

"How about you go back to your car and show Special Agent Hicks your Pinacosta County Sheriff's Posse ID then," Hauser said.

"I'm ready to leave," Garcia said. "But before I do, how about you and I talk man-to-man? Whoever you are. You're like the talking car in Disney movie."

"Give him the phone," Hauser said.

Sunny was satisfied. Garcia's knowledge of the Homeland memo was proof of his status, at least enough for her. She stepped away and stretched for her phone on the car roof.

"But don't turn your back on him," Hauser said.

What? Too late. Holding the phone, she'd already grabbed the device and was swiveling back toward Garcia. The steady desert wind seemed to pause. An electric current tickled her spine.

She'd only pulled her gaze from Garcia one second, but his former smile was a cruel line when she saw him again. And he'd drawn his over-size *pistola*, aimed the barrel at her chest.

"Turn around," he said. "Put your hands behind you."

Hauser's telephone squawking was cut short by Garcia's snatch and stomp.

5

Driving the Suburban on US Highway 8, Ray's teeth clenched. He'd never met Special Agent Hicks, but the brand new field agent was in desperate trouble. Maybe already dead. His stomach burned as he redialed Walker.

"What's up, general?"

"Agent Hicks has been kidnapped—or worse. Where are you now?"

"Oh my God. I can't—"

"Peter. This just happened. Seconds ago. Where are you?"

"Maricopa Road, a couple of miles from the access road."

"She might be in a black Chevy truck, a Silverado," Ray said. "Arizona State license three-four, three-nine."

"I'll be on the lookout."

"You're still fifteen minutes away?" Ray asked.

"Closer to ten."

"Well, hurry it up, will you? Her life's at stake."

"I know that."

Ray wanted to say something about acting like it, but held his tongue. "Call me when you get there, or if you see the truck."

"Yes, sir."

He'd crossed into Arizona half an hour ago, but wasn't sure in what county or city that horseshoe turn was located. He called the state police. By the time he explained things to the second official—who he was, what had happened to Special Agent Hicks—he realized there was no time to get a helicopter out there, anyway. The thieves and kidnappers were gone.

He hung up and called Walker.

"I'm driving up right now beside her rented Jeep Wrangler," the Air Force agent said.

"Did you see the truck?"

"No."

"Then they must have gone the other way on the access road. See any dust?"

"No, and there are other roads into the mountains close to here. We need a helicopter. The sheriff's office was working on one, going to call me back."

"So you did you call for extra help."

"Plenty. The Air Force. Pinacosta Sheriffs. Homeland in Phoenix."

"What else do you see around the car?"

"Let me get out and look. I was staying inside to talk because it's a hundred and twenty outside."

Ray didn't have much hope for Hicks after what had happened to his wife. These guys were organized and ruthless.

"No sign of Sunny," Walker said. "Both her Air Force and private phones have been smashed."

"Any blood?"

"No, and no spent casings."

"No blood is a good thing," Ray said. "Gives her a chance. Does the Air Force have a search team close? Or I'll call Homeland in Phoenix, get some people out there. We have to find some trace of that fake posse officer."

"An Air Force team is already on the way," Walker said. "And Colonel Seager's on his way from Washington. But hang on, I'm checking her car. Maybe she left us some clue."

"Don't think she had time."

"There's rental paperwork for her Jeep, a map of the train

tracks here, a close-up map of the horseshoe. Sunny's bag of samples is on the front seat."

"Nice to hear Seager's coming," Ray said.

Stretched out on the back seat of Garcia's Silverado, her hands and feet tied with strips, blindfolded, Sunny could only wonder at the incredible reversal of fortune. One minute she discovers evidence which proves her theory, another puzzle solution to make her a star in the Air Force's Office of Special Investigations. The next minute she's tied up, kidnapped, and almost certainly doomed to an unmarked desert grave.

First to worst. In ten minutes flat.

Two hours later, Sunny examined the single glow in her otherwise dark enclosure, a thin bright line against the floor. A ray of hope, she thought ironically. The long narrow space must mark the doorway she'd been dragged through. Her gut had sensed an impending grave. That she was still alive gave her a chance.

After the truck ride, Garcia and another man roughly deposited her in this dark room.

Instinct told her to keep her mouth shut. Things could get so much worse.

It had been hot in the back of that Silverado, and the cement floor cooled her. Also, it was smooth and slick. Maybe she could wiggle over to the doorway, look through that space into the next room. Or maybe not. Hard to move with her hands and feet bound.

Part of her wanted to scream in frustration and fear. But she had to stay calm. She concentrated on her breathing to calm her pulse. She considered herself smart and wary, but here she was, stretched out on a hard cement floor, hours and miles away from the train-track crime scene, the Jeep, and any potential rescue.

Garcia had to be one of the autocannon thieves. They must have been watching, as General Hauser had suggested, and she'd wandered into their trap like an unsuspecting mouse. They might torture her for information about the Air Force's search. In the end, they'd have to kill her. Garcia was a fake posse member, sure. Probably a fake license on the truck. But Sunny had seen a real face.

She drew a breath. And another, then wiggled toward the door with the light at the bottom, twisting and shifting her weight, imagining herself a fish squirming across a boat deck. First the right side, then the left. Back and forth, inching herself along the smooth cement.

Inching was no figure of speech. Her progress was snail-like.

Halfway there, maybe ten minutes into the journey, she heard voices. Her thighs, breasts, and shoulder bones burned with the effort. Her neck ached from holding up her head. She lowered her head next to the floor and listened. Men spoke to each other, but their words were unintelligible.

One man's voice carried above the others. Garcia, or the thief who'd *called* himself Garcia. Her molars pinched together as she thought of him. The way he'd tricked her.

She pressed her cheek and squinted through the crack into the barn-like, aluminum-walled space beyond. The cement turned icy as she took in the scene. Four men, twenty or thirty feet away. The view was of old, dirty blue jeans and Garcia's brown trousers, but no faces.

Then she recognized the prize.

Behind the half-circle of men's legs rested the autocannon. She'd seen pictures, but the missing autocannon was twice as big in person. Those seven long barrels were as frightening as the machine's firing specs. Imagine shooting seventy uranium-tipped sticks of dynamite every second.

What were these men planning?

6

Jessie Maris switched television stations at just the wrong time.

Her husband Nolan had warned her to stay in the trailer all day while he and his friends worked on their mysterious, weeklong project in the new aluminum barn, an order that restricted her entertainment to television or a book. And since books had to be read, visualized, and comprehended, while television did all of those things for you—including music to poke the right emotions—Jessie kicked her feet up on the couch and hit the TV remote. She watched a Phoenix shopping station until the jewelry turned artsy and boring.

That's when she changed channels and saw US Congressman Randall King on the news, the bastard standing there in person, his mean red face on the screen with a pretty blond news reporter. First, he complained about the unreasonable cost of health care in Arizona, then acknowledged the reporter's question, King saying, yes, the outgoing Arizona Governor had called him personally, told King he would have the Governor's backing to be the party's next gubernatorial nominee.

Representative sicko, Arizona's next governor? Her heartrate and blood pressure spiked, Jessie recognizing the flush, the throbbing in her arteries. Her hands clenched into fists. That crude, creepy bastard as governor of Arizona? The worst family-court judge in the state gets himself elected mayor, a congressman, and now could become the state's top politician?

Imagine the corruption and vile power he'd have *then* over families and children.

Her eyes watered, blurring her vision.

She pictured King on his bench two decades earlier, the judge sneering down from on high, staring at, but not seeing, most of the people in his courtroom. While ignoring the hurt, hungry, and sick people needing help, he focused his gooey eyes on thirteen-year-old Jessie. He hadn't cared about Jessie's mother's abuse. He hadn't cared about all the testimony, which collectively became an obvious truth. What he cared about was his bribe.

She clicked off the television and wept. She plopped on the old, tattered couch, looked around the trailer she and Nolan lived in, and cried until her shoulders heaved. Her fists wanted to pound and kill that bastard King, but she could only cry.

The judge had crushed her as a child, turned the rest of her life into hell, spoiled any chance she ever had for happiness. That's what her gut told her. King was such a horrible person. He was a monster who should be locked in prison, not running the state.

Didn't she *need* to expose him? Wasn't she obliged to tell the world everything he'd done? Sharp teeth bit her stomach from the inside, like that alien demon in the movies, eating its way out. Jessie couldn't stay silent.

She wiped her wet cheeks and hiked to the nearly barren hill fifty yards north of the trailer, the highest spot on Nolan's desert property, and the only place you could acquire a signal for cell phone service. Nolan normally called his friends on the CB radio in his truck.

From the top of the hill, she called her sister, Angie.

"Hi Jessie."

"Did you see the news?"

"What news?"

"Congressman King. I just saw him on television. He's going

to be the next governor of Arizona."

"Oh, no."

"Oh, *yes*, Angie. You've got to help me *do* something. Sue him. Get the feds to press charges. It has to come out what he did."

She recognized Angie's silence. She'd listened to her sister's disapproval all her life. Jessie was always the bad sister, never doing homework, a smartass in class, smoking cigs and blunts, screwing Tommy in the high school parking lot. The world treated her like a piece of trash because she hadn't cared about or finished high school. She had a lot more fun running off with a twenty-something biker.

"We've been over this so many times," Angie said.

"You're going to let Randall King become governor?"

"Oh, come on, Jessie, you can't be serious. It's been twenty years."

"You know they're still doing that kind of thing. He has to be exposed."

Angie grabbed a loud breath to show Jessie she wasn't happy. Her older sister was always the drama queen. Spent hours before school washing and setting her hair. A freaking Homecoming Princess.

"Remember what happened when we tried to expose Judge King back then—when it happened," Angie said. "Remember that poor lawyer."

"Ah, that punk attorney chickened out."

"I was sixteen and did the best I could, Jessie. My whole savings account to hire that poor man. He didn't chicken out. He wasn't afraid of Randall King when he should have been. You know they killed him."

"Maybe. Or he got scared and ran."

"You know King's people killed him, and you know it could happen to us."

"Not if we had the right help," Jessie said. "Some famous attorney. You know, like that Gloria whatever."

"You need to stop being a victim. Honest to God. It's two decades. Are you still seeing the shrink? I keep getting the bills."

"I am. Yes. She's helping. And you know I appreciate everything you do for me. But we can't let this happen. We can't. You have to help me stop him."

"You're still doing downers?"

Jessie's back teeth pressed together. "Screw you. Drugs have nothing to do with this phone call, my asking for help. You *know* what that man did."

"Yes, and I also know what he could do now, not only to me, but to my husband and family, if I came out in support of your accusations. Maybe he doesn't kill us, maybe he makes a phone call, pulls the unions off my husband's construction projects."

"I need you, Angie. Please? No one will ever believe me if you don't back me up."

"I'll take you to rehab, little sister, a place where you can—"

Jessie hung up and looked for Nolan's stash.

Before she swallowed two 100-milligram reds, Jessie pulled out her yellow, wire-ringed notebook and filled in another entry in her so-called drug diary. That's what the shrink called it, the woman psychologist she'd been seeing. Her job with the diary was to keep track of her drug use—write down the date, the time of day, the drug she was about to use, how much, and what she'd been thinking about or feeling before deciding to use. The first few entries didn't do much, but after looking at a month's worth...wow, talk about an eye-opener. She dropped the reds back in Nolan's bottle.

Her diary's recent entries all talked about her lousy life, how Nolan hurt her, and how depressing everything was in a desert trailer. *Nolan, lousy,* and *depressing* being the most repeated words, which was probably what the shrink wanted the diary to do, focus Jessie on specific reasons for her drug use.

Sickening, really. It made her body physically hurt to keep writing down the same bad feelings on paper every day, looking at them, staring even, Jessie getting more upset and more depressed the more entries she made. It was so easy to see why she kept burying her feelings with chemistry.

Right that second, she wanted to quit drugs and make stopping Congressman King her new focus in life. Her sister and the world were hiding from the truth, so the revelation was up to her. Why not? What did she have to lose, her whole existence these days being crap? Nolan treating her the way he did, Jessie *accepting* his treatment.

She skipped the downers to concentrate on what she'd say if she worked up the courage to ask Nolan for help with King. What words could she use?

Twenty minutes later, Jessie chugged a second can of beer and carried her third outside, against Nolan's orders. She hoped the fresh air and brewski would relax her enough to stop the strange sensations she was experiencing. Her hands trembled non-stop, and a swamp of perspiration drenched her short brown hair. Breathing had become strenuous. A desperate need to escape that stinking trailer had overcome her fear of Nolan.

The news on TV earlier had made her physically sick. That bastard King becoming a congressman six years ago had sent Jessie to bed for a week, but imagining him as Governor turned the trailer's air unclean and confining. She had to shift outside, under the sky. Where the afternoon heaven burned like a blue fire.

Gosh, it was hot. One-nineteen in the shade. She gulped her beer. This one tasted better than the first two, and the Sonora Desert's hot wind at least dried some of the sweat from her skin. She'd worn a T-shirt and cut-off jeans to take advantage, and she breathed easier than before. The trailer reeked of beer, pizza, and dirty clothes. Too bad Nolan didn't have room in his new barn for a full-size washer and dryer.

Male laughter escaped Nolan's self-constructed aluminum box. He'd called the project a workshed when trucks had delivered the unassembled kit last month, a mini-warehouse during construction, then his "barn and private castle" once finished. He'd forbidden her to go inside.

Clearly, her husband and his biker buds were up to something. Except for a couple of food runs, Nolan and friends had been working in there non-stop for over a week. Odd, they wouldn't call takeout. And then today, when Nolan had sent her to town at lunchtime, she'd come home to another black Chevy truck parked on the property. More people, including maybe a hostage or a body, because Jessie had noticed a trail in the dirt from the new truck to the barn. They had dragged someone inside.

What was Nolan doing in there?

She sighed, her curiosity making her want to peek. And she had to tell Nolan about that bastard judge, give her husband the news and ask for his help. She sipped her beer. Nolan and the guys had to be hungry. Maybe she...

The Budweiser must be making her stupid. Sure as the sun rose every day, Nolan would kick her ass if she knocked on that door. Easier, she could call out, get a big delivery of pizza, and some of those chicken salads the pizza place had been pushing on their local TV ads. She could accept the food at the trailer, then walk everything back to the barn. Maybe the sight and smell of food would keep Nolan from beating her.

Worse than risky. Improbable. But Nolan knew something of Jessie's experience with the judge and her mother. She was dying to tell him the news. She *needed* to get these feelings off her chest, not only about King, but her own sister and Angie's denial of support. That's probably what the trembling was about, the sweating. The beer and fresh air had helped, but her skin still sizzled. Something was wrong with her.

If Angie wouldn't help, she needed her husband to back her

up. Nolan had money since his uncle died. He could afford to hire her a top-notch attorney, someone who could help prepare a damning statement, maybe set up a TV press conference. Her revelations about a gubernatorial candidate could send him to prison.

Maybe what she could do, knock and ask Nolan quick what kind of pizza to pick up for dinner, did they want any chicken? Maybe did they need more beer. See if he had time to talk about King. At least she'd get a peek inside.

Do it.

She teared up as soon as she'd knocked. The sound echoed through her, a bell ringing wrong, wrong, wrong. The dumbest idea she'd ever had. Ever, ever, ever. Nolan was going to beat the shit out of her.

The aluminum door snapped open. Behind Nolan's tall frame, three other men worked on attaching some kind of big machine to a flatbed trailer. Nolan had rented one of those four-wheeled BobCats the other day, and now she saw why. Beside the trailer, the forklift helped the men reposition the odd-looking device.

Nolan hopped forward and smashed her shoulders with both hands, open-handed punches which knocked her backward, staggering like a drunk. Her spirits lost balance as well as her body. Physical attack was hatred in its purest, most simple form. How could my mate despise and hurt me? Her soul begged for answer.

She stumbled but didn't fall. Her shoulders and upper arms went numb. The contorted features on his face said he might kill her.

"What are you doing?" Nolan said. "I told you to stay in the trailer."

She pulled farther away, fighting to compose herself. The blows had shocked and frightened her. Adrenaline roared. "I thought you and your friends might be hungry. I was going to drive for pizza, get one or two of the chicken salads they've—"

"Are you crazy?" He followed her, moving outside and closing the door behind him. "Did you see anything now when I opened that door?"

"No. I was looking at you."

He pushed her again. "What didn't you understand about staying in the trailer?"

She lurched backward and burst out crying. Tears paraded on her cheeks, gathering momentum on the way down. Her nose ran, and her skin itched. She hadn't responded like this to abuse since she was a child. As she'd learned from her mother, crying only made the abuser's anger worse. But she couldn't help whatever went on inside her. Not anymore. Her distress was mushrooming. Exploding.

"Something happened." She smothered a sob. "I needed to tell—"

"You're crying? What's the matter with you? You sick?"

She teetered. Her shoulders were tender from his blows and a fiery bubble in her gut pressed against her heart. Her ability to control herself was...disappearing. "Please listen," she said. "That old bastard Judge King is going to be the next Arizona Governor. Oh, I can't even breathe."

"You need to leave me alone," he said. "I asked you nice."

"Please, Nolan. I told you about Randall King, the judge who—"

"Your mother was nuts, Jessie. It wasn't the creepy judge's fault. It wasn't your fault. But you need to leave me alone. Get out of here before I lose my temper."

"I'm going to explode. Please *help* me!"

Nolan stepped into the punch, using his two hundred pounds to drive his fist deep into her stomach, doubling her over, dropping Jessie to her knees on the dirt. The pain in her gut wasn't as bad as the shocking loss of breath. Her lungs didn't work. They wouldn't suck any air.

She toppled onto her ribs and rolled onto her back. She still couldn't breathe.

"Get back in the trailer," Nolan said. "Watch TV or read one of your stupid books. You come back, disturb me again, you'll be at the dentist all winter. You hear me?"

He stared down at her, maybe wondering why she didn't answer. Maybe not. But he finally understood she'd had the wind knocked out of her. He took hold of her cutoffs at the waist, his knuckles pressing into her abdomen. When he lifted, filling her lungs with fresh, delicious air again, she gasped with relief.

Nolan let her fall back to the dirt. "Stay in the trailer."

7

She wasn't sure how long she lay where Nolan had knocked her, curled on the ground, shaking like a dying bug. But at some point, with one of her cheeks flat to the earth, Jessie tasting the dirt, beaten without mercy, her spirit plunged to a new low, falling deeper into the dark hole of wretchedness. Deeper even than on barbiturates two years earlier. Deeper and blacker than the morning, Nolan broke her eye socket, squeezed her arm in the emergency room to make her tell the nurse she'd tripped and fallen.

As ugly as life had gotten with Nolan, and earlier with her mother, she'd never quite hated herself like this before, never thought of herself as *totally* worthless. Even that bastard judge hadn't taken all of her fight, not like this moment, lying by Nolan's shiny new barn, Jessie half-buried already, the taste of the ground on her lips and in her nose. Nolan wasn't a husband. He was an undertaker, preparing her for the grave.

And why not? She'd turned over her life willingly, accepted everything he'd dished out—like she enjoyed being brainwashed and smacked and punched and thrown into walls. After her outrageous childhood, wasn't it natural the man who loved her would also physically abuse her? The shrink said so.

Anger had been part of her nightmares as long as she could remember. So had the sensation of restraint, being held back.

Gripped by her mother's arm. Pressed down during sex. Maybe the two things went together, but she rarely lost her temper or showed any anger, as strong emotion felt like a loss of control.

But today, she was angry at Nolan, pissed at her sister, fed up with the drugs, and ready to personally crush Randall King. Lying on the ground, sore and hurting both inside and out, her self anger turned into a wrath for King and Nolan, and that turned to fury. Smelling the dirt they'd buried her inside. Her painful stomach. The emotional torture each had delivered. It's like they were the same man. When her fury burned to a red-hot rage, she scrambled to her feet, knowing exactly what came next.

Inside the two-room Airstream trailer, she knelt beside their double bed, an action which reminded her of Mama and the prayers her mother demanded of her children every night. The trips to church. Sunday school. But Jessie wasn't on the floor to thank God. She reached under the bed where Nolan kept a lock-box, a cigar-box size steel safe that needed a four-digit code to access. She got the combination right first try.

One nine eight four. The year Nolan was born.

Minutes later, she wound up and tossed a solid steel patio chair through the aluminum barn's biggest window, one of two semi-transparent panels to the left of the entrance. The glass shattered with a cascading crash, the chair, broken shards, and chunks of aluminum window frame creating an explosion of sound.

She hoped the racket inside was worse than outside, disrupting Nolan's party, showing up her SOB husband badly in front of his friends.

She placed herself twenty-five or thirty feet from the aluminum box's entrance. In the back waist of her jeans, she concealed the Beretta .45 caliber semiautomatic pistol she'd taken from Nolan's lock-box. She'd fired it and other weapons hundreds of times in their own backyard and at a Phoenix shooting range.

Nolan used to love guns and so had his father, probably why the old man had purchased this chunk of desert in the middle of nowhere, lived out here until he'd died, all that according to Nolan since she'd never met his father. One thing she knew for sure, the trailer was eight miles from their nearest neighbor.

The barn door burst open, and Nolan ran outside, his face the bright red color of beefsteak tomatoes. He headed straight for her. "I told you what would happen. You crazy bitch. This beating is on you."

Before that moment, Nolan's red face and the anger in his voice would have made her jaw quiver, her knees soft. She would have been too frightened to speak. Nolan had delivered hundreds of punches and kicks over the years. Fading yellow bruises and scars tattooed Jessie's arms and legs, not to mention the new red handprints on both shoulders.

"You're not laying a hand on me, Nolan," she said. "Never again."

Her fear had vanished, and she wasn't sure why. Sorry, Nolan. Could have been the news about King. Could have been Nolan punching her in the stomach, knocking away her air. Could be the semiautomatic. It felt really good against her back and butt.

He shook his head as he moved toward her. "I might kill you this time. You're such a stupid *bitch*."

Or maybe the change wasn't sudden at all. Like a hidden tumor, maybe the transformation, having taken a childhood, marriage, and half a life to develop, only became visible in the final stages.

"You don't have the balls," she said.

Nolan raised his right fist, spat the words at her. "You're crazy."

She slipped the Beretta out smoothly and aimed at his chest, relishing how the deadly gadget extended her reach and inflated her personal power. Instantly she had a God-like choice over this loser, life or death. The Beretta was such a cold, hard, and uncompromising tool of self-protection. Mess with me, it said, I can kill you.

Every girl should have one.

"Try to hit me, Nolan. I'm going to kill you. I've had enough."

"Sure you will."

"You gave me the guts with all the punches, Nolan. They added up. Keep coming, I'll stop you from hurting me like they taught me at the gun class. Remember the training you made me go to?"

He stopped. "Put down that weapon."

"No. Go back inside your dumb barn if you want to live."

"That's my gun, Jessie. I'm not going anywhere."

"I am. I'm packing a bag and calling Uber. Or maybe I'll take your truck. Where's the keys."

He laughed, then charged her.

She squeezed the Beretta's trigger twice in quick succession, both bullets hitting Nolan center mass. As promised, she'd executed a perfect double-tap, exactly like they'd taught her at the firing range two years ago.

When Monday nights were Ladies' Night. And Nolan had insisted she go.

As the two gunshots echoed inside their privately owned Maris Canyon, and the caustic odor of spent gunpowder scratched her nose, her skin buzzed with a crackling, electric hum of energy. She held her shooting stance until he toppled to the ground, everything about her husband loosey-goosey, his long arms and light brown hair flopping and folding like a rag as he fell, everything moving except his eyes, his pupils fixed and lifeless.

In the stillness of that gaze, a new purpose wrapped her shoulders like a comforting arm. A promise—no an oath—she made to herself. Not only would she'd take no more abuse from

Nolan, she'd take no more abuse from any person, ever again.

They'd been married six years, most of the time a torturous melodrama of assault and disrespect. Twice, when he'd injured her enough to visit the hospital—the first trip the busted eye socket, another time a shoulder separation—the nurses had begged Jessie to file a complaint. But Nolan apologized for his brutality, swore the violence wouldn't happen again.

She stared at his dead body. How had she tolerated him so long?

There had been good times, like Nolan making tacos for everybody on Cinco de Mayo, the grin slapped across his face all night while he fried corn tortillas, drank tequila, and sucked on a joint. The man could be funny, the star of the party.

But she was happy he was gone, and she was free. That last punch to the stomach, the way he hit her instead of helping her when her emotions were on fire. She'd needed a husband's comfort and instead he punched her. Somehow, that single episode had severed the connection for her.

A man's voice shouted inside the aluminum box, though Jessie didn't understand his words. She stuffed the Beretta into her waistband again and waited. The new energy, still flowing across her skin, warned her more death was coming, maybe her own.

She slowed her breathing, reminded herself the Beretta held fifteen rounds fully loaded, so the two spent on Nolan meant thirteen left. She tingled inside and out, her thinking slow but measured. She had to be ready. Nolan's friends weren't going to like she killed him.

8

Sound focused Jessie on the barn door and made her hide the Beretta.

Wearing a leather-holstered pistol on his belt, Nolan's friend Sammy hurried outside, but he froze when he saw Nolan's bloody corpse. The Beretta's hollow-point slugs had turned her husband's back into a tray of baked ziti. Heavy on the tomato sauce. Her energy and confidence buzzed like she'd snorted cocaine.

Sammy wore greasy blue jeans and a white T-shirt. No matter how hot the Sonoran Desert sun, Nolan and his friends refused to wear shorts. Only sissies wore shorts.

The gore made his mouth open and his eyes scrunch up. "What happened?"

She showed him the Beretta. She kept the muzzle aimed at the ground, but Sammy's eyes grew extra-wide, anyway. Her pulse hummed like a purring cat.

"You shot Nolan?" he asked.

She nodded. "He was going to punch me again."

He glanced right, then left, like he didn't believe her, wanted to check if anyone else was around. When his gaze came back, his right hand was closer to his holster.

"Why'd you'd throw that chair?"

The new electricity spoke, and Jessie listened. She settled into a stance and used a two-handed grip to aim at the center of his broad chest, show Sammy she knew how to conduct business. By killing Nolan, she'd found something rare and wonderful inside herself, a powerful new ally. Confidence.

He raised his hands. "Don't shoot me, Jessie, please? You know me. I have a wife and kid. My dad's president of Sacred Bones."

She kept the Beretta on him while a second man peeked from Nolan's aluminum barn. The flashy Hispanic guy, Angel, another long-time friend of her husband, and a biker like Sammy. She'd met Angel in the Pintos & Palominos Club in Scottsdale the same night she'd met Nolan. He was a *professional* criminal, always carrying drugs for sale, a large, showy revolver, and a calendar of future court dates. He liked clothes, all clean cut today in a matching brown outfit which looked like a Pinacosta Sheriff Posse uniform.

Same old scam, no doubt.

Figuring Angel might come out shooting, she readied herself, but he fooled her, strolling from the building slowly, hands high in the air, maybe hoping she didn't remember exactly what kind of man he was. He faced her easy and relaxed, a yard or two away from Sammy. Probably thinking he could trick her into letting down her guard, in which case he'd quick-draw that stupid cowboy cannon of his and put holes in her.

He had some kind of trick holster is Nolan told her.

"Hey, Jessie," Angel said. "We all know your husband was an asshole who enjoyed abusing you. Likely deserved to be shot. All the bruises and breaks, surely, what you did was self-defense. There's no need to kill."

"That's straight up," Sammy said. "We don't rat on each other around here. You know that. We're family."

Angel nodded, wise as an owl. "Hell, Jessie, we'll help bury his body."

Both kept their hands up. Angel's words had been delivered as calmly as a preacher's sermon. Sammy, almost as good.

Believable noise for the ear, but to her, both smiles came across as forced. They'd lied many times before. Fear and deception danced behind every one of their friendly words.

Worse, Angel sidestepped to his right, her left, separating himself. If Angel positioned himself far enough away, she couldn't cover both of them. She'd heard cops and a few ex-military types discuss these strategies at the range. There was a word for what Angel was doing.

She hadn't realized she'd been listening at the range so well.

"Hold it right there, Angel. Don't flank me."

Angel stopped two beats, then inched sideways at half-speed, kept his mouth shut, too, trying to pretend he wasn't threatening her. He'd already reached a spot where she'd soon have to slide her aim between the two of them. When that happened, they could draw at the same time and she'd be a goner.

"I said stop," she said. "I mean it. Stop inching sideways or I'll shoot."

Angel kept going. "Who are you going to plug first, me or Sammy?"

She shifted her aim directly onto Angel. That froze him. His hands reached higher, and his eyes grew bigger. His surprise or fear gave her own emotions a boost, but she also sensed what would happen next, saw things play out. In her peripheral vision, she caught Sammy slapping his holster.

The sequence of violence unfolded in a separate reality, a disassociation like an out-of-body experience. She saw herself and her actions from yards away and higher, a close-up on a digital screen, a tiny woman squared off against two men who wanted to kill her. She worked her controls like a video game, pointing the female character's weapon at her enemies.

Even as she yanked the Beretta's front sight back on Sammy, she knew she should have first squeezed the trigger on Angel. She'd already had him in her sights. But his hands were up, he wasn't moving, and she couldn't shoot the guy like that, even knowing the decision might cost her life.

She understood everything, even her mistakes, because of the new electricity inside her. She didn't believe in any religion, humans having a God, although the widespread Native American concept of nature as a great spirit appealed to her. The thing was, she could feel a force helping her. A smart, wicked, and fearless new engine from her center.

Sammy's gun cleared his holster, but she shot him twice in the chest before he could fire. She'd seen his face a hundred times, watched him drink, ride a Harley-Davidson, laugh at some of Nolan's bad jokes. His father was a big shot, too. But she had no regrets. He'd been drawing to shoot her, and instinct had taken over, an internal mechanism and energy source she wished she'd discovered decades ago.

She didn't bother watching Sammy fall. Her life was in danger. She dropped to one knee and swiveled her aim back at Angel, another defensive action she'd seen at the gun range. She guessed her timing was late, though. Likely, she'd be shot. She thought about it in a mechanical sense, not an "oh-dear-me" kind of pity.

The action still a digital game, seen from afar, her own potential death seemed unimportant, not even worth considering. She remembered feeling that way when Mom tied her to the tree and beat her. Like her spirit had to go somewhere else for a while.

Putting her front site on Angel, she saw he already worked his trigger. His giant revolver would fire in the tiniest fraction of a second and maybe kill her, which was too bad as she thought she'd been doing pretty good until then.

That detachment was like judging an Olympic diving contest. An objective classification of the procedures and motions. She felt only a tingle of disappointment she hadn't been ruthless enough when she had the chance.

She should have killed Angel *first*.

Her drop to one knee forced Angel to relocate his aim as he fired, and Jessie managed to squeeze off a round as Angel's first shot hit her. The pain and heat on her left side arrived instantly, like being smacked and pressed on the shoulder with a red-hot poker. She squealed and fell as the fire traveled from shoulder down her back.

Her tumble and her own shot must have spoiled his aim. His second shot missed her entirely. She rolled over ready to shoot, searching for Angel, found him squirming in pain and breathing in loud gasps. His hand rested inches from his long-barreled revolver, but he was down. She'd hit him.

She checked the blood and torn flesh at the top of her left arm. The pain and shock slowed her fingers and senses as she explored what appeared to be a minor wound, more of a gouge than a hole. The energy said it was no problem, check the other guy.

She scrambled to her feet and hurried to stand over Angel's prone figure. Her left arm hung numb-dead. Blood trickled down to her fingers. But when Angel opened his eyes and saw her, he reached for his pistol, forcing her to finish him off, two in the ribs. Her aim was unsteady, but at that range it didn't matter.

She tucked the Beretta in her waist, used her mouth and good arm to rip her blouse, double-wrap a rag around the wound. She tied the two ends to make a bandage. The bleeding slowed sharply, but she'd better find a needle and thread in the trailer, throw on some disinfectant. There was household bleach in the dirty clothes basket.

Wait. She needed to first make sure no more of Nolan's friends hid inside the barn—plus, she was curious. Four men or more had worked two weeks straight on Nolan's secret project inside that aluminum barn. That odd-looking machine she'd glimpsed.

What the hell was it?

She hesitated at the barn door. The sun melted into the desert hills behind her, casting a red glow across the barn's shiny façade. There was time enough to satisfy her curiosity before getting to work. Unless she planned on turning herself in for murder—oh hell no—Jessie needed to get rid of three bodies.

She pushed the door open. There was a place half a mile behind the barn, a dry gully, or *arroyo*, where animals often searched for water and food. If she transported her husband and his two buddies to the *arroyo*, cut them into smaller pieces, birds and animals would scatter their bones over five square miles of Sonoran Desert.

Not a pretty job, but she'd have help. Nolan had a Kawasaki Mule in his barn, plus tarps, axes and shovels. He'd never showed them to her, but she'd seen the bills. They had to be in the barn somewhere. She could roll Nolan and his pals onto a tarp, drag them back to the *arroyo* one at a time if she had to, maybe all at once if that four-wheel Mule had any balls.

If she needed to cut the bodies in pieces, she'd do it after the ride.

She couldn't think of another reason to stay outside the aluminum box. Something about going inside she didn't like, but...

Nolan and his friends had mounted something on a flatbed trailer. Whatever the machine was, the contraption's basic shape reminded her of her father's pipe, one end a large, sideways-mounted bowl, and the other end, a stem of seven barrels banded together into one long, narrow tube. Wires, chords, and feeds looped and surrounded the pipe bowl.

A folding table beside the trailer supported a computer. Jessie touched a key and a picture of the machine popped up. "The General Electric GAU-8 Avenger is a 30 mm hydraulically driven seven-barrel Gatling-type autocannon which is typically mounted in the United States Air Force's Fairchild Republic A-10 Thunderbolt II."

Gatling-type autocannon? She'd seen cowboys with Gatling guns in old movies, machine guns which fired super fast because the bullets came out of multiple barrels spinning, usually some old white-bearded guy with a hand crank.

BEFORE THE RAIN

She clicked on the blue-inked *autocannon*. The *Wikipedia* page read, "An automatic cannon is a fully automatic, rapid-fire projectile weapon that fires armor-piercing or explosive shells, as opposed to the bullet fired by a machine gun."

Explosive shells?

Ray flipped on his rechargeable flashlight. In the high, rocky center of the horseshoe turn, the ground shadows grew long and dark. He checked underneath each rock carefully before flipping it, and the precaution was prescient. Tucked under the third and largest rock he flipped was a black and orange Gila monster.

The lizard's hiss made him leap back awkwardly.

He stumbled and toppled on his butt.

The two Air Force agents searching with him, one of them Peter Walker, broke out laughing, as did Ray. Their guffaws attracted glances from other searchers. A few shouts. Ray knew he must have made quite the sight. Such a big man to be scared of a lizard. Frightened, jumping away, and falling down.

A poisonous reptile, but smaller than Ray's boot.

Once more he laughed out loud at the picture of himself. A toppled giant. He believed in laughter, both as a self-soothing, self-healing therapy for all ills, and as a marvelous form of human communication. Everybody can sense the goodness. Unless humor has been beaten out of you. Etta made sure the Hauser kids watched funny TV shows.

Grinning, he scrambled to his feet. "Looks like I met my match."

The Air Force agents laughed again, Ray's antics maybe breaking some of the tension surrounding Special Agent Hicks' disappearance. It did for him, anyway. They'd been intensely discussing, planning, and hunting for hours. They'd found no evidence yet where she and that truck might be now.

He glanced at the surrounding tracks. Homeland and the Air Force had rounded up maybe thirty searchers, all of them looking for Hicks and evidence. Good people. Wanting to help find the young agent on her first field assignment.

Flashlights popped on like stars.

Ray picked up a stick. "I was half-expecting the darn thing, and it still looked like Godzilla. You two want to help me pull the rock away?"

"The one with the lizard?" Walker said. "Why? You don't need to kill it."

"I'm not going to kill him. I want to see what else is under that rock."

Walker and the other special agent glanced at each other. Ray wondered if they thought he was nuts.

"I thought we were looking for crawler tracks, signs of big equipment," Walker said.

Ray nodded. "Yeah, but this terrain doesn't look so good for equipment. And there's an even better kind of fulcrum for this work."

He slowly poked his stick beneath the rock, into the hole where the lizard had retreated. Instantly, the beast grabbed a hold of the dry wood with its mouth, refusing to let go. Ray pulled him from the hole and gently tossed the wood and lizard to the side. Even then the Gila monster remained attached.

"Guardian of the realm," he said.

Walker and his friend rolled the big rock over. With his foot, Ray kicked at the flat patch of sand, dirt, and pebbles previously covered by the stone. A gust of wind cooled his neck. The temperature must have dropped thirty degrees in a few hours. The Sonoran Desert wore a different mask without the sun.

His toe uncovered steel.

He brushed away the soil and examined the mechanism—two swivel rings made of one-inch steel, a forged, square steel base. The device was bolted in concrete, buried in a circle cut into the rock.

He stared at the steel rings and wondered if this was the place where Alissa had been murdered. Special Agent Hicks hadn't looked for it, but maybe Alissa had. She could have figured everything looking at the semi-circle in the tracks. Even found this fulcrum.

"Looks old," Walker said.

Ray nodded. This particular horseshoe turn in the railroad tracks avoided the tip of disappearing rock deposits. The railroad must have calculated it cheaper to build the extra tracks than to cut through the solid rock. But whatever the railroad saved in construction, it had lost in operation. The gang of thieves who'd killed Alissa and kidnapped Hicks had been stealing railroad cargo here for decades.

He breathed out between his lips and watched the sun disappear. The old, established pivot mechanism ruled out foreign terrorists. Not that the thieves wouldn't sell to anybody, but the bandits had to be a local.

Stealing from trains for decades.

Murdering women for years.

9

Sunny pressed her cheek to the cement. What she saw this time didn't make sense. She'd peeked beneath her prison door earlier, after an explosion of glass, some shouting, and two gunshots. But then seven more gunshots made her roll away from the door, Sunny hoping Navy SEALs or a local police unit had located her.

Optimism was maybe one of her faults.

The cavalry turned out to be a single, five-foot-tall woman in a black bra, cutoff shorts, and a make-shift bandage around her upper arm. Maybe most of the missing blouse. She was alone but walked inside the aluminum barn carrying a semiautomatic pistol aimed down beside her thigh.

Was this the *Jessie* she heard mentioned when the glass broke, her name used in a way like she might have been responsible? One act of violence suggested another.

Hey, she didn't care who freed her. The plastic strips around her ankles and wrists dug painfully into her swelling flesh, and her elbows and knees screamed from hours in their locked position. The kind of torture that worked.

But after glancing at the door hiding her, the woman—call her Jessie, who couldn't have weighed a hundred pounds—strolled straight to the barn's main attraction, the Air Force's stolen autocannon. She acted as if she had no clue what it was.

Sunny needed to think. Jessie looked neither tough nor dangerous, though Sunny had only a distant half-profile of her face, and the thirty-something, frail-looking woman with the short brown hair had to be the winner of whatever gun battle took place. No men walked around. No engines had started up. Nor did Jessie appear worried about anyone sneaking up behind her. Her complete attention focused on a computer beside the cannon.

Instinctively, Sunny wanted to yell for help, take a chance Jessie would free her. But maybe Jessie was part of the gang who'd stolen the autocannon. Maybe she'd killed everybody else to take the biggest share and wouldn't hesitate killing any witnesses.

Maybe she should keep quiet. Her pulse spiked, realizing any decision might be final.

If she kept quiet, she'd probably die of thirst. Maybe no one alive knew she was in the closet. All three of the men must at least be injured, maybe dead, and were all villains, anyway. How would she ever free herself from the plastic strips in time to save herself? Dehydration already stalked her. She'd fall unconscious, probably die in less than seventy-two hours.

She filled her lungs and gave the scream everything she had. "*Help!*"

Under the door, she watched Jessie duck her head as she approached the closet. The woman's sandals clicked on the cement, but her face stayed hidden. Red welts marked both her shoulders, from armpit to bra strap. A third red mark discolored her belly. Someone had physically abused Jessie.

To avoid being bumped or stepped on, Sunny slid away from the door. She held her breath when the footsteps stopped, but the door didn't open. Seemed like a bad development.

"Who needs help?" Jessie asked. The door muffled her voice.

"United States Air Force Special Agent S. Hicks. The man in the brown uniform kidnapped me. I really need water."

"What's the S stand for?"

Unbelievable. "Sunny."

"No kidding?"

"No kidding."

"Are you wearing a blindfold?"

A *seriously* bad development. "Not anymore," she said. "The guy in the brown uniform took off the smelly oil rag when he threw me in here. I need water."

"Why did he kidnap you?"

That sounded better. "I found evidence pertaining to that stolen Air Force weapon, the automatic cannon on that trailer behind you. The man in the uniform was part of the gang who stole it."

"He was watching when you found the evidence?"

"He must have been, yes," she said. "If you shot him, you might get a reward."

Silence.

"Did you shoot the whole gang?" Sunny said.

Silence.

"I'm not a cop," she said. "Remember, I'm Air Force, hunting for that weapon."

"I need to think a minute," Jessie said. "I'll get you some water."

The beat of Jessie's sandals clicking away sent cold arrows into her gut. Not untying her right away felt like major trouble, as did her asking about a blindfold. Jessie may or may not have been involved in the crime, but one thing she knew. Jessie was a killer. Nine gunshots and Jessie wounded only once.

Jessie's footfalls resurfaced a few minutes later. Her pace measured and quick this time, not the hotel-lobby stroll from before. Determined. Busy. The clicking sandals came to a halt inches beyond Sunny's door.

Sunny's pulse picked up. To stay calm, she concentrated on her breathing, in through the nose, out through the lips. A technique Uncle Sal had taught her, Sal a friend of her father.

"First," Jessie said, "before we talk about this water, I need you to promise you won't run, or take off the blindfold I'm going to make you wear. If you do either, I'll have to shoot you like I did my rat bastard husband and his friends."

"You killed four men?"

"Three. Somebody left."

"Why?"

"I don't know. But a motorcycle was gone."

"No," she said. "I mean, why did you kill three men?"

"My husband abused me for six years, and I got scars and broken bones to prove it. The bastard was mad again today, about to punch me. This time I shot him."

"And the other two?"

"His two friends came out of the barn, both carrying. They flanked me and drew on me. I had no choice."

Sunny believed her. "Then all you have to do is call the police."

Jessie scoffed.

She was so thirsty, talking scratched her throat. "You didn't murder anybody. It was self-defense."

"Maybe," Jessie said. "Except I don't think I'm done shooting people."

She kept her mouth shut. Not an easy trick after Jessie asked her to turn her face away from the doorway. She half-figured she'd be shot in the head. But when the closet door opened, Jessie applied a Halloween blindfold or old-fashioned sleep aid to her skull, not a bullet. Rubber bands wrapped her ears and held the mask snugly in place.

She heard the light switch flip on. A stripe of brightness appeared on her cheeks.

"Can you see anything?" Jessie said.

She nodded. "A little light at the bottom edge of the mask. A thin strip."

"That's okay. If you were tied up like this all day, I probably don't have to worry about you getting physical when I untie you, do I? At least right away?"

She shook her head. "Never."

Jessie snickered. "Okay, then. Here we go."

The plastic ties around her ankles came off first. Then her wrists. She rubbed her aching muscles and tried to push up. Pain stopped her, her elbows and knees both crashing as supports. The sensation of freedom was powerful and encouraging, but Jessie had good reason to kill her. She stayed wary.

"Push up onto both knees," Jessie said. "I'll help you stand."

"Can I have that water first?"

"Sure."

She worked up to her fiery knees. The pain traveled the length of her spine when Jessie pushed a plastic container into her hands. Thin, flexible plastic, like a large Dixie cup. She smelled nothing. She sipped, then gulped the freshest, best water she'd ever tasted. She needed only one break for air to empty the cup.

"Are you ready to stand?" Jessie said.

"I'll try."

Jessie gripped her elbows from behind. The water bringing her back to life.

"Let me help," Jessie said.

Her hands and wrists easily pulled Sunny erect. Should she scream for help? She couldn't make out other voices, and nine gunshots hadn't brought a cop or even a neighbor.

Better shut up. No one would hear.

"I need to sit here a minute," she said. "You mind?"

"Maybe a minute. But we have to leave. My husband has other friends who could show up. He liked to brag."

"Can I have more water?"

"Soon as you can walk. The faucet is by the trailer. Ready to try again?"

"What trailer?"

"Never mind. You ready or not?"

"Not really," she said.
"Try anyway."
"Where are we going?"
"Outside to a truck. If you behave yourself, keep the blindfold on, I'll drop you off where you can call for help."
"Sounds good," Sunny said. "But I still think you should call the police. I don't see you've committed any crimes—yet."
"Really? That's what you think?"
"I'm no lawyer, but—"
"Man, that's for sure."
"Holding me, driving me somewhere *is* a big crime, though—kidnapping," she said. "Plus, I told you the weapon was stolen Air Force property. Not reporting stolen items makes you an accessory, maybe receiving stolen property, too."
Jessie grunted. "You and Snoopy with the five-cent advice. Come on, let's get out of this closet. Watch yourself going through the doorway."
She usually had more success at logical persuasion. She'd majored in communications at the academy. Written a lot of Air Force press releases over her two tours of duty. Taken several base commanders to the toolshed for a verbal whipping on media relations.
Jessie's hand guided her forearm, steering her with pressure, or tugging to go forward. "You probably should stop mentioning my serious crimes," Jessie said, "giving me reasons to shoot you. You seem smart otherwise."
Good advice, and the two-minute, staggering hike across the barn floor brought fresher air to Sunny's face. Also, the walk gave her time to worry about her mistake. Jessie *said* she'd drive her somewhere, but would she really leave a witness alive? She'd killed three men. Why not another woman?
She wondered when to make her move. She was determined to try something. She couldn't take the chance Jessie would keep her word. Jessie was tiny, and despite her grip, couldn't be *that* strong. She hadn't practiced her martial arts much, but she

knew how to strike hard, adding power by turning her hip, using her weight.

And she knew debilitating spots to strike.

The only snag might be her muscles. Would they work well enough—say enough to take Jessie's weapon—after spending the day tied up?

"You're moving better," Jessie said. "I'll have to tie you in the truck. I promise I won't hurt you if you go along."

"I promise."

"Okay, we're almost there," Jessie said. "We'll take Nolan's truck."

Shuffling beside her captor, Jessie's hand still on her forearm, she realized her plans were total crap. Martial arts required training and rehearsal, working out with instructors three or more times a week. She no longer practiced.

Plus, no kick or punch was going to stop a bullet.

But despite her fears about disarming Jessie, she decided she didn't have a choice. No matter what Jessie said, or how nice she acted, her intention could easily be to kill her, not drop her off. That meant a surprise move had to come soon.

Before Jessie wrapped Sunny's hands again.

Jessie pulled her outside the barn, a hand on her forearm. Warmer but fresher air caressed her face. Through the slit at the bottom of her blindfold, she watched her sneakers land on reddish, grainy soil.

She lingered at the barn's threshold, deeply inhaling the better air, encouraging Jessie to move ahead. She hoped Jessie would take the lead and reach back for her arm. Jessie's tug would aid in shifting her weight and guiding her kick.

Her heart quickened. She knew what rumbled in her gut. But she stuck by her decision to fight, even wearing the blindfold. By slowing down and stopping in the doorway, she'd forced Jessie to yank on Sunny's right arm.

She gripped Jessie's wrist in return. Then tugged and kick—

What happened in class when you grabbed the target, the

target naturally pulled away trying to free themselves. That's when the aggressor—in this case, Sunny—would throw a strong sidekick into the target's exposed ribs below the armpit, never letting go of the target's arm. Broken ribs were pretty much guaranteed. Incapacitation. And the best part, the blindfold shouldn't matter to the kick because she held Jessie's wrist and knew where to aim.

Unfortunately, Jessie didn't pull away.

Like an instructor demonstrating the perfect defense, Jessie stepped *toward* the tugging, crowding and blocking the launch of Sunny's sidekick. For a split second, she hung awkwardly, off balance with all of her weight on one foot. One knee and leg in the air, all limbs helplessly contained by Jessie's hip and elbow.

That's the moment Jessie shoved her to the dirt.

10

Maybe because Sunny was off balance, the drop felt like two stories. She flapped like a wounded bird, illogically searching the air for a grip. While training taught her how to fall, there was no cushioned mat to land on. She sat down, dropping on her rear end, then spilled hard, smashing her shoulder, disrupting her senses. She figured she would soon die, and the thought produced more anger than fear. Mad at herself for being over-eager, impulsive.

Why hadn't she waited for Walker to show up?

Jessie poked a foot in her ribs to roll her over. In the crack at the bottom of her blindfold, a stripe of stars popped on like welcoming lights to heaven. She wanted to fight back, but couldn't think how. Her breathing was thick and labored.

Jessie stood over her. "You want to die? Really?"

"No, I don't want to die. That's why I tried something desperate. I think you're going to kill me like you did those men."

Jessie grunted. "You're not a man, first thing. My relationships with men got screwed up when my father left."

Sunny snatched a deep breath, hoped Jessie told the truth. Wished she could see the woman's face so she could judge, but the revelation about her father opened a serious opportunity for an ex-communications officer.

"My dad killed himself when I was six," Sunny said. "I

know how you feel."

"Bullshit."

Sunny shook her head. She wasn't lying. "Blew his brains out on my parents' bed with his old Navy Colt .45, let me find him. I can remember the coldness of his skin sometimes when I hold a semiautomatic."

Jessie was silent. "Are we having a girl's moment?"

"Looks like it." Sunny risked a smile.

Jessie shrugged. "My mom was meaner than a rattlesnake, so in a way I understood why Daddy left. She was a beauty queen, then a stage actress for a while. Thought she was God's gift to men. My father had to save himself, I guess, but I wish he'd taken me with him."

"My mom died less than two years after my father," Sunny said. "I've been an orphan almost as long as I can remember."

"Wish my mom had died."

"Really?"

"Definitely. I felt worse than an orphan—more like a beaten dog."

In the following quiet, she had a hunch Jessie remembered something painful. Maybe Sunny could slip in a question.

"What was your husband going to do with the autocannon?" she asked.

"Sell it. A machine which can kill so many so quickly must be worth millions."

"You don't think he wanted to use it on anybody?"

"He's not *that* stupid," Jessie said. "Blowing up stuff would attract some serious attention from law enforcement. I don't see how anybody could expect to use that thing inside the United States and not get caught."

"That's good thinking."

"Maybe if someone felt they had a good enough cause," Jessie said. "People who didn't mind getting caught or even dying."

"Did your husband have a cause?"

"Nope. Money and oral sex were his causes. So how you feeling? Ready for a trip?"

"You're not going to kill me?"

"If I was going to kill you, I would have already done it. Why bring you water?"

Sunny pushed up onto her elbows. Despite the fall, her body ached less. *Every* muscle no longer groaned, only a few. Her pounding head had eased dramatically. How could...

She frowned. "Did you drug my water?"

"A sedative to make you relax. Don't worry."

"You sound like Bill Cosby."

"Plus a pill which makes you forget."

"Forget everything?"

"Well, not everything. Nolan tried to give me the pill one time, thought I'd forget when he raped me. Can you imagine?"

"No."

"He beat me so bad once, I wouldn't sleep with him, so he got pissed, tried to put...oh, forget it. That SOB doesn't matter anymore. What the pill does, you don't forget who you are, or your education and stuff. You only forget what happens for an hour or two after you take the pill."

Sunny still lay in the soil, blindfolded and dumbfounded. "I never heard of such a thing."

"Anesthesiologists use it in case you wake up during an operation. Looks like you're already sleepy, huh?"

"Maybe."

"Like you don't really want to get off that dirt?"

"Maybe."

"Sorry, Sunny Hicks, you gotta get up."

In his Phoenix hotel room that night, Ray's sister Etta checked in on his private phone. He could have ignored the call, but she was probably worried after their talk earlier that day.

"How's that gorgeous smile holding up?" Etta said. "People

being nice?"

She didn't sound worried. "Everybody but an ex-college footballer I had to dismiss from an investigation. The guy bullied a sharp woman under his command."

"Sharp woman? Did you meet her?"

"Oh, stop, Etta. I'll start dating again when I feel like it. I meant sharp in the sense she'd figured out something no one else had for many, many years?"

"How can there still be assholes like her boss in the military? Must cost the country millions in lawsuits."

"Billions. Almost as much as generic Viagra."

Etta's hearty laughter echoed his own, adding to the pleasure of their conversation. For a few minutes, he'd been able to forget about Alissa.

"How's Brianna's doll?"

"Okay so far."

"That arm will come off again if the cat pulls on it. I can only glue it so many times."

"Love you think it's the cat. Not your precious Brianna."

Ray smiled, thinking about his grandniece. "She told you I said she was precious?"

"She made a nametag for her dress."

They laughed again. Maybe why Etta called.

Her throat tickled, coaxing Sunny awake. The touching wasn't inside her mouth, like she had to cough or gag, but feathery touches lingered on the exposed skin at the collar of her T-shirt. Ghostly fingers stroked her neck.

"Want me to get that off, lady?"

She blinked and opened her eyes. The voice belonged to a smiling older man who badly needed a bath, a shave, a toothbrush, and a new jacket. He smelled like the blue and white fungus on old oranges, rotten and antiseptic at the same time. The sky and the man's face loomed above her, grinning, trying hard to look friendly.

Wearing a dirty, D-Backs baseball cap. There was something in his hand.

"I could flick it off your face with my newspaper," he said.

Behind the man's head, white stars still blinked in a fading night sky. She'd been out all night. Sunny lay stretched out on a hard surface. The tickle had shifted to her jaw. An orange-to-red traffic light glared. A green neon LIQUOR sign and a tall gas station marquee called to drivers, all the lights poking her eyes with bright color.

"Get *what* off?" she said.

"Pretty sure it's a tarantula."

An hour later, after enduring an unnecessarily detailed physical inspection, Sunny curled up in a corner chair of the ER waiting room. A sign at the nurse's desk said the medical facility was part of Davis-Monthan Air Force Base in Tucson.

Col. Seager had phoned the facility and spoken to her briefly while the doctor examined her. So had Homeland Security, a newly assigned *fixer*, he'd called himself. A replacement for Seager, Marine Corps Brigadier General Ray Hauser. He spent ten minutes listening to her tale, and with more empathy than her own CO. General Hauser was a nice guy.

"Great work finding the crime scene," Hauser had said. "Out of the box thinking. Glad you're okay."

Col. Seager and Hauser both promised visits this morning, and could arrive at the hospital any minute. Identification of the sedative Jessie had used on her, plus her official medical release, might take longer. She'd been given Tylenol for her bruises, sore joints and minor pains. The spider hadn't bitten her.

But she fought a losing battle rating her own job performance, second-guessing her earlier decisions. Waiting alone in the Air Force medical facility's uncomfortable plastic chair, she fumed at herself for starting her search of that potential crime scene alone. She should have waited.

Her hand balled her into a fist. She hadn't *believed* in herself. She should have *expected* to quickly find proof. *Expected* the tracks there to be a crime scene.

She hadn't planned for success.

Maybe she *did* belong among the OIS analysts, behind a computer and a telephone, reading online news stories, researching crimes and criminals and making up theories to solve oddities. Taking her turn with the coffee-room supply checks, updating delivery orders. Putting notes on the staff refrigerator about eating other people's lunches.

Yesterday's mistake could and should have cost Sunny her life.

Ray waited for Seager near the medical facility's main entrance, the morning pleasant compared to how hot yesterday had been. A soft breeze whipped around the corner of the one-story brick building to brush his cheeks. The fresh, moving air was hot, but not stifling. He hoped Seager wasn't bringing bad weather.

He didn't need extra hurdles in his search for Alissa's killers.

There seemed reason to worry. Seager had come out to Arizona from Quantico, if not to take a punch at him, then something just for fun. Ray didn't want him around, and earlier had sent formal notification Seager was off the investigation. Seager pretended it was too late to change his flight plans. Said he was coming to see Sunny.

From their previous conversation, he was pretty sure Seager was a complete, lifelong Adam Henry. Therefore, he had a hunch Seager wanted to be fired in person. Maybe start a fight. Sounded silly in the military, and of course it was extremely rare among officers. But with his job, he'd seen plenty of physical resistance.

Every other car arriving at the hospital contained at least one Air Force officer, but because Seager had already identified himself as a big-time college football player, the former defensive lineman was easy to spot climbing out of his BMW. He was as big as Ray, but thicker around the gut. He had an Air Force captain beside him. Maybe a friendly witness.

Seager saluted with a sneer. "Aren't you going to call me asswipe? Say it to my face?"

Ray grimaced. His gut was already sour on the guy, thanks to Seager's treatment of Air Force Special Agent Sunny Hicks. Endangering her life. Not better supervising her first assignment. The F-ing Romeo. Lucky the thieves hadn't made Hicks disappear like Alissa. Seager was a jerk. Nothing close to a gentleman.

He made himself loose and ready. "I wasn't *planning* on calling you asswipe, but why not? Asswipe."

Seager's right hand shot out to slam Ray's shoulder, the open-palm thrust a juicy target for a practicing martial artist. Standard exercise, so Ray's responses were reflex and instinct, ingrained in muscle memory. Seager's attempted shove was still two inches short of making contact when Ray snatched Seager's attacking wrist and forearm, used the momentum to spin him and force Seager's arm behind his back.

A rear wrist lock. Bada bing, bada boom.

Seager's pal retreated a step. Lips grim, Ray guessed he'd made up his mind to remain an observer.

Ray sighed. "Assault? Bill, please. What kind of response is that to being removed from an investigation? Ask yourself, how does this look on your employment record, ace?"

"Go f—"

Ray bent his wrist hard. "What you did to Special Agent Hicks was maybe the worst conduct by a commanding officer I've run across. Her first field assignment, and you let her almost get killed."

"I didn't—"

Ray goosed the pressure. Talked to the back of his neck. "Shut up. Say another word, I will arrest you for assault on a

Homeland Security agent. Take you to the nearest Federal Detention Facility."

"You're going to need help," Seager said. "Even with handcuffs."

He couldn't believe Seager said that. The man bringing himself additional pain and embarrassment. But true Adam Henrys were special guys. They didn't understand much of anything, this one having no clue women hated taking crap as much as men did, especially from a boss. Someone you thought was a friend. No human of any gender likes being pressured into action or choice. Women and men and every variation want to make their own picks, free of intimidation.

It was his sister Etta who taught Ray to be a gentleman at thirteen, before his first dance. She made him sit down and listen and repeat her rules. Don't offer to shake a woman's hand. Let her offer her hand to you. If seated, stand when a woman walks in the room. Introduce yourself, and say, yes, ma'am, yes sir, to parents and all adults. Thank your friend and her mother for inviting you into their home. Threat all living things with respect. As you would like all living things to treat you.

He understood every man couldn't be a gentleman. Most men didn't know the rules or didn't care, had no interest. They equated the word with sissy. Plus, there had always been men who believed women wanted to be aggressively pursued and directed. These guys were asswipes, one stage below Adam Henrys. The red line was making the disagreement physical. Take a swing at Ray or try to shove him like Seager did, that made you an Adam Henry.

A loser deserving of being twisted into a knot and arrested.

Delivered to the local federal authorities.

He had to be a hardass sometimes. A bully imposing his personal rules on others. But he was good at his job for the opposite trait—being friendly and gently guiding men and women to make the right decision. He was a large, intimidating man. Sure. With a big title, US Marine Corps general. But he knew being a gentleman usually won the battle, often before a conflict started. Not so much with Adam Henrys, maybe. He'd given Colonel Seager the chance to shut up and step back, even after the loser had taken a swipe at him. But no, this non-gentleman with violent tendencies, abuser of his authority over women, still wanted more.

Ray bent Seager's wrist harder, made him squeak, kept him on his toes as they fast-walked down the sidewalk. "You have a tiny dick, a small brain, and a big mouth," Ray said.

He hustled Seager fifty, sixty feet to where Ray's black Suburban sat parked. A young man and woman, both with long, black hair, stopped to watch the two men struggling.

Seager's witness, the Air Force captain, followed at a fast walk. Ray bet Seager would pick a better wingman next time he started a fight. What a jerk.

Ray clicked a button on his key ring and the Suburban's back door popped open. Using his hands and a knee in the nuts, he forced Seager's head through the opening, showed him a close-up of the back-seat, one-man jail.

Ray Hauser's Steel-Tube Ride for the Ungentlemanly.

"I've only used this lockdown seat twice," he said, "but it usually makes a serious impression." He hiked the pain in Seager's wrist, elbow, and shoulder. "Or does it?"

"I'm impressed. I'm impressed. Let me go. I'm gone without another word."

Ray eased up. "Stay out of sight. You can see Sunny when I leave. And she'd better tell me later you apologized."

"For what?"

"Everything."

Sunny looked up from a *People Magazine* when General Hauser walked into the waiting room. The general was as big as Colonel Seager, tanner, and better muscled, especially his

Popeye-like forearms and wrists.

She saluted. He returned the gesture, then asked familiar questions rapid fire, prodding her into rehashing the story, start to finish in less than five minutes. She expanded her information from their earlier phone call, but this time she finished with an apology. "Sorry I didn't wait long enough for my partner. I never imagined I'd find evidence so quickly."

General Hauser offered her a fist-bump. "You discovered an extremely important crime scene, special agent. Your imagination and determination have finally put us on the trail of the thieves. You're a hero."

She touched his fist with her own. "That's nice of you to say, sir. But I feel bad I almost got myself killed. Over-eager beaver."

Hauser shook his head. "Every investigator walks into bad situations alone sometimes. It happens. Luckily, the guys who took you ran into somebody even tougher, somebody who didn't want or need to kill you to cover their crimes."

"Jessie. What a woman."

"For sure. How good a look did you get at the autocannon? Could you tell how far along they were with installing the cannon on a trailer?"

"They'd mounted the cannon, hydraulic motors, and the ammunition drum, set the weight off-center, too, like in a Warthog aircraft. So the torque won't flip the plane over."

"You know a lot about these autocannons?"

"I read about them two nights straight and there isn't that much to read."

They laughed together.

"Sounds like they plan on using it," Hauser said.

She shrugged. "Or they've been making it more attractive to sell."

"If she killed or shot three men," Hauser said, "do you think this women Jessie had military or law enforcement experience?"

She wasn't so sure. "She used the term *flank*, said that's why she knew her husband's two friends were going to kill her. They flanked her. But she didn't come across as the military type to me. Undisciplined. A pill popper, I think."

Hauser's cell phone beeped.

"I have an idea," Sunny said.

Hauser pulled his phone and stared at the screen. "My boss. The CIA identified overseas chatter about an American weapon arriving into *yad Allah*, the hands of God."

She decided to rephrase. "General Hauser, sir. I know how to find that aluminum barn."

He cocked his massive head. The one-star general was as big as the hulk, only he was tan, not green. At least six-foot-seven. And thick. "Tell me, please," he said.

"That aluminum building was brand new. The bolts and nuts were shiny, almost polished."

"That's a good lead," he said. "We can contact manufacturers. Distributors."

"I was thinking of something faster. You're with Homeland. Do our spy agencies keep old satellite photos?"

11

A faded red car drove onto the Maris property, Jessie watching from the trailer as the unfamiliar sedan rolled tire marks across her newly raked dirt near the barn. She'd been packing clothes, personal items, equipment, deeds, wills, and other important papers in cardboard boxes, getting ready to bug out, but she quit all that when she heard the car approach. Gripping her holstered Beretta, she walked outside.

In her mind, Jessie had already assumed sole ownership of the property's new aluminum barn, Nolan's Ford truck, the five-year-old Airstream trailer, and the near-eternal two-hundred acres of surrounding Sonoran Desert, not to mention the forty-five caliber weapon she wore, the semiautomatic in front, directly over her belt buckle and the zipper of her cut-off jeans.

The sun looked brighter today, a shine which worked on her insides as well as her skin. Not since she was a young child had the Arizona daylight embraced her with such warmth, or had the pale blue sky cheered her soul. Today, as she had thirty years ago, Jessie loved the desert. Her first morning without Nolan felt like the best day of her life.

She'd never seen the sputtering old Dodge before, but she recognized the driver when he ducked out into the sunshine. She shaded her eyes to confirm the features of Hamza's young mug.

The Pakistani man worked at a convenience store in Gila Bend, where Jessie and Nolan bought gas, beer, candy, and cigarettes for their weekend binges. Hamza Yusin, who did not like being called Ham, also sold potent Afghani hash, and ranked as only one of two people in all of Arizona who could make Nolan laugh out loud.

She wondered why he didn't tune his car.

"Greetings, Mrs. Maris," Hamza said. "I was hoping to see my friend Nolan on this beautiful August day."

She stuffed her hands in her pockets. She liked the Pakistani, too, maybe because he always called her Mrs. Maris and looked directly in her eyes. "Hi, Hamza. Nolan and Angel and Sammy took off for Colorado last night. They said they were going hunting, but I think the trip was more about pot seeds."

"Hunting? That surprises me. Did Nolan say how long he would be gone?"

"A few days, I think, maybe a week."

"Oh, my. Hunting marijuana seeds?"

"I don't know for sure. They took Angel's Ford 150 with the extended cab and lots of rifles. Maybe they were going to rip off some pot dealers. Or shoot Bambi. Those guys, you never can tell."

"This strikes me as extremely unusual," Hamza said. "Nolan and I spoke yesterday. We made plans to meet today. He said he and his friends had recently acquired equipment I might want to buy."

She studied the Pakistani with new respect. "Really? You must mean that big machine in the barn. How much were you going to pay?"

Hamza smiled. His incisors bent in separate directions and one was broken, but the crooked grin added to his likeability. He was such a humble man, devoid of the macho, controlling crap so many of Nolan's friends dumped on her. She liked his clothes, too, Hamza always in bright, primary colors. Today, his loose-fitting shirt was solid, bright blue, and his Bermuda shorts were canary yellow.

"We had not agreed on a price," he said. "Your husband said I should first look at the machine, and then talk."

She thought a minute. She'd cleaned up the property last night, working until sunrise to shift the bodies way back in the arroyo. She'd transported the bloodied soil and Angel's truck there, too. Their DNA remained inside the barn, sure, but that proved only Nolan's friends had visited. No obvious trace of murder and mayhem where the shootings had occurred, and she hoped no blood or DNA could be found within a square mile.

In other words, she saw no reason not to take Hamza inside, observe his reaction, and hear out his offer. She hadn't considered selling, but Jessie knew her big idea for using the cannon was slightly outrageous. Maybe taking cash would be smarter. She could do a cost/benefit analysis, see if donating Hamza's money to a woman's shelter would do more good than what she'd been thinking about.

"So you collect—what?" she said. "Automatic cannons?"

He stared at her. Maybe he was surprised she knew exactly what was being offered. He took three or four beats to make up his mind what to say. The guy had a lot of wheels and levers working up there.

"In a manner, yes," he said. "I have a customer and friend who acquires antique and used American weapons of war. In the past, I have earned a profit by buying and selling such things to him."

She stared with skepticism. Total horse manure. Somebody wanted a cannon to mount on their wall? Part of their cannon collection? As nice as Hamza seemed, as humble as he acted, maybe he was a terrorist.

"Do you want to see the cannon?" she asked.

He blinked. "Yes."

She hooked her left arm through his elbow and escorted him to the barn, her right thumb tucked in her waist, fingers touching the Beretta. She understood danger existed in showing the autocannon to Hamza, but wasn't worried while she carried.

Compared to most amateurs, she'd turned out to be quite the gunfighter. Not proud of herself exactly, but aware she'd been calm and precise under fire. Probably because she didn't give a rat's ass. Apparently, that meant a lot when firing deadly weapons—and being fired *at*.

Inside the shiny barn, she flicked on the lights. The thirtyish Pakistani froze when he glimpsed the autocannon. In addition to the odor of gasoline, grease, and gun oil, she faintly tasted spent gunpowder in the air. Remnants of yesterday's battle must have drifted and stayed inside and lingered. She wondered if Hamza noticed.

Or was the smell in her imagination?

"Oh, my," he said.

For a second, she wondered if he meant the odor. But, no. He was practically drooling, his eyes and lips glossy over the autocannon. She told herself to stay calm and walked closer alongside him. "Big sucker, isn't it?"

Guns and rifles fired bullets, Jessie had learned the night before, while cannons fired explosive shells. She pointed at two different types of unused cannon shells in their casings, which had been set out on the trailer's edge.

"Look at the rounds it fires." She used both hands to lift and offer the larger round to Hamza. "Over eleven inches long, weighs a pound and a half, despite the casing made of aluminum."

He hesitated, reluctant to hold the unspent shell. She imagined tossing it to him. She'd woken up that morning in such a strange mood, almost content—her new life loose and easy without a mean husband.

"No, thank you," he said.

She no longer had so many worries. Nolan wouldn't hit her today, and she had a decent idea of what she wanted to occur in her limited future, where a good plan could take her, what kind of newsworthy trouble she wanted to get in.

She didn't want his money. "So, what's the deal, Hamza? How much do you want to pay?"

"Nolan said I should speak about these matters only with him. He also agreed we would talk today. I cannot understand why your husband would go hunting just now."

"Nolan told me before he left two or three potential buyers might stop by today. He told me to set up an auction, get the best price I could by tomorrow night. You're supposed to give me an opening offer."

He shook his head. "Oh, Mrs. Maris, this strikes me as extremely unusual."

"Why? Valuable items are often sold at auction."

The Pakistani walked to her left, examining the autocannon from a different angle. Nineteen and a half feet long with the ammunition drum attached, it barely fit on the twenty-five-foot flatbed trailer. She wondered what the cannon sounded like with its belts all humming, those long barrels spinning, firing seventy shells per second. Throwing bombs like a firehose sprays water.

Hard to miss your target with an Avenger automatic cannon.

On the opposite side of the trailer, he strolled behind the big ammunition drum. She listened to his footsteps and voice, but for a moment couldn't see him. "Nolan did not mention he planned to hold an auction, and I am sure that, as a friend, he would have mentioned this."

She touched her Beretta. "I'm sure you're not calling me a liar. Nolan probably made a last-minute decision."

He came back into view, hands hanging at his sides as before, circling the cannon, pausing at the trailer's coupling apparatus, and again beside each of the trailer's front tires. She was ready if he tried something.

His travels finished beside her again, a circle completed around the autocannon. He spoke softly, looking carefully. "There is a cheap suitcase within the trunk of my car, and in this container, I have one-hundred thousand dollars in cash—the highest price I could have negotiated with your absent husband."

He checked her face for reaction. She tried to give him none, but greed wasn't easy to hide. She had access to all of Nolan's monthly income, which was plenty to live on, but one hundred thousand was a lot of cash. Especially since she was taking off.

She nodded. "That's a good bid."

"Nolan is not here," he said, "and the smell of gunpowder hints of recent trouble. Because of this, I will give you the money now in exchange for the equipment later, when I return with a truck and men to help me."

"I can't do that, Hamza. I *promised* Nolan to sell the cannon through auction."

He smiled at her. "One hundred thousand dollars is a fair price, Mrs. Maris. Nolan will believe you are the world's greatest auctioneer."

"Hamza, I promised. If Nolan finds out I jumped at the first offer, he'd slice me up and toss my parts on the barbeque."

"Did you shoot him, Mrs. Maris?"

She frowned. "Of course not. He went hunting. Why would you say that?"

"Nolan told me that we would make a deal today, but he is not here."

"He'll be back. But I'm selling the autocannon tomorrow night at eight o'clock to the highest bidder, like I told him I would. Your one-hundred-thousand opening offer is duly noted. Come back tomorrow, see if that's high enough."

He shook his head. "This is, for me, a monumentally unhappy occurrence, Mrs. Maris. Extremely."

"I'm sorry, Hamza. But I don't know how I can make you happy until tomorrow."

"Please accept my money now. Accept my payment as your husband has agreed. Acknowledge we have a deal."

"My husband agreed to nothing. You said yourself the price

was still to be negotiated. I'm only asking you to wait one day."

He left shaking his head.

Jessie completed her errands that evening, including packing her clothes and equipment, purchasing and installing a GPS device on the cannon, all the while pretending she hadn't yet made up her mind about the cannon. Pretending she might take the cash. She sat down and popped a can of Budweiser.

Day two without Seconal.

To pull off the stunt she'd been imagining for more than twenty-four hours—couldn't get out of her mind, actually—she'd need help. Only two or three possibilities existed, and the one guy she'd need for sure was an ex-friend of hers—and Nolan's—named Tommy Moon. To earn Tommy's cooperation, she might have to hide her purpose, and she'd definitely have to sleep with him.

Not the worst situation, and besides, she'd made up her mind. She was determined to put a rain of hell on that SOB Congressman King, send him back to Satan. Sure, there were excuses if she wanted to chicken out. Anything as big as a cannon was difficult to hide, and even harder to move around. To install such a large and actively sought stolen government weapon in the right place at the right time would be nearly impossible.

She chugged half the beer. One government agent already had seen the weapon in her barn. No doubt the whole Sonora Desert would be crawling with cops by tomorrow or the next day. But taking the cannon for herself, ridding the world of a terrible, disgusting man, making a forceful statement about the abuse of women worldwide, well...that was too worthy an idea to ignore. Imagining success made her body purr.

The task would require many skills she didn't have, though, a kind of critical planning she'd never done. She'd need tons of information about the congressman and his schedule.

She drank a second beer while reading an article online about moving with stealth, then shut the computer off with a loud exhale. Silly to think reading could make you a ninja, which was what she figured keeping her cannon and destroying Randall King would take. But what else was she going to do with her life now she'd killed her husband and two of his friends, chopped up their bodies and buried them?

The Feds would be coming for her soon. And before them, maybe Hamza. Maybe tonight. Funny how that was kind of exciting, too.

Later, as the sun disappeared, she half-filled a black plastic garbage bag with two boxes of forty-five caliber ammo, a noise-suppressor for the Beretta, one box of squirrel-shot cartridges for the pump-action shotgun she'd found in the new barn, four, double-bar Snickers, three bottles of water, and a thermos of black coffee.

She wasn't sure what to expect that night, but the uncertainly wasn't unpleasant. She'd tried to prepare for anything—from campout to shootout to bugout—and the kick it gave her was undeniable. Being a little frightened had its rewards. Plus, waiting outside for hours, maybe all night if Hamza didn't show, her stuff packed and ready to split in her Ford 350 pickup, she'd have time to plan the assassination.

She wasn't selling that cannon, or letting Hamza steal it, either. That hissing dragon—she'd watched a YouTube training film over a dozen times—belonged to her.

She hauled the plastic bag, the scattergun, and a jacket for later when the temperature dropped forty degrees, carrying everything up the three-story hill south of the barn. Besides offering superior elevation and an excellent view, a five-foot-tall creosote bush grew near the top, a thick and natural cover where Jessie could monitor the trailer, yard, and barn.

When she replayed in her mind the way Hamza carefully

checked out the cannon, especially how closely he'd examined the trailer hitch and the condition of all four trailer tires, she decided the Pakistani might be back that night with a gang and a truck, like he said, only with no intention of paying her one cent.

He didn't act macho, but she saw a greedy man inside Hamza. Greedy, ruthless even in the search for money. Violent. She figured he'd probably kill her, or *try to*, that is.

She gazed at the stars, sharp and bright in Arizona's desert sky. Could she carry out the terrible deed she imagined? The autocannon was so powerful, innocent people could die. She glanced from the stars to the Beretta. Maybe the innocents were like Jessie. Expendable. The new electricity came for important but costly reasons. An example the world needed to re-focus on the eternal and deadly abuse of women.

12

Before midnight, Hamza's Dodge returned to the Maris's canyon property with its headlights off, a dark sedan on a lonely desert road. Even from her hiding spot on the hill, Jessie recognized the car's mis-tuned, sputtering engine.

The Pakistani pulled over on the paved, two-lane highway instead of turning into her parking area beside the trailer, a level spot Nolan had created with soil from digging the barn's foundation. Jessie had been right about Hamza. If he couldn't buy the cannon, he'd take it.

Three, dark-dressed men exited the Dodge. Moonlight, clear skies, and the high panorama gave her an excellent view of the intruders. They spread out as they crossed the blacktopped county road, all carrying long guns. On the far right, the last man headed directly toward her hill, south of the barn.

She hugged the creosote. Its pungent odor stung her nose and added to her excitement, but she had to stifle a sneeze. During the squelch, masking the noise, she lost sight of the man headed her way. But footfalls soon scuffed rocks near the bottom of the hill, close to where she'd begun her own climb.

She aimed the Beretta where the sound came from but kept her forefinger on the trigger guard. If she fired and gave away her position, even killing this first man would not be enough to save her life. She might have handled Nolan, Angel, and

Sammy, but this team looked different and likely carried fully automatic weapons.

Perspiration beaded her neck and gathered into droplets which rolled between her breasts. She slowed her breathing. Tasting fear, she realized the old Jessie still existed. Nolan's punching bag had shrunk in size but remained a part of her.

But if she closed her eyes and fully focused on the Beretta in her grip, she could feel the new power or electricity running through her, even experience pleasure at the prospect of a gunfight. She'd been reluctant to admit it so far, but killing Nolan and his two friends had been the most exhilarating thing she'd ever been done.

The electricity also fought her fear by reminding Jessie she had nothing to lose. Like the tubercular Doc Holliday at the OK Corral, the law was coming for her. The presence of the cannon made this a fact, not a possibility.

In her excitement, or fear, she'd forgotten to attach Nolan's noise suppressor. She slipped the legally purchased equipment—a form to fill out, then a wait—from the garbage bag and screwed it on the barrel of her Beretta. She checked the magazine and chambered a round. She'd been taught to keep the safety off, always, but she confirmed that, too.

The Beretta was ready to fire. She was more than ready. She was psyched.

She waited twenty minutes for someone to walk up the hill. Nobody came.

Instead, voices eventually drifted up from the yard. She peeked from behind the creosote bush, saw Hamza and his two men regroup near her Airstream. One guy who wasn't Hamza slipped inside.

He quickly found the light switches. Instantly the trailer and surrounding yard glowed, the curved Airstream door hanging wide open. Nolan's fancy outdoor sunlamp illuminated half the parking area. You could read a book.

All three men wore black clothes and wool caps, Hamza's face the only one she recognized. No happy blue shirt tonight. They each carried an AK-47 assault rifle, a Russian model with a down-folding, metal butt-stock. She recognized the fully automatic rifle from the time she'd fired one at the gun range.

The Lady's Night graduation party.

She sipped water from her bottle. Assault weapons and black clothes meant these men qualified as serious professionals, maybe soldiers in a terrorist organization, Hamza their Mr. Nice Guy public contact. Or maybe Hamza and these two accomplices were CIA operatives, US government killers getting their weapon back, using AK-47s to mask their identity.

Either way, confrontation was out. Not caring too much whether she lived or died was an advantage, for sure, but she couldn't win a shootout with three better-armed professionals. Her death now would accomplish nothing.

She smiled. Maybe she wasn't crazy. Despite the new energy or electricity or power, whatever it was, the thing telling her she was Superwoman, she still had a little common sense.

That didn't mean Arizona could afford Randall King as Governor, or that women everywhere didn't need to hear what the bastard had done. Something her plan would guarantee. She'd have to follow Hamza and his men, take back the trailer carrying that cannon later.

Her cannon.

Another vehicle—a heavy-duty, six-wheel, Ford 350 pickup like Jessie's—drove onto the Maris property, the driver backing his truck close to the barn's garage door. The wide and tall opening lifted bottom to top, twenty-five feet from the regular doorway.

The place she'd gunned down Nolan.

All four men disappeared inside the barn for fifteen minutes, then showed up again, pushing the trailer-mounted cannon outside. The weapon had been camouflaged with neatly stacked cardboard boxes and two over-stretched tarpaulins expertly disguising the load. The trailer looked to be stocked with square containers of goods.

That answered one question. If Hamza could disguise and transport the weapon, she could, too. She watched carefully as they hooked up the Ford 350 to the cannon's trailer, the ball hitch easy to work. A heavy duty, seven-prong electric cable came next, and finally the safety chain.

She waited five minutes after Hamza left, in case he'd forgotten something, then dragged her plastic bag of ammo and trash—she'd munched both Snickers—down the hill to her Airstream. One more job, and she was ready to leave this rathole forever.

Her plan was to take back the cannon early this morning while Hamza and his men slept, then give the job of blowing up Randall King everything she had—one grand deed she *knew* would make a positive difference. What she imagined, destroying King would make her like Jonas Salk, the man who invented a vaccine which rid children of polio. King was another children's crippling disease to be exterminated.

Inside the Airstream, she plucked a ballpoint pen and her paper notebook from a kitchen drawer, put herself in a chair at the round wooden table to write a note to S. Hicks, the Special Agent she'd met the day before. Her first letter of several, she figured. She'd retrieved the agent's name from Hicks' purse.

The feds would find her words in a day or two when they came back looking for that cannon, maybe even Hicks herself. The two of them had quite a conversation the other day, weird really. But Jessie kind of liked her.

When she finished the note, she hiked three-quarters of a mile to where she'd hidden her 350 pickup. She re-connected the truck's CB radio and scanner, then set-up to the GPS device, letting her monitor the low-frequency transmitter she'd stashed beneath the stolen cannon's ammunition drum.

She started the engine and checked the monitor, everything

working perfectly, the cannon's transmitter showing up like emergency lights on her dashboard. Originally, she'd tagged the trailer, but later decided if they changed transportation methods, she'd be screwed.

The cannon was the treasure to keep track of, not the flatbed. She put the transmission in DRIVE and took off after her prize.

The eastern horizon paled on a gauzy line, stirring Jessie with the second day of her brand new life. She'd parked directly behind the bankrupt auto shop where Hamza and his celebrating men switched off the lights an hour earlier.

The dash clock read 5:30. She'd waited long enough.

She opened the truck door and slipped outside with a grin on her face. Her pulse was slow and steady, the electricity circulating inside with a strong and exhilarating sense of purpose. Totally calm. She'd never done anything like this before, anything this important. Or as risky, single-handedly going after the cannon against at least three professionals.

But taking back her autocannon to assassinate a despicable ex-judge and Congressman was a worthy cause, justification which gave her courage. Although wouldn't it be nice if she caught Hamza and his pals fast asleep.

The thieves had taken the autocannon into Gila Bend on a back road, arriving minutes after 4 o'clock a.m. in a ramshackle part of the city. Each building on the north side of the street stood adjacent to the Southern Pacific main railroad tracks, including the old auto shop and junkyard where they'd taken her autocannon. Two weed-cluttered used car lots occupied the wide street's south side.

She advanced slowly along the junkyard's perimeter. Her senses had never been more alive. She was tense, on edge, but having fun, too. A stalker.

She'd followed Hamza from eight miles behind, watching her

cannon's progress on the truck's radio-controlled GPS. When Gila Bend's cell towers came back into range, she'd switched from the truck's GPS to her iPhone so she could reference Google Maps, see Hamza had picked a closed auto and truck repair business as their hideout.

She circled the block, clinging to the border fence. Her steps were steady and quiet, her breathing the same. At the front entrance, a chain-link fence on wheels blocked cars and trucks from going inside, but the space between the rolling section and the solid post had been sloppily chained.

She squeezed her head through. No cameras, no dogs, no sentry, as far as she could see, about as bad a security set-up as she could have hoped for. Just three or four men with AK-47s, hiding somewhere close. But sleepy men, tired men who'd had their adrenal glands pumping much of the night. The grounds offered no light but the stars overhead.

She slipped through the gate like a caterpillar, her passage taking four full minutes. Patience and care were the only skills required, not ninja training, the book said. She listened for an alarm, but heard no change in the silence.

Inside the blacktopped lot, she dropped to her gloved hands and knees and crawled toward a two-story, tin-roofed building at the left rear of the property. The cannon had to be inside. The structure was the only place big enough to conceal a thing so large.

Birds began their dawn chorus in a dim but brightening sky as she found an unlatched bathroom window and slipped inside. The air was cooler. Vague sunlight flooded the space—big as two basketball courts—through high, narrow windows. Only the thieves' Ford 350 and the still-attached trailer with the cannon were parked inside.

A snore tickled her ears. She followed the sound, crawling closer to the dark, opposite corner where two sheet-rock walls jutted out at right angles and connected, making a square in the big room's corner for a small office. The box had a single doorway which hung open.

She crouched in the doorway. Two men slept inside, each on separate right-angled sofas, their backs to Jessie and the big room. She couldn't see the other two men or the AK-47s. The light was dim.

She hesitated. A truck or bus traveled past noisily out front. She smelled donuts. Gila Bend was waking up, and for the first time in a day and half, Jessie experienced hunger, a pang in her empty gut, a cry for a maple-glazed cruller. Weird, but there was a shop...

A toilet flushed within feet of her. She jumped. Her heart raced. Maybe her black Sketchers didn't actually lift off the cement, but her head and shoulders shifted half-a-foot, hard left, an instinctive recoil from the sound. Must be a bathroom next to the office, although no light came from any door crack.

Two beats later, one of the missing men nearly smacked her opening the door, her pulse spiking as she hopped out of the door's reach. She drew her Beretta with the noise suppressor, told herself not to panic over surprises. Focus on control.

The bathroom nightlight silhouetted a short, stocky man. She couldn't see his face, but no matter. The presence of the cannon proved his association with Hamza, evidenced his guilt. She slid into his path, aimed the Beretta at his nose. He pulled back so quickly he lost balance.

"Where are the keys for the truck?" she whispered.

The man shouted, "Ahmed! Wake up."

The door to the square office rested open, Jessie remembered, meaning there was no chance Ahmed and his friend weren't waking up and seconds away from shooting her. Their AK-47s must be close.

She dropped her aim and shot Paul Revere once in his thigh. The *pop* echoed inside the empty garage as she twisted, snapping her Beretta toward the cubicle. Ahmed and his friend wrestled to raise their automatic rifles.

Dawn light entered through a dusty, rectangular window.

She hopped inside the office and pointed her weapon at the closest man's chest. "Raise your hands."

Both Ahmed and his friend froze, then left their automatic rifles on the floor. Slowly, they lifted their hands above the shoulders.

She waved her Beretta like a pointer. "Take off your pants and use your feet to slide the weapons to me."

One shook his head, maybe saying no, or he didn't understand, but the other one complied perfectly, stripping to his bun-huggers and kicking his AK-47 up against her shoes. When she aimed at the man who couldn't understand, he copied his partner.

"Now throw me those keys," she said. She'd recognized the Ford 350 ignition key on a ring of keys on the office desk. She left one just like it on the rear wheel of her Ford 350 before sneaking in here.

She placed their automatic weapons inside their Ford 350, the truck still attached to the cannon trailer. The electric garage door lifted when she pushed a big red button on the wall.

She pretended to hop inside the truck, but stepped back down to catch them running toward her. She fired two shots over their heads, and they scrambled, first getting out of her firing line, then hiding somewhere on the far side of the trailer.

She jumped in and started their truck, chugged out of the building.

When she reached the street and wheeled the cab left, the rear-window glass exploded. Two holes with extending cracks appeared in the truck's windshield, the two bullets maybe missing Jessie's neck or head by twelve-to-fifteen inches.

Hamza's men had other weapons.

She checked the mirror. The two guys looked pretty silly in their tighty whiteys, running barefoot in the street, one of them shooting with a long semi-automatic, the other a pistol. For Jessie, the memory of this night, this best-ever expression of her will and courage, would always be defined by a few crazy sights.

She soaked up the image.

Two men shooting at her in their underwear.

Ducking lower, she stomped the gas pedal. She'd already busted through the loose fence and started her left turn, probably causing someone to miss their shot, but she knew the extra speed posed a real danger turning, especially to trucks towing a heavy load.

Jessie's quick pace forced the cab's left front wheel to lift, making Jessie ease up on the gas, extending the circumference of her turn. To keep the truck and trailer upright, she *had* to, but as a result, the truck crushed two street signs, a mailbox, and a despondent roadside planting when she crossed the far sidewalk. The line of clay flower pots shattered into a thousand pieces.

Her butt bounced off the seat when she nicked two junk cars in the cross-street auto lot. Behind her, the trailer with her cannon rolled and bumped through the hairy turn on two wheels. Inches from disaster. She'd held her breath the whole way.

She'd never had so much fun.

Hamza's men quit shooting when she'd traveled a block, and she turned at the traffic light as if she were headed back to the Maris box canyon and her Airstream, back to the home where she'd lived six years with Nolan.

But she wasn't going home. Any luck, she'd never see that property again. She did need her own Ford 350, however, the one she'd left two blocks away.

Still in Gila Bend where she could use her iPhone, she called Tommy Moon.

"Jessie? This really you?"

"Sure the hell is. How you been, stud?"

"Better now that you called. Where's your old man?"

"Nolan ran off with the waitress at the Chinese joint, calls her his *geisha goombah*."

"What a douchebag."

"Yeah, I'm still in semi-shock, although Nolan always was a numb-nuts."

"I told you," Tommy said. "Listen, you need any help moving, a place to stay a few nights?"

"Maybe. I've been thinking about you, Tommy. I have a moneymaking project for us."

"Really?"

"I'll get to that, but first I need a favor. I had to leave Nolan's truck behind, and it would mean a lot to me if you'd pick it up in Gila Bend. Doesn't have to be right this morning, but the quicker the better."

"The Ford 350?"

"Yeah. I left the key on top of the back right tire."

"Where do you want me to bring it?"

"Got a pencil? I'm going to give you a new phone number, a number no one has but you, okay?"

"Sure, what's the big deal?"

"Oh, Tommy, you won't believe what I'm towing. Wait till you see it. You and I are going to make a fortune, enough to live on a tropical island somewhere. Or Mexico, at least. Anyway, when you have time for Gila Bend, get there and call me on the new phone number and I'll tell you where to meet me. I'm on my way now. We'll have a party when you get there. Like we used to. Remember? Bring the whipped cream."

"You serious?"

"Absolutely. My old man left me for a waitress. Think I'm going to stay home and pine over the son-of-a-bitch? I always liked you, Tommy. You know it's true."

"I am *so* ready," he said. "I'm not working for two days. I'll pack some crap and head into town."

"Can't wait to see you, Tommy. Ready for the number?"

13

On forced rest for the afternoon, Sunny went shopping. The local retail stores didn't provide much choice in jigsaw puzzles, but she found a five-hundred-piece farm and barnyard scene she liked well enough. The animals hid in corners or behind bushes. Goats, lambs, pigs, and a horse. Her interest in puzzles began after her father killed himself. Six years old, she'd spent whole days alone, watched by nannies, and the concentration required by a box of unassembled, odd-shaped picture pieces—total focus for Sunny—produced a better escape than television, books, or even the other kids in San Marino, California.

As she spread out her farm puzzle, her new phone rang. Colonel Seager.

"Pack your bag," he said. His tone matched his words.

"Why? Where am I going?"

"I'm pulling our personnel. No way any of us are working for Hauser."

She glanced at her puzzle. "I liked General Hauser. I don't mind working for him. It is our equipment, so wouldn't it be good for us to keep—"

Seager cursed under his breath, but not softly enough so she couldn't hear.

"You work for me," Seager said. "Pack. We're going back to Quantico tomorrow."

He hung up.

This stolen autocannon case was hers. It was Sunny who figured out the how, used that to figure where. She wasn't leaving the investigation. Her jaws pressed together as she dug out the business card General Hauser had slipped her at the Air Force base medical facility. His private cell was on the back.

"General Hauser, sir, this is Special Agent Sunny Hicks."

"I recognize your voice," he said. "Must be the reason they call you Sunny."

"Sunny's my given name. It's really not that uncommon."

"Maybe in California."

"Well, I don't know—"

"Forget it," Hauser said. "I was ten minutes from calling you. I'm hoping you have *another* brilliant idea."

Sunny rose from her puzzle-working chair. "What I mentioned to you in the hospital worked out? You know, the current versus year-old satellite photos?"

"Worked out doesn't come close. My boss's staff found three new aluminum barn buildings. One seems likely. It's in Maris Canyon."

"Why likely?"

"Nice size plot, way out in nowhere land, owned by a biker with a rap sheet, Nolan Maris. Property's been in the family for generations. The most recent satellite shot caught people, bikes, and multiple trucks milling about."

"Jessie said her husband's name was Nolan. I forgot."

"Really? That's big. Here's another clincher—Nolan Maris has a wife named Jessie with two arrests for drug possession. I'll text you her photo."

"When are you going to check out the Maris place?"

"I'm waiting on a warrant. Probably not until tomorrow. You want to go?"

Her shoulders sank. "My CO expects me back in Quantico tomorrow."

"Sunny, my CO is General Eric Johannsen, Homeland's

Principal Deputy Under Secretary for Intelligence and Analysis. He gives me whatever I need to do my job, in this case, you. If I ask, he'll throw Colonel Seager behind bars until he signs your transfer."

"Sounds great."

"It's as good as done, and please call me Ray. I like you figured out this theft. I like you're still alive after being kidnapped. And you pointed us to the aluminum barn which most likely has or had our cannon inside. For the rest of this investigation, agent, you're my ace investigator."

"Ok, Gen—I mean Ray. If you can arrange it. Please call me Sunny."

"Great. You should be getting Jessie's photo."

She checked the two-year-old mug shot of a thin-faced woman with the same short haircut. She easily could be the woman who'd claimed to have shot those men and let Sunny go. The woman in the photo had nice features, pretty even, but plain and unkempt.

"I can't be a hundred percent," Sunny said, "but I think that's her. Everything fits—especially the hair and her size, the profile."

"All right, maybe your tentative ID—that's what I'm going to call it—will get us the warrant quicker. I'll phone in before we meet for lunch."

"Lunch?"

"I want to seal the deal, get to know each other. If we're lucky, our warrant comes through while we're eating. You like enchiladas?"

Ray found her waiting just inside Lucy's Mexican Restaurant on the Highway 85 cutoff, halfway between Phoenix and Gila Bend. The cooled air soothed his hot neck, the walk from his air-conditioned SUV to the air-conditioned restaurant a long one thanks to a totally full parking lot. The joint was popular and packed, but the hostess found them a booth near a busy, brass-railed bar.

Ray liked Sunny the moment he looked into her eyes at the medical facility. Her intelligence showed in the way she examined him, the way she assessed without judgement or bias. The depth of her awareness. The fact she'd figured out how and where the thieves had taken the cannon, and how to find the barn, well, that said a lot, too. He'd need a partner to help him discover who'd taken his wife and the autocannon. He was almost certain that person was Sunny.

"How long have you been a cop?" he asked.

"I joined the Air Force's Office of Special Investigations four years ago as an information specialist, then an analyst. But my CO wouldn't send me for special agent training until a year ago."

"What about before the Office of Special Investigations?"

"I graduated from the Air Force Academy with a major in communications," Sunny said. "Spent my first tours working as an assistant public spokesperson at two air bases in Europe, then for various Air Force projects and departments back in the states, the latest being Special Investigations in Washington."

"And you liked investigating?"

She nodded. "Even with no law enforcement training, I wanted to become a special agent about two days after I arrived. So many interesting crimes to figure out. I like puzzles. It surprised me how many bad guys there are in the services, how smart they can be at stealing things."

"And Seager kept you out of special agent school?"

"No, that was another CO. Colonel Seager's the one who got me *into* Glynco."

He frowned. "He thought that gave him an excuse to make moves?"

Sunny blushed. "How did you know about that?"

He wanted her to work beside him. But that meant he wanted to know nearly everything about her. "Sorry to probe personal stuff," he said, "but your comments about him inside the Air Force were leaked to Homeland's Human Resources Department, then me. I need to push this off the table."

"Sure."

"You liked him at one time?" he said. "You were friends?"

She blinked. "Before he was my CO, but I found out he had a wife and two kids in Maryland. He didn't wear a wedding ring, claimed they were separated. He's divorced now, but nothing was ever going to happen between us. I've been seeing a newspaper reporter for a while. Although he just moved to Los Angeles."

"I don't like that guy. Seager, I mean."

"Me either. How about you? How long have you been in the military?"

"Since nine-eleven. I joined the Marine Corps out of high school, then applied to Homeland over a decade ago when a friend asked me to join him."

"By friend, you mean Eric Johannsen, Homeland's Principal Deputy Under Secretary for Intelligence and Analysis?"

He stared with new respect. "Touché."

They both laughed, and Ray sensed a good connection. She was smarter than him, maybe. Probably. Either way, he knew an asset when he met one. Special Agent Sunny Hicks would help him locate Alissa's killers and that autocannon.

"You grew up in New Jersey?" she said.

"Yup." He lifted his diet soda. "My dad owned a specialized, antique auto repair business in Red Bank. Had me pounding out dents for him all summer. *Every* summer since I was eleven. Maybe that's another reason I joined the Marines."

"Your father was...a big man, too?"

"My dad was bigger, meaner, and a drunk. If I fought him, he'd take it out on me *and* Mom."

Silence filled the space between them like a fog, the low cloud holding still while the waitress delivered their food and they ate. Ray was finishing his beef enchiladas when he got a text and glanced up. "The search warrant has been signed."

They both pushed back from the table, Ray reaching for his wallet. "I'll follow you back to Gila Bend to drop off your car."

She finally pushed outside her Gila Bend motel. Ray leaned across the front console and yanked the chrome door latch, clicking open the SUV's shotgun seat entrance. He guessed what she'd comment on first.

"Just the two of us?" She'd done a barely perceptible double-take at the holding chair, but her words were not what he'd expected. Maybe she'd seen a backseat jail before.

"We don't need an army," he said. "Latest satellite photos show the property deserted, and our job is reconnaissance. See if you can identify the interior of the aluminum barn."

"If I do, then what?"

He accelerated into modest traffic. "If the place is familiar, or we find other evidence the autocannon has been there, we'll call forensics."

"What if it's the right place, but instead of deserted, we run into Jessie Maris?"

"That's a major score. We bust her. And it means we could also find the cannon."

"What if we find armed terrorists?"

"Same, only we call for a helicopter gunship with a dozen SEALs."

"That sounds better."

Sunny worried too much. After her eager mistake the other day, checking the crime scene by herself, she was overcompensating. He might have said something if he hadn't of been raised by his sisters. They'd taught him to shut the hell up when women voiced concerns and anxieties men thought silly and unnecessary.

***

She tightened her seatbelt. Ray's SUV handled the broken desert road like a bouncing rock. If Sunny held a container of fresh cream, the ride would have made butter. Two lanes of cracked, potholed pavement carried them deep into a remote canyon in the South Maricopa mountains. What she could see of the western sky collected afternoon gold.

"There it is," she said.

Ray braked. The seatbelt strap pressed tightly against her chest.

He eased them into a dirt parking area between an Airstream trailer and a shiny new aluminum barn. Even the cement foundation had been recently poured. This was the building Homeland's staff had spotted on satellite photos. No vehicles. No people.

She hopped out into a steady wind. A tickle traveled her spine. Tailbone to neck, a twisty trail of smoke whispered familiarity.

Ray must have seen. "Smell something?"

"Maybe. Let's go inside the barn."

He reached out to open the aluminum door, but a loud buzz stopped him. He and Sunny turned at the same time. Like a swarm of monster, car-sized hornets, the noise soared in volume as whatever it was approached.

"Is that what I think it is?" he said.

From the road behind the property's silver trailer, the hornets pulsed into view.

"Were you thinking motorcycle gang?" she asked.

14

Led by a man Sunny judged handsome enough to be a Hollywood movie star, five motorcycle riders roared up the Maris' dirt driveway. They idled their Harley and Indian motorbikes around Ray's black Suburban, parading in a ragged circle, showing off their colors and craziness. All the men were barechested underneath traditional sleeveless denim jackets, the jean material open in front, a stitched skull and crossbones on the back.

Above and below the pirate emblem, stitched print read *Sacred Bones M.C.*

The Hollywood-handsome leader with his long blond hair pulled his bike out of the circle. He curled off toward Ray and Sunny, the two agents propped together at the barn's entrance. Her heart surprised her, skipping a step, like a young girl, over the biker's good looks. She hadn't experienced a physical reaction to a man like that in a while.

Hollywood skidded his bike within six inches of Ray's tan leather boots, the general's kicks as big as small golf bags.

Without apparent concern, Ray glanced at his feet, then Hollywood. Sunny decided she'd learn a lot working with him. The general was cool, tough, and confident.

The rest of the gang parked beside Hollywood, two on each flank, all facing the barn. She hoped they'd taken note of

Hauser's SUV's special white *US Government, For Official Use Only* license plates. Four of the five riders wore holstered weapons. To Sunny, open-carry states seemed like the wild west two hundred years ago.

Ray held up his badge, rested the other hand on his belt, inches from his holstered weapon. "I'm Ray Hauser with the Department of Homeland Security. Beside me is Special Agent Hicks. You gentlemen are trespassing on a federal crime scene. We must ask you to turn around and go back the way you—"

Hollywood had been giving Sunny his movie-star smile. All teeth. Beaming eyes. "Why, Ray, I was about to say the same thing to your partner, Agent Hicks. Mind turning around...so I can see a little more of your ass?"

His friends laughed, and Sunny nearly joined them, barely managing to maintain her grim stare. Hollywood was so disarmingly good looking. Wavy blond hair hanging all the way to his muscled, thick shoulders. Square jaw. Prominent cheekbones. Those deep blue eyes. His mouth and mood existed in a constant state of rebellious smirk.

"Nothing funny about a Homeland Security crime scene," Ray said. "Hanging around after I've explained you need to leave could potentially land you at a nearby FCI—that's federal correctional institution. There's a nice one in Phoenix."

Hollywood opened wide his sky-colored eyes, dropped his jaw like a flabbergasted old lady. The guy even had great teeth. Maybe he *was* an actor.

"He's offering us a free trip to Phoenix," he said. "Sound like fun, bros?"

They cheered.

"You won't have much fun," Ray said.

While Hollywood let his men make noise, he focused again on Sunny. Air Force special agents wore what they wanted to work, depending on conditions and the assignment. For the search of the potential crime scene, she'd changed from the business attire into comfortable, loose-fitting blue jeans, sneakers, and a short-sleeved, western blouse colored light green and white. Hollywood examined every fold and wrinkle within certain areas. She tried not to blush, but heat touched her cheeks.

"You hear me, butthole?" Ray said.

Hollywood exaggerated a new regard, pivoting his head and shoulders as he transferred his gaze away from Sunny. His expression flipped to cold and dark.

"We don't need to hit Phoenix for fun," Hollywood said. "We could throw a party right here, right now, with Agent Hicks. Couldn't we, boys?"

Amid the cheering, Ray's right hand touched his weapon. "We're federal agents on a criminal investigation, you mopes. If you don't leave right now, Agent Hicks and I are going to place every one of you under arrest."

Hollywood tilted his face, and his eyes changed back to happy. He liked Ray, or his words, or maybe his guts. She did, too, even though her heart raced and her palms were wet. She fingered her holster like Ray, waiting for one of the crazy bikers to draw and shoot.

What a partner she had today.

"There are five of us, two of you," Hollywood said.

Each of Hollywood's armed scruffy henchmen touched their holsters. She eyed Ray, looking for guidance. Should they draw? She noticed Hollywood's menacing voice hadn't lost tension the way his eyes had. Have *fun* with her?

"Then you'd better draw and start shooting," Ray said, "because our forensic team truck and backup will be here any minute. I wouldn't count on those favorable odds for long."

"Something else," Sunny said.

All five men and Hauser stared at her. She forced back an urge to swallow. She'd surprised herself speaking up, but what the handsome blond needed was a succinct summary of the facts. Much of the time, Air Force colonels and generals didn't listen, and as one admiring teacher had called it, Sunny's "Crisis

Overview for Dummies" was one of her best public relations strengths. She'd written an article for *Forbes*.

Ray had already made up his mind about Sunny. Wanted her for a partner. But when she said, "Something else," taking attention away from the confrontation, he wanted to hug her. Maybe a kiss. Five guys with pistols was not a fight he wanted. He'd already gone through how he'd kick, punch, then kick and punch again. But guy number five had time to shoot. Maybe guy number four. Ray was real happy Sunny had chimed in. He couldn't wait to hear what she'd say. He hoped her words were as good as her timing.

"Forget our approaching backup," Sunny said. "Here's what matters. If we shoot you, it's called federal agents using self-defense. You shoot us, it's called murder of a federal officer. Every lawman in America will hunt you down. And because I'm a woman, half of them would rather kill you than bring you in alive."

A man with a big belly and dirty black hair, including chest-length, curling ropes and a shaggy, untrimmed beard, sat up tall on the first bike to the right of Hollywood. He grunted before he spoke. "If they never find your body, bitch, how would anyone know who raped and killed you?"

Ray's neck turned red. He looked ready to pop.

She touched his elbow and laughed. "Homeland is pulling up your rap sheets right now, gentlemen. How do you think we found this crime scene?" She pointed to the sky. "We've been taking satellite photos every ten minutes since dawn this morning. You five members of the Sacred Bones Motorcycle Club have *already* been identified."

Hollywood's smirk came back. "Horse crap."

"How else would I know this property—owned by Nolan

and Jessie Maris—includes two hundred acres of creosote, rocks, and, by actual count, one-thousand, two-hundred and fifty-two saguaro cactus, half of them near a gully. I was examining photos all night."

Hollywood stared at her unblinking. The charm evaporated.

"Nolan Maris a friend of yours?" Ray asked. "Maybe you could answer a few questions for us?"

Hollywood gunned his Harley-Davidson, backed the bike up for a K-turn, then idled across the dirt lot toward the broken desert highway. His crew followed single file, all five members of The Sacred Bones M.C. now pointing to the sky like Sunny had, except using a different finger.

When they left, Ray offered his fist for a celebratory bump. "And I thought *I* was a good liar."

Walking with across the barn's cement floor in plastic booties and gloves, the smells, sounds, and sights fit Sunny's memories of her time spent there. So did the inside of the walk-in tool closet. But the clincher was pressing her face against the cement and peeking underneath the closet door into the aluminum barn's main room. The computer was gone, but the bench it rested on remained. So did the chair. Broken window glass. In fact, everything about the low and narrow view corresponded, save for the missing autocannon and the trailer it had rested on. The memories caused by the cool cement gave her a nasty shiver.

She jumped up quickly and followed Ray outside. He approached the house trailer, removed a pocket-knife-size device from his belt, and poked open the Airstream's locked door.

"Cool," she said. "I want one of those."

Sig Sauer drawn, he led Sunny carefully inside. "I'll text you the requisition form."

The house trailer was empty of people, photos, and women's clothing, but the kitchen table displayed a sheet of yellow-lined notepaper with handwriting. Signed by "Jessie," the note was addressed to Sunny.

To Special Agent S. Hicks,
　At first I didn't believe my husband when he said I was helpless and stupid, that without him I'd end up a whore and a junkie. But after years of Nolan hitting me, telling me those awful things, I couldn't help but think I'd wind up on the street like he said. No one ever told me I deserved to be treated with warmth and kindness.
　I'm writing this note, maybe others, because I know I'm not alone and nobody's doing anything. Three times a day in America—365 days a year—a current or former partner murders a woman. Maybe a million times a day, some manchild throws a punch. Girls and young women need to know they deserve consideration and affection, to speak out when they're abused. Maybe defend themselves. Fight back.
　I'm going to do something, probably next weekend. Me, Jessie Maris. I'm going to expose one of America's worst abusers by destroying him, a savage act I hope will call attention to an American system of justice which still treats girls and women like horses and pigs. Everyone knows this person. But they do not know all he has done.
　I shot my husband dead the day before yesterday. Two of his friends tried to kill me in revenge, so I wasted their asses, too. And I'm not done killing. Not by a longshot—hint, hint.
　A Rain of Hell is coming because America won't wake up!
　Jessie

Ray repeated the last part. "'Not by a longshot, hint-hint?'"

"How about 'rain of hell?'" Sunny said. "Sure sounds like she plans to fire our Avenger autocannon."

He pinched the note with gloved fingers and slipped the

yellow paper into a plastic bag. "She had to write this a day or two ago. And probably *next weekend* means what? We have a week to find her yesterday. If we don't, maybe she kills half of Arizona with an automatic cannon."

Sunny nodded. "America's worst abuser. Who do you think she means?"

Ray drove them back toward Gila Bend in the dying sunlight, the Suburban's air-conditioning on full, Sunny checking her cell phone. Except for the saguaros, and the tarantulas by the road, he thought the famous Sonoran Desert looked pretty much like a thousand barren dirt lots he'd seen in Jersey. Less weeds, maybe.

He slowed and pulled over. There was an arriving message on his encrypted device, something he'd been waiting for. The second time he read it, he did so out loud. "Eric says, 'As of today's date, Air Force Special Agent Sunny Hicks is temporarily assigned to the Department of Homeland Security under the command of General Ray Hauser.'"

"I'm receiving the same email," Sunny said.

Ray pulled back onto the road. "Told you."

In her motel room, resting in bed with the TV on, wearing her double-X Dodgers T-shirt as pajamas and wishing vaguely she wasn't alone, Sunny's new cell phone buzzed. The number was unfamiliar, but her caller ID said *The Los Angeles Times*, so the call had to come from her missing boyfriend.

"Jordan?"

"Hi Sunny. How are you?"

"Surprised," she said. "I haven't heard from you in a month."

"You told me to stop calling, find an actress girlfriend, remember?"

She sat up in bed. The advice to Jordan seemed like a good idea at the time, although she didn't remember putting things quite so starkly. Girlfriend? Truth was, she wouldn't mind Jordan with her right now. He'd been a reporter for *The Washington Post* and lived near her in Quantico when they'd met. But after a fun and progressively close, six-month relationship, he'd taken off for the new job.

"I remember," she said, "and dating other people *still* sounds like good advice. Why call me now?"

"I heard your employer, the US Air Force, lost a dangerous weapon and you might be on a team looking for it."

Her heart-rate soared. How the heck...she considered several responses, none which would look good in print, which is what happens when you curse at reporters. What *exactly* had he heard?

"Sunny? Come on. I won't use your name or even call you an Air Force source."

"The story reeks like bad cheese, Jordan."

"That's not a denial."

"Really? Sounds like one to me."

"Yes or no, is the Air Force searching for a lost weapon?"

"You mean like a rifle or a pistol? I think it's safe to say the Air Force is *always* looking for missing equipment, including—"

"You know that's not what I mean."

"How do I know what you mean?"

"I mean like a GAU-8 Avenger," Jordan said, "a Gatling-gun like, automatic cannon that fires explosive shells at the rate of seventy per second."

How could he have possibly found out? "I have no comment."

"So it's true," he said.

"No comment means no comment." The investigation was supposed to be semi-classified, but maybe that bulletin Homeland sent out to local law enforcement along the rail line popped the cork on secrecy. Still, Sunny had to protect the Air

Force from criticism.

"If this story were baloney," Jordan said, "you'd explain why it's not true, not say 'no comment.'"

She changed the subject. "I have no comment other than to say, screw you Jordan Scott for finally calling me after a month, not to tell me you miss me, but to ask about a lousy fake *news* story."

"Oh, Sunny. I've been crazy busy with the new job. My new editor here hates me because I make more money than him."

"We're a world apart."

"Not even six hours by car."

"You know what I mean," she said.

"So if you're not looking for a missing cannon autocannon, why are you in Gila Bend, Arizona?"

"How the hell do you know that?"

"I'm an ace reporter, remember? Plus, you have your location services turned on."

Damn. The new phone. She fixed her settings.

"Yeah, well, it's still no comment."

"I have other sources, Sunny. I know this story is true. Two Navy SEALs told me about a new assault boat they wanted to build around an Avenger, only the Air Force never delivered the weapon as promised, claimed the autocannon was stolen off a railroad flatcar."

He knew way too much. "Stop right there, Jordan. I know nothing about Navy SEAL weapons or plans."

"But you know something about a missing autocannon. I have two reliable sources. You'd only be confirming something I already know."

"No comment."

"I'm going to publish this—with you or without you."

"Sounds like an old song."

"Ha. Come on, Sunny. Are you looking for that autocannon or not?"

She hung up and turned out the lights.

If Jordan's paper ran a story about the Air Force's missing weapon, everyone would think Sunny leaked it. Colonel Seager knew Jordan Scott had been Sunny's boyfriend.

15

Back at his motel in Phoenix, Ray changed into a T-shirt and shorts, went outside to the empty pool area and stretched out on a lounge. His idea was to admire the stars, let his mind wander, forget Alissa's case for an hour. Maybe coax his subconscious into joining Alissa's search team. He'd learned he couldn't guess what his subconscious might know or suspect. He had to relax, let his thoughts drift on random topics.
Let the tool do the work.

After teaching karate night classes on the base, he often hiked across the freeway to spend time alone on the beach, under the bright stars. There was wonder and hope for him in the glowing, distant lights, a calming dose of spirituality in the eternal crashing of ocean waves. He could think clearly at those times, make decisions. He'd been beside the water when he'd decided to propose.

Or maybe he'd already made up his mind back then, he and Alissa having talked that evening about living together, maybe joining up for private investigations after he left the service and she gained more experience on the business side. He told her the number of years on the job didn't matter, but she said she wanted to feel like an equal, not a junior partner.

He'd understood. He grasped almost everything Alissa said because he'd had grown up with three sisters in a four-room house. Women were not a mystery.

Stretched on the lounge, the stars so close, he pulled out his private phone. His oldest sister was set up as a one touch.

"Ray?"

He didn't know exactly what to say. He wanted to talk about Alissa.

"Tell me something, Etta. When I was away on an assignment and Alissa visited you, what did you two talk about?"

She took a second. "Mostly your genitals."

He laughed. "Come on. I'm serious."

"When Alissa came to see me, she talked about my health, asked questions. She was here to see how I was doing, how she could help me battle the cancer."

"She really cared about you."

"I know that. I loved your wife. I don't know if I could have finished the chemo without her. And it saved my life."

"Did she ever worry a lot about me when I was working? Was it unpleasant for her when I went away?"

"No, she was an investigator, too, remember? She understood the risks, but she also knew you were good at what you do."

"Really? She didn't worry?"

"Not that she talked about. I'm no mind reader."

"I worried about her every time she had to go away. I wanted to go with her that time to Arizona."

"Of course," Etta said. "Men want to protect."

Etta had been more of a parent to him than their alcoholic mother, buying and preparing his food, checking his homework. After Alissa disappeared, Etta was the one who showed him what a deadly trap his sadness and drinking had become, what a circle of despair and loss. Dragged him to his first AA meeting.

"You making any progress on your investigation?" Etta asked.

"A little."

"Like what?"
"I can't say, Etta. Give me a break."
"Then why you'd call?"
"I wanted to talk about Alissa."
Etta's sighed. "Okay, poor baby brother. Did you know I asked her once if the two of you ever considered opening up your own private investigation business?"
"No."
"Well, I did, and your wife said being together day and night probably wouldn't work well for you two."
"Really? She say why?"
"She claimed the sex was too good. She couldn't keep her hands off."
"Really?"
Etta laughed. "Said no wife. *Ever*."

Sunny noticed him first thing when she hit the lobby for coffee the next morning. Hollywood's long blond curls on top of those cantaloupe-size, bare shoulders were an eye-grabbing combo. Especially before breakfast. He sat off by himself in a stiff lobby chair, blue-jeaned legs in a Grand Canyon man-spread, a muscled, naked chest under the sleeveless, blue-jean, motorcycle club jacket. His attention zipped back and forth between his cell phone and the occasional motel guest arriving in the lobby for free rolls and coffee.
He was waiting for her.
When he caught her staring, he nodded and headed over. He sauntered bowlegged, like a cowboy, stashing his phone in his back pocket as he arrived beside her. Hollywood stood at least six-foot-four. His manner came across as apologetic, though, not intimidating. His face carried lines of worry.
"Can we talk a few minutes?" he said. "I have information you'll want."
Information? What she wondered most was how those

wrestler's arms and shoulders would feel wrapped around her. The guy was a hunk, for sure. Dangerous. She laughed at herself.

"Where shall we go to talk?" she asked.

He grinned. "How about breakfast across the street?"

"Juanita's?"

"Yeah. I bring women there all the time for breakfast. Nobody will think I'm ratting to the Feds."

How romantic. "I think first you should tell me your name."

"Dennis Williams."

She had on comfortable jeans, no bra, but her oversize pajamas, the Dodgers T-shirt, hid everything but her knees. She needed to change, but Mexican breakfast sounded good. She had time. Maybe she'd go, but two things bothered her. "Who are you going to rat out?"

"Nolan Maris told me he stole something from the Air Force, and now he's missing."

Verification. And Hollywood might know a lot more. But there was still one more issue she had to clear up before she'd be comfortable eating with him, even across the street.

"Tell me how you found me."

Hollywood grinned. "There're only two motel possibilities in Gila Bend for a working federal agent, and I know the woman on the other overnight desk."

Sunny chewed another fork of *machaca*, swallowed, then sipped the deliciously thick black coffee. Dennis, AKA Hollywood, had introduced himself as an ex-US Navy Warrant Officer and concerned citizen. His motorcycle club brother Nolan had bragged of stealing and having plans to sell a powerful weapon from the Air Force. Subsequently, Maris and two of his friends—Samuel Polanco and Angel Alcides—had failed to answer telephone calls.

Hollywood also worried Nolan's Pakistani pal could have

been involved—Hamza Yasin—who maybe was the weapon's planned purchaser. Hollywood said he didn't want to sound like a racist, but he worried the Pakistani could be a terrorist. See something, say something, he mentioned. He gave a brief description, including the Pakistani's penchant for brightly colored clothes and selling hashish.

Sunny nodded. "Write down your email or phone number for me. I'll let you know if and when we have solid news on your friends. Tell me what Nolan's wife is like. Was Jessie tough and bossy?"

"The opposite."

"Explain." She already knew plenty, but an essential part of any investigation was confirmation. They'd taught her that at special agent school in Georgia.

And Hollywood was so nice to look at.

She handed him a business card.

"First time I talked to Jessie, she had a black eye," he said. He stuffed her info in his pocket, used the back of a restaurant card to write his name and phone number. He pushed his details across the table. "Another time, she had a cast on her wrist."

Sunny dropped the card in her purse. "So Nolan Maris was physically abusive?"

"One-hundred percent. I know for a fact he broke her arm. And once she tried to fight back, he told me, Jessie ended up with a broken nose and a busted shoulder."

"Who taught Jessie about guns?"

Hollywood blinked. "Guns?"

"There's evidence she trained with pistols," she said. "Was Nolan into guns and shooting? Target shooting maybe?"

"Yeah, but more when I first met him, a couple of years ago. Did Nolan get shot?"

"We don't know what happened yet. Tell me about Nolan and his guns."

He frowned. "I remember something he said a year ago

when he sold most of his weapons. Claimed he kept one Beretta in a lock-box because he was afraid Jessie might go crazy again and shoot him. It was the *again* that made me remember his comment."

"Why would she shoot him after accepting his abuse for years?"

"Nolan said she went nuts when he broke her nose last year. She tried to not sleep with him. That's the way he put it."

"*Tried* not to? You mean he made her have sex, anyway? Raped her?"

"Nolan? Oh, hell yeah. He doesn't like really women."

"No kidding. You think Jessie tried to kill him earlier. Or threatened him?"

"He said she went at him with a knife as revenge for breaking her nose. That's when he dislocated her arm. He had to take her to a different hospital because it was the same day."

Sunny could only shake her head as a familiar face walked in. Men like Nolan Maris needed to be in jail. Or worse.

Hollywood showed Sunny a warm, sexy smile. "Now me, I *love* women."

"I know you do, Romeo, but that's a conversation for another time. Here's my new boss, headed to the table."

Hollywood's shoulders pivoted. "Whoops."

Sunny waved for Ray to join them.

Seeing Sunny across a friendly table from the motorcycle gang leader made his brow pinch, even if Ray thought she'd have an investigation-related explanation. He'd trusted her immediately and instinctively, and her performance so far only reinforced that natural confidence. But Ray knew when his forehead wrinkled.

He stood by their table and kept the frown. "What's going on?"

"We're finishing breakfast," Sunny said. "You remember

Mr. Dennis Williams, ex-Navy Warrant Officer?"

"The man who suggested his biker brothers could have fun with you?"

Williams, who at least wore cleaner jeans than yesterday, raised both hands to ear-level. "Sorry about that."

"You ought to be," Ray said.

Sunny smiled. "Mr. Williams was waiting for me this morning in my motel lobby. He said he had information about his friend Nolan Maris, and since you mentioned eight-thirty, I figured I had time to listen. Plus, you know me and Mexican food."

He offered his hand to Dennis Williams. They shook. Firm and friendly. Williams was a good actor or a decently raised man. Ray's gaze fell back on Sunny. "Find out anything?"

"Nolan Maris has a friend named Hamza Yasin whom we need to check out. Works at a convenience store a few blocks away."

"Anything else?" Ray asked.

"Maris bragged about stealing a government weapon, plus he and two friends have been missing a couple of days."

"That it?"

It was Sunny's turn to wrinkle her face. "Something up?"

"Yes. Ready to leave?"

He worried about Williams knowing Nolan Maris and the others who'd disappeared. How much did the guy *really* know? Williams could easily be part of the gang who'd stolen the autocannon and earlier kidnapped Alissa, the guy only trying to throw them off by acting helpful. His deceit was at least as plausible as wanting to help federal officers.

Of course, being female and attractive, Sunny wasn't your average Fed.

But she probably didn't trust him either, only acting to get the info.

He liked and respected Agent Hicks. Smart, educated in subjects Ray was not, and she didn't hesitate speaking up, so far exactly when her ideas were called for. An officer who respected the truth and doing the right thing. A person Ray could admire and work closely with. A complete asset but for her inexperience.

Not a little thing. But manageable.

He tried not to make a face when Sunny tossed twenty-five dollars on the restaurant table. Williams showed no objection to her paying. The half-naked heartthrob took women out for Mexican breakfasts and made them pay.

What a bum.

Near the exit, he leaned closer as he opened the restaurant door for Sunny. "They found human remains on the Maris property. At least five separate DBs. Looks like everything Jessie wrote in that note is true. And more."

"Hollywood gave me the names," Sunny said. "Nolan Maris's missing pals are Samuel Polanco and Angel Alcides. We can check them with the DNA when we get it."

Ray shook his head as she walked past him into the brilliant, sizzling sunshine. "Did you just call that guy Hollywood?"

She nodded. "You have to admit he's handsome."

"I knew who you meant. But he's not my type. Too pretty."

Soon as they walked through the convenience store's double glass doors, Sunny in front because Ray held the door, one of the two counter men ducked behind a wall of stacked cigarette cartons. Maybe he was retrieving goods from the storeroom, but the motion appeared surreptitious. Her pulse spiked. Ray agreed because she saw his eyebrows merge.

He guided her back outside. "Cover the rear," he said. "Don't let anybody leave."

Heart thumping, she reached the side of the building in time to see a man running from the back, the guy in a total sprint. He matched Hollywood's description of Hamza Yasin right down to clothes "like a box of crayons," blue shorts and a yellow camp shirt printed with green palm trees.

He ran to an old red Dodge. Sunny was no car aficionado, but the automobile's grill emblem—a five-point star surrounded by a pentagon—reminded her of a car her aunt had driven much of the time Sunny lived with her. A Dodge Omni.

She picked up her pace. Hamza was quick on his feet, and if what Hollywood said was true—that Hamza might be a potential buyer of stolen autocannons—she had to catch up and detain him. She wanted to do her job. She wanted to keep impressing Ray.

The boxy red sedan rested against the property's fenced rear border. Beyond the chainlink, dry, brown weeds and one tall, yellow sunflower bordered a railroad spur. The tracks ran parallel to the street and the rear fence. There was no back way out for Hamza. She had him cornered.

Her fingers trembled as she unsnapped her holster. She carefully avoided touching the pistol itself. Not until she absolutely had to.

16

Sunny slowed to a fast walk as she approached Hamza's car. Around her in the convenience store parking lot, brakes squealed and two pickups honked over the center exit lane. The desert's powerful sunlight baked the blacktop and humans alike, her exposed arms and neck glowing in the morning heat.

Hamza started his sputtering engine with her five or six feet away. She charged her last few strides and stretched for the door handle.

The car jumped backward, out of reach.

Her momentum slammed her thigh and hip into the moving front fender, spinning her, stealing her balance and tumbling her across the ground like dice. Her vision shrunk to a thin line. The parking lot sounds stopped, replaced by a loud drumbeat, an unworldly, unsteady thumping she eventually identified as her own heartbeat.

Full of flight or fight juice, she didn't feel the pain of her crash landing. She knew her shoulder and hip would be bruised and stiff tomorrow, but who cared. She had a job to do. Detain Hamza. Impress the boss. She was down, not out.

She scrambled to her feet. Hamza was getting away, the car backing into a K-turn, its nose pointing at the street. In the corner of her eye, she saw Ray exit the back of the store. He had his hand on his weapon. Jogging toward her, seeing that their target was escaping.

Her skin glistened with perspiration. She reached for her weapon. "Stop the car or I'll shoot."

Hamza glanced at her, no fear in his eyes, only determination, and he stomped on the car's accelerator one beat later. His rear wheels squealed and spun a wisp of blue smoke.

She smelled the burnt rubber as she yanked the Sig Sauer from her leather holster. The pistol's size and shape intimidated her sense of touch, and halfway out, her damp fingers lost their grip. The weapon slipped from her hand.

For the slimmest of a split-second, her semiautomatic floated loose, the weapon in mid-air. She made a desperate, last-second clutch before it fell to the ground, a coordinated and masterful snag, kind of, her fingers re-capturing the barrel, not the grip.

With care, she re-grasped the Sig Sauer with both hands, two thumbs on the same side, sucked a deep breath, and assumed a low-ready stance. "I said stop or I'll shoot."

She was bluffing, exhibiting her weapon to achieve compliance.

Hamza was a better poker player. He kept going. His Dodge bounced out of the lot and landed hard on the highway, sparks flying as the frame hit asphalt. He barely missed a passing green panel truck with ladders on top.

Ray arrived at her side. "You okay?"

She examined herself. Her pantsuit was soiled, torn at the hip and shoulder. Underneath all the material, the scrapes on her skin appeared minor. No serious bleeding.

"I'll call in the license number," Ray said. "We'll have him by the end of the day."

On the way to meet with Department of Homeland Security's General Johannsen in Phoenix, Ray drove them north on Arizona Highway 85, along the Gila River and never-ending acres of manicured commercial farming property. During a silence, Sunny worried her new assignment with the DHS hadn't launched well. Ray hadn't said anything, but he must have seen her mishandle her weapon.

"Don't worry about what to say at the meeting," he said. "All Johannsen has time for is to shake your hand. Everybody there is crazy looking for Jessie Maris, but Eric is managing other crap as well, of course."

Besides her clumsiness, there was something else on her mind. "Do you think Jessie's really going to fire that cannon at somebody?"

"It wouldn't be easy," he said, " but I bet she's making plans to sell it."

She felt Tommy Moon amble up behind her, Jessie working intently on her laptop. She'd logged into a dark website, but the onionizing tool—which covered up her identity and IP address beneath layer after layer of IDs and addresses—was complicated. Afterward, she could work almost anywhere online without being traced.

"What're you doing?" Tommy said. "Thought you said there were more vents to open."

She kept working, switching sites. Jessie could use a computer-aided design program—CAD for short—like a junior engineer. Before marrying Nolan, she'd spent seven months as receptionist for a Phoenix mechanical designer, and the lazy bastard taught her to input and run most of the CAD software while he drank and ate long lunches. A good job she never should have quit for Nolan.

Because of that boss's training, she knew how to create a basic design on the computer, including materials, processes, dimensions, and tolerances. After that, a few clicks and you had a complete mechanical drawing. For actually building cannon mounts, she had Tommy. For additional planning and info, she knew she'd need more help.

With Nolan's old passwords and apps, she'd hoped to find help on the dark web. The site she'd logged into first, mostly to use the onionizing tools, belonged to Nolan and his friends—the Sacred Bones Motorcycle Club—and was part of a national group.

"Did you hear me?"

Tommy grunted after a beat or two, walked away to open the refrigerator for another beer. The two of them had been in the isolated rock cabin and attached mineshaft over twenty-four hours, Jessie not having enough time earlier to completely open up all the vents before Tommy arrived. Stashing the autocannon had been a bigger priority, and it had taken her over an hour to work the truck and trailer inside the century-old mine's entrance.

"This place stinks," Tommy said.

Although the hill above them had been hollowed out by previous smugglers, making room for Tommy's truck took another hour.

The attached cabin's hand-built stone walls, which camouflaged and neighbored the old mine's entrance, also kept the two west-facing rooms cool in the summer. The stone walls had been constructed during Prohibition by bootleggers, Nolan's great grandfather included.

"I mean stink with a capital S," Tommy said.

Those old bootleggers had stocked the mine with illegal booze from across the border in Mexico, set up a distribution from the mine shaft. All within half an hour's drive of Phoenix. Nolan had inherited everything, the desert canyon in the south nearer the border, this fifty-acre mountaintop with the abandoned mine, plus a nasty, mean streak—all from Uncle Jack Maris, who died in prison.

"No wonder Nolan never brought anybody out here," Tommy said.

Poor ventilation kept anyone from living in the cave-house permanently. Plus, there were no municipal electric or gas connections. A small generator ran a few lights at night, the internet and refrigerator, but air-conditioning had been nixed because electric usage had always been a target for tax collectors and cops.

"The place smells like gopher crap," he said. "No way I'm living here."

Jessie glanced up. "Only *you* would know what gopher crap smells like."

The natural flow of air and insulation efforts had been improved many times, according to Nolan's uncle, but without a stiff outside wind sucking on the exhaust grates, the air inside was stale and smelly.

That reminded her of something. "I'll be right back."

Jessie closed the computer program, went into the old mineshaft and opened every last air intake, even the ones only reached by crawling on her back in the dark. More important, she connected what she'd forgotten—the stone hideout's latest addition, a solar-powered air pump.

Nolan had driven up last summer to install the device, which was, as far as Jessie knew, the last time the grates all throughout old mine had been opened. The job was a pain in the ass, but Tommy was right. The place smelled like an animal hole.

Back at her computer, the air beginning to freshen, Tommy walked close again and popped another beer. "What are you designing on the computer? I thought you wanted to sell the gun."

"It's a cannon, not a gun," she said.

Jessie had no intention of selling, but Tommy didn't need to know that.

"I know," he said. "Just a shorter word."

"We can sell the cannon for a lot more money if a shooter can manipulate the line of fire, side-to-side a little."

"Okay, but why are we in a freaking cave?"

"We're not *in* the cave," she said. "The trucks and trailer are."

"You know what I mean. Getting buyers to drive out here is harder than inviting them to a private warehouse in town, is all I'm saying. You and I could be snuggling in a nice hotel room."

She touched his hip. "We have the internet for sales and marketing. Hamza offered me a hundred thousand dollars, but it's worth at least half a million. Maybe a full million if we use it first, show buyers the destruction a cannon can cause, get the media talking."

"We could also get caught and spend the rest of our lives in prison."

"Not if we're careful. You know Nolan and the gang had connections to the sheriff's posse. Some of them are my connections, too. I've hooked up with one or two on the dark web."

Tommy shook his head. "I think we should take the hundred gees."

"Maybe I will, but it's my autocannon, not yours. I'll share anything we get fifty-fifty if you keep helping me, but it's my decision when and who to sell it to, and at what price. Okay?"

Tommy stared at her with his soft brown eyes before nodding. The six-foot, three-hundred-pound man was like a furry-animal carnival prize, squishy and something to cuddle, but not a teddy bear because they made bears too safe-looking and nice. Too agreeable. Tommy was more like a gray and white fuzzy shark, a wicked grin exposing nasty teeth. Tender and huggable, but dangerous. Jessie had to treat him with care.

She rose from the computer table again and wrapped her arms around his neck.

He rose a foot taller and was twice as wide, had gigantic ears he let Jessie hold onto and guide for oral sex. What a treat to have orgasms again. Sexually, they'd always been as compatible as a man and woman could get.

"Let me finish this," she said.

When she closed her laptop, Jessie pulled Tommy outside and

screwed him in Nolan's truck, once in the cab and thirty minutes later in the Ford 350's extended bed. Jessie couldn't do what she wanted without him, at least for a while yet, so she had to keep him happy, and with Tommy, sex worked. So would home cooking, airing out the cabin, and the promise of a big paycheck.

She needed to make sure he stayed responsive to her needs.

Maybe an hour in front of midnight, Tommy snoring in the bedroom, the inside air almost tasty, Jessie went online to check Representative King's public appearance schedule, particularly his upcoming campaign stops in Phoenix. She wanted to find out, if she could, where he'd stay, which roads he might travel.

Her body hummed with excitement. No way could she sleep.

She discovered little information, the campaign website and independent news stories claiming the King campaign still sorted various dates and appearances, but going back in time, reading a one-year-old profile in the *Phoenix Times-Merchant*, the reporter mentioned the interview had taken place at King's "new favorite" hotel, the Sonora Desert Golf and Dude Ranch.

She'd heard of the fancy, overpriced place. A map check showed the luxury golf complex was outside the downtown area, a large piece of property on AZ 101. But the resort wasn't too far from US 17 and the old bootlegger hideout.

Wouldn't that be a piece of luck, King speaking in town but staying only miles from where she'd stashed herself and the autocannon? Too much a piece of luck, probably, and definitely nothing to count on. She had to be ready for anything.

She'd killed one friend of Nolan's—Angel Alcides—who'd been a member of that volunteer group, the Pinacosta County Sheriff's Posse. But there was another man Nolan didn't know about, a friend of Angel's and also a former posse member. The man who'd talked to Jessie with kindness one night after Nolan slapped her around at a Colorado river weekend. He'd told her to call him if she ever needed help.

With Jessie using Nolan's dark web account, even with a different tag-name, the man might guess who she was. She hadn't seen him since that night over a year ago, and the idea of making contact felt risky. He might not remember her, or be mad because of what happened to Angel. If he didn't hunt Jessie down for a reward, he might want to steal the cannon.

A lot to worry about, for sure, but how else was she going to get info on Representative King? She needed a friend inside that posse group.

Hamza was on the bikers' website, too, Nolan had told her. Maybe she'd hear from him. If either one responded, she'd offer them a piece of the cannon like she had with Tommy, pretending her stolen cannon could be sold, even after use.

Which there was no way. Jessie already knew she'd die firing that cannon. She hoped for it—as long as death meant she'd blown up that bastard ex-judge.

Using the moniker HAPPYWIDOW, Jessie posted to the biker website seeking help in "demonstrating" against the congressman on his upcoming trip to Phoenix. She asked for a long list of skills, ideas, bits of information, and any knowledge of King's plans, but never mentioned the cannon or intended violence.

Within thirty minutes, she received a dozen messages of support, most with expressions of dislike for King, a few with locations and times of the governor's weekend events. As a gesture of goodwill, one new contact—the self-described DESERTFLYER—offered one of Jessie's requested bits of information, a bona fide email address for Air Force Special Agent S. Hicks.

Thrilled, she used the onionized tool on the website to send Sunny a second note. Her first letter hadn't been shown or talked about on television, so Special Agent Hicks must have buried the news. This time, Jessie would email both the first and second notes to every newspaper and TV station in Phoenix, Tucson, and San Diego.

To Special Agent S. Hicks,

Me again. I know the terror of abuse, first from my mother and then from my husband, but sadly, I'm not that special. At some point, every woman knows. Murder, assault, rape, bullying, robbery, threats, and insults against females unfold daily wherever humans live and work.

Husbands and boyfriends, present and ex—the same people who claim love—cause most of the physical injuries, but bosses, cops, doctors, coaches, teachers, and salesmen exploit and mistreat women in a hundred different ways every day.

In what turned out to be a good example for my sisters worldwide, a few days ago, I decided to no longer accept the abuse. I refused my husband's physical assault, used a weapon to kill him in self-defense. I wish I had not been forced into violence, but failing to reject his brutality would have been worse.

I'm done with it. Other women must follow me. Protect yourself.

I was afraid to leave both my mother and then my husband because each convinced me I couldn't survive without them. The truth was different, and available, but I didn't ask for help, the single most important thing I could have done, reached out to a teacher or a friend. Someone would have offered me a hand, but I didn't believe I was worth saving.

My mistakes are clear to me now my head is free of him. I needed to take responsibility, first for protecting myself, doing the things I needed to do to be healthy. Now I'm gonna set an example, calling attention to the suffering.

I want to show my sisters we can fight back and destroy a wicked abuser. Doing this deed publicly and dramatically will alert all abusers what awaits their own bad behavior. Violent abuse must be called out, challenged, and confronted. Sometimes publicly revenged. And this weekend, I will get even with one sick bastard and his fans. The people and teammates who support him are enablers, nourishing and sheltering an evil human being.

I will take them all for a ride on the Highway of Death. (Big hint)

Google it.

The Rain of Hell is coming soon.

Jessie wasn't sure yet where and when she would attack King, but let them think everything was planned, and let them guess wrong about her target. To pull it off, she'd need last-minute information on the governor's whereabouts, and DESERTFLYER at least claimed the ability.

She'd have to be careful not to get played, robbed, captured, or killed. Risky people might know who she was, what she possessed, what sat bolted onto a truck trailer. But nobody but Tommy knew where she *was*. That was her safety net.

Jessie pushed away from the computer and poured a double shot of clear tequila into a clean cocktail glass. She carried the double shot outside and hiked to the hilltop rim of the circular depression which hid her stone-faced mine entrance and cabin from the highway. A warm wind at her back, she gazed south into the brightest lights of Phoenix.

She lifted her glass in a toast. "Justice stalks you, Randall King."

FOUR DAYS BEFORE THE RAIN

17

Sunny set her alarm early to survey her internet inquiries, but she saved twenty minutes to drink coffee in her motel lobby, read online media headlines. Jordan Scott's page one story that morning in *The Los Angeles Times* punched her in the nose like a ruthless mugger. About her missing cannon, Jordan's account was headlined "Air Force Loses Weapon of Mass Destruction."

Jordan hadn't quoted her, but the story mentioned a Quantico, VA-based, "military investigator" mysteriously visiting Gila Bend, Arizona, a "normally talkative source" who'd refused comment.

Talkative source?

Sunny's molars ground. He'd been deliberately hurtful. That wasn't information he'd normally include in a news story. A source *not talking* isn't news. A government official or a corporation head not talking about a specific issue might be. But not an anonymous source. Ridiculous. And since there was currently but one Quantico, VA-based military investigator staying in Gila Bend, that piece of information could get her spanked.

She capped her coffee and carried the paper cup outside as Ray's black Suburban pulled up. She wondered if he'd read the story, what he thought, but couldn't see his face through the dark glass. Not until she opened the door. Oh boy, yes. Ray had definitely read the news. Her spirits sank.

"What the hell were you *thinking*?" he said. "Why would you *ever* talk to a reporter?"

She hopped into the shotgun seat. "Jordan Scott is the boyfriend I told you about."

He had yanked the gearshift back into PARK. *"What?"*

She examined the special door locks, then eyed the restraining chair in the wide-open space behind her. She hoped he wasn't going to arrest her.

"You heard me," she said. "I mentioned him at the Mexican place, told you I'd dated a reporter for a couple of months when he worked for *The Washington Post*. Before he took a job in Los Angeles?"

Ray scowled. "Jordan Scott is *that* boyfriend?"

"Probably not anymore. I hung up on him. Plus, he's a loser for mentioning Gila Bend and a military investigator together in the same story. I could get in trouble."

"Sunny, you have no idea. But you may have dodged a bullet on the timing. Have you read Jessie Maris's second letter?"

"What?"

"It's on the Phoenix newspaper's web page this morning," he said. "And like her first communication, it's addressed to you."

When he pulled away, she checked the local paper's website on her iPhone. There was her name, under a subhead which said *Developing Story*. She skimmed the first half, then glanced at Ray. She wanted to speak, but her constricted throat barely passed air, let alone words.

She gave up and checked her email, found Jessie Maris' second note buried in spam. Jessie had sent her a direct email. Maybe Homeland could trace it. She flashed the screen to Ray.

"Jessie dumping this investigation on the media has one

benefit," he said. "Your boyfriend's big scoop dies today, and therefore, so does some of the heat on you. Johannsen's called a press conference for the afternoon."

"But my name's on the note. In the paper. Won't the press want to ask me questions?"

"Sure. And that's why Johannsen says you're *not* showing up. You're working an important case. You do not discuss ongoing investigations. And obviously, you don't talk to the press ever again, including Jordan Scott."

"All I said to Jordan was no comment. Practically."

When they reached the highway, Ray shook his head. "We have to skip these side issues, find our autocannon by identifying Jessie's target."

"Yes, we do," Sunny said.

"Quickly."

Sunny thought a minute. "Jessie's mention of Google and the Highway of Death means Johannsen will have to come clean about the cannon being missing. Pictures of the Warthog and that infamous Iraqi retreat will be all over the internet and the newspapers, even before the news conference because of Jessie's note. But maybe we'll get a tip from all the publicity. Johannsen's press conference will extend the coverage."

Ray wrinkled his nose. "Optimistic. I wouldn't count on tips, and you're still in hot water if you leaked *any* info to Scott."

His words didn't help her spirits. She liked and wanted the Homeland giant to like her. "I didn't leak anything, Ray. Jordan claimed two Navy SEALs he knew in San Diego told him about the secret boat project, how the Air Force failed to deliver the weapon."

"I believe you. He mentioned a SEAL Team source in the story."

Their eyes met, and Sunny's mood improved. Ray made her feel trusted.

"Thanks," she said.

"You and I are a team for the duration of this investigation.

I've already checked into another Gila Bend motel so we can call Scott's story false."

"Thanks, boss."

"Don't thank me yet. There's something else we need to talk about, and you're not going to like one word."

In two beats of silence, both sipped their coffees. They had a date that morning with a used-car lot owner, a local resident who reported "automatic weapons" fire and "a wild truck" to the local cops earlier. The Gila Bend police report turned up on her daily law enforcement scans, and it wasn't the gunfire or truck that caught her eye.

The witness had a familiar last name.

"What else did I do wrong?" she said.

Ray kept his gaze on her while a loud bus passed. "You fumbled your weapon in that convenience store parking lot. It could have easily fallen and discharged."

"It slipped in my hand."

"The situation looked worse than that to me. I could see your hand was unsteady from forty feet away. You were lucky you didn't drop that semiautomatic. Only a lucky snatch saved you."

"My hands were sweaty."

"It was more than perspiration," Ray said. "You're afraid of weapons, aren't you?"

"Not afraid. A little nervous holding one, maybe."

"I can't believe no one noticed this before."

"It caught the attention of my instructor at Glynco. He worked with me, made me put in twenty or thirty extra hours of practice. I finally qualified only because of him."

"Tell you what. You and I are going to the shooting range after work this afternoon, maybe right after we check this 9-1-1 caller. A couple of times this week, every week. The more you handle weapons, the better off you'll be."

"Okay. I've been spending time at the gun range in Virginia."

"Good. Let me tell you what's also worked for a couple of

women I know. Men, too."

"What?"

"Sleep with it."

She pretended shock. "What?"

Ray's cheeks reddened. She choked a giggle. A brigadier general blushing?

"Teach yourself to fall asleep holding your weapon," he said.

"Sounds mystical," she said.

"Ever hear of Isaiah Thomas?"

"Sure. I'm more a baseball fan, but I know Isaiah's a famous basketball player."

"It's what he and a million other kids did, players who wanted to be great on the court. In fact, it's how Isaiah prepared for every new season, even as a star."

"He slept with a Sig Sauer?"

"No, smartass," Ray said. "He not only carried a basketball everywhere, he slept with one."

Ray found the witness's address on an old commercial street in a worn-out part of Gila Bend. Sunny had discovered a woman had called municipal 9-1-1 early in the morning, the day before, claimed a truck towing a loaded, flatbed trailer had roared out of the repair shop. The truck almost turned over, the female witness reported, because two men from the repair shop chased the vehicle on foot, both firing guns.

"Machine gunners in their underwear," was how the woman had described the scene to the dispatcher, Sunny said. And the woman's name was Mrs. Polanco, same tag as a deceased friend of Nolan Maris.

Ray parked his Suburban inside Mrs. Polanco's used car lot. Hard to tell if the place was open or closed. In business or bankrupt. He hopped out onto old asphalt, cracked and broken, with irregular chunks missing. Torn pieces of paper and cigarette butts filled the cracks and holes. Torn remnants of red plastic pennants flapped on a wire above their heads.

"Have any luck with the online records this morning?" he asked.

"Something to chase," Sunny said, "but nothing useful yet."

They reached the shabby entrance of what used to be the car lot's sales shack, probably a desk for signing contracts and a toilet for the salesmen. These days, the dollhouse-size cabin served as Mrs. Polanco's home address. Gold-colored numbers had been nailed above the door.

He let Sunny knock on the screen.

"Other than traffic tickets and the drug raps we knew about," she said, "I couldn't find anything new on Jessie Maris. But under her maiden name, Costello, I—"

"Any relation to Frank Costello?" Ray asked.

"Who's that? The short guy in Abbot and Costello?"

"Frank Costello's a legendary gangster from the nineteen-twenties and thirties. Took over the Luciano family when Vito Genovese went to hide in Naples."

"If you say so. You a mafia historian?"

"I got interested when I was a kid—after seeing The Godfather."

"Well, Jessie is no relation to anybody famous whom I'm aware," she said. "And I only found one listing at the courthouse for Jessie Costello, a Pinacosta County juvenile court case, permanently sealed by the judge. I petitioned to have it unsealed, but the clerk emailed not to hold my breath."

She opened the screen and knocked loudly on Polanco's door.

In two beats, heavy footsteps ambled toward them. Didn't sound like an older woman. Ray backed up and unbuttoned his holster, tugged on Sunny's arm to do the same. Half a dozen crows picked that moment to screech from a dead tree next door, fly off as one flapping black cloud. Sunny flinched.

The front door rattled open to reveal the long-haired biker.

"Mr. Williams?" Sunny said.

"Special Agent Hicks," he said. "Boy, am I glad to see you."

Williams pushed them back by stepping outside, shutting the door behind him. "And you brought the big man with you. Perfect. You detectives need to help me find my mom."

Ray frowned. "Your mother's name is Polanco?"

"Yeah. My dad died, and she married again. Polanco is my mom's new married name. New-er, I guess is the way to say it. There were more than two."

"Why don't we all step away from the doorway here and have a little chat," Ray said. "Maybe even a heart-to-heart."

Williams shuffled off the steps. Loose and coordinated, like an old Fred Astaire movie. He wore the same jeans and sleeveless M.C. jacket over a bare chest he'd worn when Ray had seen him eating breakfast with Sunny. His standard dress code.

"I'll answer questions, sure," Williams said, "but my mom could be in trouble. She reported two guys firing weapons across the street, and now she's missing."

"*You* say she's missing," Ray said.

Hollywood scowled. "I told her I was dropping by to see her today. She said she'd be here. She's not. When you showed up, I was trying to decide if I should call the cops or go check out across the street myself."

"Why across the street?" Sunny said.

"Mom will be seventy this year, but she's feisty," he said. "That's her property over there, too, or it was until the bank foreclosed. There's still a bankruptcy case, and she says she hasn't lost everything *yet*. She also said the cops never followed up on her 9-1-1 call, so if I know her, she wants to take a peek at her property."

"Seriously?" Ray asked. "Your mother?"

"Oh, yeah, seriously." Hollywood pointed back inside the car-lot dollhouse. "She might have taken a shotgun with her, too. Usually sits on steer horns on the wall in there, but it's gone. She kept shells in the kitchen."

"Okay, Mr. Williams," Ray said. "Please raise your hands."

"*What?*"

"Raise your hands and allow my partner to search you for weapons."

"Not a chance."

Sunny touched Ray's shoulder, gazed at him in a way that said to let her handle him. She'd explained earlier to Ray about her famous 'Crisis Overview for Dummies' speeches, and he'd agreed testosterone often produced a negative effect on some men's common sense.

He nodded for her to proceed.

"Listen, Dennis," Sunny said. "This is the *second* crime scene you've turned up at. On what could be the same case. My boss here is suspicious, okay? Me, too. You're not stupid. You should have no trouble understanding that?"

Hollywood raised his hands like signaling a field goal. "Okay, I get it. Fine. But while you're scratching my balls, Agent Hicks, could you update me on my friends, Nolan, Sammy, and Angel?"

Ray watched her check inside Hollywood's black motorcycle boots, press her hands against his ass, examine his armpits, and pat down the inside of his thighs. She clearly brushed his junk twice, on both sides. Her training required contact, and since her attraction to the guy was obvious, Ray decided to have some fun.

"Anything dangerous in there, agent?" he asked.

She laughed. "Nothing special for a man his size. I mean, a guy six-four, you're not expecting a cocktail sausage and peanuts."

Ray laughed. He loved she'd played along.

She faced Williams, not far from nose-to-nose. "All I can say about your friends is our lab is testing DNA samples which could help. I'll let you know."

"You found their bodies?" he said.

"I can't discuss that," she said. "But they are your friends, I understand, and you helped with the case. I'll let you know if I hear something definite."

"Sammy Polanco is actually a cousin," Williams said.

Sunny nodded like she'd known all along. New to investigations, sure, but she was razor sharp.

"Can we check Mom's auto shop across the street?" Williams said. "I'm worried about her. Like I said, I told her I was coming, and Mom said she'd be here."

Ray was skeptical. "Sounds like that property belongs to the bank."

"Not in my mother's mind."

"Right," he said. "I get it. We're worried about your mom, too. But the thing is, our job requires us to search these premises first. Where the 9-1-1 call originated, and the place you were inside before we got here."

"I already checked the place out. Mom's not here. Why would I lie?"

"All we know about *you*, Mr. Williams, you keep showing up at crime scenes."

Williams' face went red. He pointed across the street. "You need to check over there for my mom right now. If you don't, I'm going by myself."

"No, you're not," Ray said.

"Try and stop me, asshole."

"Whoops. That's crossing a line." Ray pulled handcuffs. "Please turn around. I need to restrain you while we search these premises."

Storm clouds crossed Williams' eyes as he took a step back. "Good luck putting those on."

18

Studying Williams's scowl, the lightning in his stare, his partner's internal alarms must have sounded. Ray watched Sunny recoil with rookie angst, her blood no doubt flooding with adrenaline. She drew her weapon, but at least kept the Sig Sauer in the low-ready.

Her finger off the trigger.

"Easy there, Agent Hicks," he said. "Mr. Williams has no intention of disobeying my request, do you, Mr. Williams?"

Before the golden-haired biker could answer, Ray laid a hand on Hollywood's shoulder, near the neck, gripping William's flesh like he'd clenched and swung that two-pound ball peen hammer all summer as a kid. He squeezed. About a seven on his private scale of ten. The man's knees wobbled, but he didn't go down.

The guy Sunny called Hollywood was thorny.

But when Ray eased his grip, the biker let the handcuffs lock on him with a quiet *click*.

Sunny exhaled loudly and slid the Sig Sauer back in her holster. Hauling Williams to the Suburban, Ray wondered at her attraction to the guy. Yeah, Williams was tall, handsome, and a long-haired bad boy. At least one of his three sisters found that combo sexy. But he could not understand how any woman trusted a man like that.

Ray deposited Williams in the Suburban's floor-mounted restraint chair. Handcuffed behind his back, locked in the seat from overhead and both sides, Williams would find any movement difficult. Escape was impossible, or at least hadn't happened yet, according to the manufacturer.

Inside Mrs. Polanco's auto sales shack, Ray opened the slide-out, top drawer of a six-by-three-foot desk, one of two matching worktables. He told Sunny to check the bathroom and closet, then search the matching desk across from him.

He found brown, manila folders and stacks of papers he tossed on the mutuallyshared top, then picked through each, one-by-one. Mostly expense receipts, including property tax bills with red, screaming headlines, OVERDUE.

By the time Sunny got to work on her desk, he'd turned up copies of marriage and divorce certificates from the early 1980s, documents confirming what Williams had said a few minutes ago. Georgiana Williams Sutcliff had married King Polanco, Jr. after divorcing Ernesto Williams. And Williams was listed as the father on Dennis Robert Williams' birth, certificate.

"He told us the truth about this being his mom's house," he said.

Busy with her own reading, Hicks barely nodded. "Okay."

He picked up a yellowed newspaper photo, a head and shoulders portrait of an older Hispanic man. Handsome and distinguished, he wore a scowl and a three-piece-suit with a collar and string tie, a watch chain hanging across his vest. A thick gold loop.

The caption said, "King Polanco Denies Charges."

The headline had been sliced off, so only the yellowed photograph topped the four-paragraph story. Mostly a rehash of the civil charges contained in a private lawsuit, including extortion, embezzlement, and fraud. Not a flattering slice of publicity for Mr. Polanco. Particularly the last line.

Polanco denied any relationship to New York mobsters.
At least Polanco looked distinguished.

Sunny glanced up. "What did you just say?"

"I said Williams told us the truth. The lot and shack belong to his mother."

"We should we take him out of that chair before we go across the street," Sunny said. "How do we keep him in custody for occupying his mother's property?"

"Is that good or bad? That he drove his gang to Nolan Maris's property *and* showed up here is tough for me to swallow as coincidence, but you know what's worse? That his mom owns the joint across the street where men fired weapons on a stolen truck."

"The shop's bankrupt," Sunny said. "Anybody could sneak in there."

"You like the guy, don't you?"

She smiled. "His concern for his friends seemed real to me. I think we have to let him go, or take him with us across the street."

"He is admittedly friends with the thieves."

"Doesn't mean he's a thief."

"Because you've had so much experience with criminals?"

"Hey."

"Sorry. You're right. You performed at a high level with that group of bikers at the Maris barn. You deserve, and have earned, your own opinion."

"No problem."

"But let me ask you, did you grab a feel during that weapons search?"

Sunny issued an odd cackle, almost a bark.

The sound made him laugh. She joined in, and twenty or thirty seconds passed before they stopped.

"Okay," Ray said. "We'll take him with us. But on one condition."

***

Crossing the street, he talked Williams into leading the way. The biker could show him and Sunny where Mom might be located inside the bankrupt property. Being the first one in made him point man, Ray explained. Make your mother proud.

Williams bit like a starving trout.

Ray trailed on Williams' right, Sunny on the worried son's left, both officers staying ten to fifteen feet behind. Because Williams earlier had reported his mother's possible possession of a loaded shotgun, both Homeland agents kept their weapons drawn.

Two-handed grip. In the low-ready.

Ray thought Sunny's hold looked steady and firm.

Bent, busted, and knocked to the side, the front chainlink gate confirmed one part of Mrs. Polanco's report to the police—that a flatbed truck had knocked a fence down. Earlier, Ray had noticed broken curb cement and scarred asphalt across the street—at Polanco's car lot—again details matching the police description Sunny had obtained.

Williams led them toward a decayed, two-story rectangular building. Yellow stucco. A Spanish, red-tiled roof. Three tall garage doors and one man-sized door faced the street. Williams opened the people's entrance and walked inside.

Ray signaled Hicks to cover the back, then followed the biker. He'd seen dozens of older car garages, this one bigger because it had been built for trucks. But typical with red-painted equipment on the floor, hoses hanging from the ceiling, and dirty work rags scattered across most of the bench work surfaces. Three lifts pushed heavy vehicles in the air, and the air smelled like grease, oil, and gasoline.

Sunny grunted. Ray always sent her to the back.

She hurried first to her left, her strides carefully targeting bare spots between risky trash—boxes, bags, boards—plus chunks of broken concrete. Her preferred foot path featured oily gravel and dirt. The sun burned hotter by the minute.

She turned the corner and headed back along the stucco wall, past a broken window, toward the chainlink fence in back. The barrier prevented easy access to railroad tracks, and beyond the raised bed of crushed rock, unplowed acres of sandy dirt and sparse brown weeds spread into acres of desert. And a half-concealed, parked car.

Hamza's Dodge.

A train horn sounded as she called Ray. "I found a broken window, a way into the building. But I also see Hamza's red Dodge parked on the other side of the fence. Across the train tracks."

"You sure it's the same car?"

"Yes. I can see the license."

"Anybody inside?"

"Looks empty," Sunny said.

"Can you get in through the building window and meet us?"

"Yeah, but I haven't been all the way to the back fence yet."

"There's no one running," Hauser said. "Meet us inside, but be careful. I can't see your window."

With a flat-sided rock, Sunny swept away all glass remnants from the sill. The train horn sounded again, closer, the loud noise goosing her pulse and excitement. A feeling something big was about to happen.

When entry was safe, she hiked her butt up onto the window and dropped one leg through the opening. Perched half in, half out of the window, Sunny glanced at the railroad tracks. She gasped. A vise pressed her chest.

The blue shorts. A yellow camp shirt with green palm trees. There was Hamza Yusin, using a blanket to roll over the barbed wire on top of the chainlink fence, not more than twenty-five or thirty feet from Sunny. He must have exited a back way.

The world froze, her mind caught between. As train whistles shocked the air and boxed her ears, Hamza dropped clumsily onto the far side of the fence. He hopped and jumped his way across the train tracks, tripped, then staggered to his feet and lumbered toward his car.

Four locomotives exploded from right to left, blocking Sunny's chase route. She'd been leaning out the window to view Hamza. The shattering blast of sound rocked her perch. She was less than thirty feet away.

She yelped and nearly fell, clutching the window frame to save herself.

She considered chasing Hamza. But four locomotives indicated a large and lengthy freight train. Hamza would be long gone by the time she saw a caboose.

She rolled inside the men's bathroom, heard Ray's voice, and found him quickly in the near-empty garage, a cell phone pressed against his ear. He had a great smile, but his mouth currently was set firm in concentration.

He waved when he saw Sunny, but continued listening intently.

She invaded his space. She felt her information was important. "Hamza Yusin just crossed the tracks in front of the train, got to his parked car there. We can't pursue until the train passes."

The train still roared by outside. Ray shook his head and didn't stop listening to the phone. When Sunny didn't move, he stepped away from her, raising his hand, asking her to wait. He showed her his back.

Hell with him. She slipped into the garage's corner business office. Huddled together on one of two green sofas pushed at right angles against the wall, Hollywood held his mother in his arms. She leaned her cheek on his shoulder, her thin body still, eyes closed. Sunny guessed her age to be mid-seventies.

Hollywood caught Sunny's eye, nodded at his mother with his mouth pinched. "That F-ing Hamza knocked my mother down."

Sunny sat on the other sofa, closer to Mrs. Polanco. Hollywood shifted closer to let his mom sit up straighter, but she kept her weight against him. She'd been pretty in her youth, shared Hollywood's handsome blue eyes and Viking facial structure. She wore baggy blue jeans and a white-flowered, blue muumuu. Cheap and dirty white sneakers. Sunny saw no bandages or visible wounds.

She opened her eyes. They were already staring at Sunny. "Who are *you*?"

"Special Agent Sunny Hicks. I'm with the Air Force, but on a case for Homeland Security."

Mrs. Polanco grunted. "On the case, huh? Sunny Hicks on a big one?"

"Yes, ma'am."

Mrs. Polanco patted her son's leg. "And you *like* the big ones, right?"

Sunny's cheeks flushed, but she couldn't convince herself the woman was actually *trying* to be suggestive. Better to ignore her comments. "Your husband was an extremely handsome man, Mrs. Polanco. I saw his picture."

The woman's wrinkled face screwed up tighter. Especially her lips.

"We found a newspaper clipping across the street," Sunny said. "King Polanco was your husband, right?"

"You think I'm a hundred?" she said.

Oops. "Oh, that's right. Polanco Senior. So sorry. You were married to his son?"

"You went through my papers?"

"Your son said you were missing."

"Hey," Hollywood said. "Don't blame me."

Mrs. Polanco glared at her. "Get lost, Sunny."

Some old lady. Quick as a whip and mean, too. "Can't you tell me what happened? Why was a man running out the back? Why did he knock you down? Did he hold you against your will, threaten you?"

Mrs. Polanco nestled into Hollywood's shoulder. "Like I told the other one, some man I don't know jumped out of the dark, grabbed my shotgun, and knocked me down. I thought he ran out the back ten minutes ago. That's everything I know."

The Polanco woman seemed odd. Sunny wanted to talk more. But Ray waved to come outside the office. Oh, sure. *Now* he had time for her.

She excused herself and joined Ray. That woman had been weird.

Ray still had the phone to his ear. "Of course. We'll drop him from our radar. Let him operate without interference."

He tucked the phone in his coat pocket and glanced at her. "That was Eric. Hamza Yusin works for the Central Intelligence Agency."

19

Ray found Eric where he said he'd be, hunched over a martini in the Phoenix Hyatt's off-lobby cocktail lounge. The Homeland Under Secretary commanded the loneliest stool at the end of a cheerless bar. And as he'd guessed from the hour, the place, and the fact Eric's secretary had called to arrange the meet, his friend's body language suggested the news wasn't good.

He slipped onto the next stool and pried loose the knot in his gut. "What happened?"

Eric wouldn't or couldn't speak. From an inside jacket pocket, he produced a double-folded, single sheet of letter-size copy paper. He pushed the paper in front of Ray.

His breathing slowed. His gut told him the information was about Alissa.

He took his time unfolding the paper.

On the sheet were typed five names. Nolan Maris. Angel Alcides. Samuel Polanco. James Dawson. Alissa Hauser. Even sensing her name would be there, Ray's heart stuttered as he read it. He could guess who these people were. He swallowed twice before he could ask. "Forensics identified Alissa's remains at the Maris Canyon crime scene?"

Eric's eyes stayed on his drink. "Yes."

He straightened his back and drew in a long breath. There were half a dozen connections between the Maris property and

Alissa he wanted to explore, other questions to ask. Emotion prevented him. That human response his military training told him to ignore. Think with your head, not your heart.

Block that anger, Ray.

"Who's Dawson?" he asked.

"An attorney missing twenty years."

Though Alissa had disappeared two years earlier and under circumstances which made Ray believe she could no longer be alive, the word *hope* existed for people like him. Men and women who wanted to believe something that couldn't be.

This matching DNA from Alissa's bones clarified any self-induced dreams. He sensed the death in his throat and behind his eyes. Like a kid again, wanting to cry. The physical perception of impending tears. He blinked and blinked again.

"Have a drink," Eric said. "Now we know for sure the gang who took the cannon is the same group of killers who took Alissa. This time, we'll find them, Ray."

He asked the bartender for a Diet Coca-Cola. The small bones meant they had spread out Alissa for the animals, presumably after they'd murdered her. He tried not to think about the other possibility, or what they might have done before. Rape and torture. Nor was it productive imagining how long she'd waited for him to rescue her.

The guilt made him—

"Ray? You okay?"

He glanced at his hands. They were fists.

Picking up the clear bar of Neutrogena again, Sunny decided clumsiness was a fitting end to the day. She'd banged her elbow, bumped her head, and three times dropped the soap. However, she finished shampooing, showering and drying off in the cramped motel bathroom without permanent physical damage, so there was hope.

She slipped into her Dodger T-shirt, used the hairdryer and

toothbrush, applied moisturizer, and headed for bed. Only one more thing she had left to do that night, and the task created an interesting ambivalence.

Sitting on the edge of the saggy mattress, she searched her purse for the Juanita's Restaurant card, then called the number Hollywood had written down at breakfast. With strong, big hands and long, delicate fingers. Something about the man persisted in her thoughts. Maybe lots of things.

He answered on the third ring. "Who's this?"

"Special Agent Hicks. How's your mom?"

A full beat of silence. "Sunny, sure. Hey, thanks for asking. She's good. I brought her to my house a few hours ago. You catch that guy?"

"No, we didn't. Colors was long gone by the time the freight train passed. Did your mom ever explain why—"

"Why do you call him Colors?"

"I like to make up nicknames to remember people."

"Did you make one up for me?"

"Sure thing, Hollywood."

"Hollywood?"

"You look like a movie star, Dennis. I think you know that very well."

"Some women think I'm okay. Others don't. Too pretty. Calling me Hollywood says you might be the first kind."

She sucked in a quiet breath. She could have this man up here in minutes if she wanted him. If she were ready to suffer whatever consequences might arise. Offer men a decent chance for sex, they appeared out of barren deserts, empty forests, and even fell from the sky. A part of her *did* want him that way. For sure.

That long golden hair to play with. The muscles.

She broke off those thoughts by imagining what Ray and Eric Johannsen would do if she slept with a witness. Maybe a suspect.

"Did your mother explain what Hamza wanted?" she asked. "Why he was on her property? She told us practically nothing."

"Mom said Hamza asked her about Nolan's wife, Jessie. Said she cheated him, or something—didn't say how."

"How does your mom know Jessie Maris?"

He was quiet for a second. "I don't know that she does. Maybe Nolan worked for the Polanco family once. Most of the guys around here did at one time or another."

"Any idea why Hamza was hanging around when the three of us came over."

"Mom thought he'd left earlier. She said he was looking for something."

"Looking for what?"

"No clue."

She cleared her throat to tell Hollywood about his friends, the official reason she'd called. She wondered how he'd take the news.

"I should tell you something I heard at a biker bar yesterday," Hollywood said.

The reprieve from spilling her announcement was a relief, if temporary. "What?"

"People think Nolan's dead, that his wife killed him. A friend of a friend was at the Maris place first of the week, said Nolan's wife acted weird and the barn smelled like gunpowder.

"It's true. Nolan's dead."

"Ah, hell."

She couldn't tell much from his response. She needed him to talk more. "There's a press conference tomorrow morning, so I can give you the news now. Nolan Maris's DNA matched human remains we found on his property."

"Damn."

"We discovered other bodies as well, matched them with the DNA of Angel Alcides and Samuel Polanco."

Hollywood groaned. "All three?"

Homeland's forensics team had found the remains of five bodies in that gully, Sunny knew, a man and woman buried years earlier.

"Sorry, yes," she said. "Didn't you say Sammy Polanco was your cousin?"

"Yup."

"So, your mom did know Nolan, through you and Sammy."

"I don't think so. Nolan has never been a big friend of mine, and I quit hanging with him when I saw him smack Jessie at a river party. That was it for me. Only assholes hit women. Excuse my language."

"If Nolan Maris wasn't your friend, why did you and your boys come looking for him?"

"He said he had a new toy to show us."

Sunny glanced at the clock. Quarter of eleven. Her body soft and relaxed because of the hot shower, but tired as well. Seconds passed. "I'm sorry about your friends, Dennis."

"Thanks. Hey, you want to have a late dinner, talk more about the case?"

There's the offer. That was her chance. "Thanks, Dennis, but not tonight. In fact, not while I'm working this case, or any other you might be involved in. We need to keep our discussions on a professional level."

"Sure. That's all I was suggesting, Special Agent. Info on your case."

"Of course. Now, before we say goodnight, tell me something I don't know about Jessie Maris."

"I told you. I hardly knew her."

"Who might talk to me about her?"

"Nobody in the club. None of the women liked her, but Sacred Bones is still a club, you know. We don't rat on each other."

"Why didn't the other women like her?"

"Jessie wasn't around the parties much. When she was, she didn't talk to the other women. And once she got caught with somebody's fiancé. Those parties were wild, but partners were supposed to be off limits."

"You never saw her speaking with anyone else? Jessie didn't

have a girlfriend she talked to?"

"The only human I remember her talking to more than two seconds was Nolan, plus the man who got caught banging her. One of the club's big river runs. He and Nolan had words that first time, then months later, much worse—like maybe the guy and Jessie had been sneaking behind Nolan's back. I don't know. I haven't seen the guy since that fight."

"So he and Nolan had real fisticuffs over Jessie?"

"The second time, yeah. Fisticuffs. I love it. The girl I was dating loved it. Lots of blood. Nolan pulled a hatchet from his hip pocket. Girls were screaming."

"You have to remember the man's name, a fight like that. Come on, Dennis, what was it? Think."

"He was a big guy, heavy. Yanked away Nolan's hatchet and whacked him on the head with it. Sideways, not with the blade, thank God, but you should have seen the blood. Knocked Nolan cold."

"His name?"

"I never talked to the guy much, only…wait…Bobby, Jimmy, Tommy. That's it. His name was Tommy Moon."

Jessie rested a chopping knife on the counter, abandoning her ham and potato casserole preparations, determined to follow her ears and discover what made that the hammering sound so late at night. She and Tommy would be extremely busy today and tomorrow, and she wanted to cook a couple a one-pot meals tonight. The banging noise disturbed her. It had to be Tommy, but she couldn't imagine what he was doing.

She squeezed carefully from the space Nolan had called a kitchen, a rock closet offering no door and not much of an entrance, only a narrow, twenty-nine inches between hand-hewn walls of sharp granite. It was like living in a *Flintstones* cartoon, the surfaces almost impossible to keep clean.

She found Tommy in the bathroom—another edgy-walled

rock closet—in the process of hanging a mirror, of all things, the man with no clue. Guess she'd never told him how she felt about her reflection. Even Nolan hadn't insisted they hang one.

"Where did you get that?" she said.

"At the welding supplies place," Tommy said. "The owner's getting divorced. He was selling his wife's furniture in the parking lot. Thought I'd surprise you."

"How nice," she said. "Thank you."

He encouraged Jessie to come inside the bath, see his work. She stayed still, away from any potential self-image, but kind of wanting to see herself again, see if she'd changed. She'd acted differently the last several days and felt different. Stronger. Better without Nolan. Except she hadn't looked in a mirror in so many years. What if she saw the same person she'd always been? Miss Punching Bag. Maybe she'd fall right back into her previous ways, like having a cigarette after you quit smoking.

"Something wrong?" Tommy said.

"No. Thank you for the present. That's sweet."

Her image had been entirely non-descript the last time. She hadn't seen her hair, her eyes, her skin, the makeup, or the way her nose and mouth pushed together. What she'd seen instead were specific words her mother had used to describe her daughter, letters printed on the glass. *Plain. Average.* And *stupid*, because Mom said any woman who didn't worry about her appearance was ignorant and dull-witted.

"I thought women liked mirrors," he said. "You're so pretty, too."

"That's nice, Tommy. I appreciate the compliment. Really."

"Come see if I hung it at the right height."

She sighed. Better to put the truth out there. "I have a thing with mirrors, Tommy. Okay? I thought I told you before, honest. I'm sorry."

"A thing?"

"I can't look in them. My mother used to use them as a weapon against me. Most of my friends already—"

"What friends?"

Jessie's chest felt the bite in his words. It surprised and stung her. "Don't be mean," she said. "I had lots of friends before Nolan moved us to a trailer in the desert."

"If you say so."

Ouch. She counted to five, staring at the chopping knife on the counter where she'd been slicing potatoes and a left-over ham. That blade was as sharp as a razor. She could gut fat boy here with one fast swipe, Tommy not feeling much pain until his intestines plopped onto the stone floor.

She refocused. "That's really mean. What's the matter with you?"

"You're the one acting mean, like a big boss lady, making me build some engineering marvel on the back of a flatbed trailer."

"You're angry about your work on the autocannon?"

"If we're going to sell it, why don't we just sell it? Let's go spend the cash in Cabo. We could have big fun for a year down there with a hundred grand."

"I want to get what it's worth."

"What you're making me build isn't easy, Jessie. The mechanicals you gave me aren't really complete. The measurements seem off. It's like aliens designed it."

"'Engineering marvel' was good. I liked that better than 'aliens.' Geez, Tommy, I asked you to help me install the autocannon on a platform."

"A swiveling platform."

"No, a swivel allows for three-hundred-sixty-degree turns. The blueprints I gave you call for a shift of fifteen degrees. Don't you understand how this is going to zoom our price when we show people what the cannon can do?"

He tossed his hammer on the bathroom floor, cracking two of the one-inch-square ceramic tiles installed a century ago. Shaking his head, he squeezed past her into the stone cabin's den-slash-living room. He plopped his massive frame on the couch and switched on his smart phone, sticking plastic buds in his ears.

She lived in a cave where the walls were bare rock. But her man was denser.

She picked up his hammer, held the tool in her hands, palmed the weight, gripped the handle, decided a good description of the steel mallet included well-balanced. She carried the hammer with her, joined Tommy in the next room. He couldn't walk away now. Not until he'd finished the platform. A few more lies were needed.

"Okay," she said. "When you're right, you're right. We'll sell the cannon this weekend, rain or shine. Instead of a riskier public demonstration and open negotiation, we go for a private and quick auction. We accept three or four potential buyers, people we know have the cash, show them what a fifteen-degree shift can do. We'll get a line of old cars or something, mow them down like ducks, sell that night to the highest bidder."

Tommy sat up, worry crossing his face like a cloud. His features were growing plumper, too, Jessie cooking so much. Breakfast, lunch, and dinner. The man could eat, including a full pound of pasta when she made spaghetti with meatballs or macaroni and cheese.

"So, I still have to finish the platform?" Tommy said.

"Can't you? It will double our price."

He nodded. "Okay—if we sell it this weekend."

"Promise."

He seemed puzzled. "Something else?" Jessie said.

"How can we trust strangers not to rob us at the auction? Or maybe undercover cops show up, bust our asses."

Jessie shook her head. Poor man. Good thing he could drive big rigs and weld.

"Come on, Tommy. People won't come in *person* to the demonstration and auction. What did you think? We were going to throw a big dinner party and show?"

He shrugged.

"We'll livestream the demo and auction from an undisclosed location."

"You can do that?"

She leaned over and kissed him. "On the internet, Tommy. Ever hear about the *dark web*?"

"Yeah, but I don't know what it is."

"Onionland."

"Huh?"

"Messages are hidden inside in layers of encryption, like an onion," Jessie said. "They're transmitted through a series of onion routers, each of which peels away a single layer. The sender stays hidden because each layer only knows the two layers on either side."

"Who taught you this stuff?"

"Nolan showed me how to buy pills."

THREE DAYS BEFORE THE RAIN

20

Ray knew the caller was Etta before he checked his phone.

Who else would poke him at sunrise?

He could also guess why she'd called. Yesterday's press conference by Homeland Security in Phoenix still dominated the media. On top of his Gila Bend-motel double bed, he'd watched talking heads repeat Homeland's news about the missing autocannon, while behind them on a screen, airborne Warthogs destroyed three tanks on a video loop.

"Hi, Etta. How you doing? How's my grandniece?"

"Brianna is the same as she was yesterday and the day before that. Are you working that missing autocannon case, Ray? Potential terrorism? I saw the Homeland Security news conference in Arizona."

"You know I can't talk about what I do."

"Ray. You called *me* to say you might have a lead on Alissa. And the Homeland Security official I saw on television said he worked for Intelligence and Analysis, same as you."

He pulled a long breath. "I'm not talking about *that* case, or *my* case, Etta. I'm not talking about any case. Everything is going well in my work. I'm not in Phoenix." Not a lie. Ray had moved to cover for Sunny. "And most of what I'm doing involves making losers do their job. You know that."

"Don't give me the cover story. A *Los Angeles Times* reporter came on after the Homeland man, said his Navy SEAL sources confirmed the missing autocannon was stolen off a train."

Ray closed his eyes. He was going to hear Etta talk about his dead wife again. She was going to use Alissa's name, and hearing it would make him remember the feel and smell of her, the warmth of her heart against his, the taste of her lips. How much her disappearance two years ago still hurt inside.

Hearing of the DNA match crushed hope he hadn't believed existed.

"Are these the same thieves who took Alissa's generator? Because that's what she thought, too. You told me she was searching the train tracks in Arizona."

"I can't say, Etta. I can't talk about my cases."

"Damn it, Ray, stop telling—"

"I have to go."

"Tell me about Agent Hicks. The woman you're looking for writes notes to Hicks, so you must have at least met her. They had a picture. She looked pretty."

"No comment."

"So, you *are* working with her, using her on the investigation."

"Come on, Etta."

"It's all on television, Ray. Agent Hicks. The missing autocannon. An assassination threat."

"Damn."

"Don't curse."

"Sorry. But it's a crime for me to talk about a case. I have to go."

"Don't you hang up on me, Ray Hauser. If these are the same people, and you catch them, do you really think you could just—"

He pushed cancel.

His insides didn't hurt like he'd lost the love of a woman. His heart and lungs twisted around his ribs as if he'd lost the love of *all* women. Forever. As if mating were no longer for him. Like the bullfrog with a broken leg.

Too bad for you in the genetic stew.

Not today, General Ray.

His Alissa. His one chance at happiness, murdered because she'd discovered a crime scene as had Sunny. Probably both smart ladies figuring out how centrifugal force could pull a four-thousand pound package from a rolling train.

Besides brushing her hair, scrubbing her teeth, and applying a light coat of lipstick, Sunny prepared for the morning teleconference by studying every case note she'd taken. She got up extra early to compose comments and questions for the internal Homeland Security-sponsored event. She wanted to look good and sound good.

Didn't everybody?

Besides Ray and his boss-friend Eric from Homeland, who ran the morning meeting by iPad, the electronic gathering included representatives of the Central Intelligence Agency, the Federal Bureau of Investigation, the Defense Department, the National Security Administration, and Seager's replacement at the Air Force's Office of Special Investigations.

But when the male-dominated confab was a half-hour old, Sunny wished she hadn't bothered attending. Her questions about lifting the court-ordered seal on Jessie Maris's juvenile record earned nothing but the repeated phrase, "The Department of Justice is working on it."

In fact, Sunny learned nothing new about anything. *Nada.* Half the men in attendance were suspicious, wanted to know why Jessie had addressed the letters to Sunny. She'd wasted much time reminding them she and Jessie had several conversations at the crime scene, and Jessie had released her unharmed.

Worst thing about the information-sharing event, the CIA wouldn't share a freaking thing about Hamza or his actions. What was that about?

The group only discussed the obvious. Jessie Maris was an armed killer and almost certainly had control of the cannon. Besides her confession to the shootings of three men, traces of Jessie's DNA could be associated with clothing remnants from three of the five bodies, and inside another truck hidden on the property, the Chevy used to kidnap Sunny. Registered to Angel Alcides. Nolan Maris's Ford 350 hadn't turned up on traffic cameras.

Sunny's lead about Tommy Moon seemed to be their only workable thread. She and Ray planned to check out Moon's home address after the meeting, but with so few leads, and so little time, the whole group needed to get off their ass. According to Jessie's notes, they had three or four days to find that cannon and prevent potential mass murder.

But who was Jessie's target?

"Her use of the words 'fans' and 'teammates' focused us on a professional football game Sunday," the FBI rep said. "The Arizona Cardinals play an exhibition game in State Farm Stadium. Over sixty-thousand in attendance. The visiting quarterback was sidelined by the league for domestic violence. The upcoming game is his controversial return."

"I think her use of those words is a diversion," Sunny said. "I believe Jessie is targeting someone from her childhood."

"You're the only one in the room who's talked to her," Eric said. "What makes you say that?"

"Jessie told me her world turned bad when her father left. That her mother was cruel and abusive." Sunny considered her words. "Trying to identify, I told her my story—that I'd lost my own father at six, and was an orphan soon after that."

Two new people inhaled loudly enough to make Sunny pause.

"And Jessie replied, 'I felt worse than an orphan—more like a beaten dog.' I believe she's seeking revenge against someone from that childhood, not current events."

"Sounds like you had quite the conversation during your kidnapping." the FBI spokesman said.

Sunny nodded. "She called it a girl's moment."

"Other possibilities besides the quarterback?" Eric said.

A political candidate also seemed possible, the CIA and others agreed, but there were so many choices. America was coming up on November elections, and several candidates had been accused of sexual misconduct at one time or another. August fundraising parties bloomed like flowers in spring. In the Phoenix area alone, the FBI identified eleven political fundraisers scheduled for Saturday and Sunday.

The FBI passed out a list. The Sheriff of Pinacosta County was holding a chicken and waffle dinner. A local Congressman, Randall King, now a candidate for Arizona's Governor, had four different events, two of them expecting thousands. With him, at least they'd have security help from State Troopers.

After the teleconference, still in her motel room, Sunny's cell buzzed. *The Los Angeles Times.* Jordan. A flicker of curiosity burned her, and she answered, but immediately canceled the call. She was still angry about his stupid story.

He called back. She answered and hung up again. He called back. On his fourth try, she answered. "Stop calling me."

"I need to apologize," Jordan said. "I should never have put that line in my story about Gila Bend and the talkative source. I am so *sorry*. It was dumb. Got edited out in the print edition and I got yelled at. Guess I was angry you wouldn't help me. And...I miss you. I know ¡that's no excuse, but I owe you the truth."

"You owe me nothing, Jordan. Just stop calling. I don't want to talk to you."

"Did I get you in trouble?"

"Unclear. A friend covered for me."

"Thank God. I'm so sorry."

"Why did you do that? It was so *mean*."

"I don't know. I was angry."

"You expected me to give you classified information? Risk a prison sentence?"

He cleared his throat. "Well...no, not when you put it that way. But I had the story. I was looking for confirmation. I wouldn't have—"

"Anything I know about it is classified information. You don't give a crap about me, my career, or my future. All you care about is yourself. Ace newspaper reporter. I'm hanging up. Don't *ever* call me again."

Sunny turned off her phone, went to her purse and exchanged the cell for her holstered Sig Sauer. Time to finish dressing. Ray was picking her up in ten minutes. She checked the load, slipped the weapon back in its leather, and clipped the holstered semiautomatic onto her belt.

She hurried downstairs. She liked being there when he drove up.

Phone in hand, she froze entering the tiny motel lobby. A TV camera crew and a reporter waited for her on the sidewalk. Her name was all over the media, linked to the fugitive Jessie Maris, confessed murderer of her apparently abusive husband and two other men. Coverage had escalated after Homeland Security's press conference had acknowledged Jessie Maris was a person of interest in the disappearance of the Air Force's cannon.

Thanks to Jordan's story, the poor Homeland spokesman had been unable to deny the autocannon's theft, or Jessie's connection. Jessie had attached the "Highway of Death" photo to her latest online press submission.

She used her cell to dial the front desk. "Hi, this is S. Hicks in room 202. I need to avoid the TV reporters on the sidewalk. Is there—"

"I made them wait outside."

"Thank you," Sunny said, "but is there a back way out of here?"

"Is that you by the elevator?"

Sunny waved. "Yes."

"Take that hall straight back, turn left, keep walking until you see the EXIT sign. Your friend in the SUV is waiting in back."

Must be Ray.

He unbuckled his seatbelt and hopped out. On the other side of the black Suburban, Sunny did the same. They'd easily found the Malago Street address Thomas Moon listed on his Arizona driver's license. Not the fanciest part of town. A nasty-looking yard of hardpan dirt surrounded a four-room, single-family, vinyl-sided box. All the houses on Malago Street had given up on grass lawns, although half sported an unhappy palm tree or two.

He pushed through the sidewalk gate, a narrow break in the four-foot chain fence which surrounded the Moon address. The dirt lot was scattered with toys, a barbeque, a broken cement birdbath, and a motorcycle without wheels. Didn't feel like the kind of place he might learn something about Alissa's death.

But you never knew.

"Remind me who lives here," he said.

Sunny checked her notes. "Tommy and his widowed mother. Caron Moon. She owns the house and at least one gun, a .44 magnum Desert Eagle, this according to a Gila Bend Police incident report from last year. Mother and son attracted attention with a screaming match. When the confrontation devolved into pistol waving, neighbors called the police."

"Stand over there when I knock," he said.

The hum of an air-conditioner partially muted his rapping, but footsteps soon squeaked on loose floorboards. A shuffling kind of walk.

The wood door opened behind the screen. He could see only half the figure obscured in the house shade, but that was enough to recognize a possible threat. The two-hundred-pound woman had short hair, wore a loose-fitting, dark-colored housedress, and kept her right hand hidden behind her. Didn't have to be a gun. But Arizona was open carry.

He held up his shield. "Hello. I'm Ray Hauser with the US Department of Homeland Security. This is Agent Hicks. Are you Mrs. Caron Moon?"

Nothing.

"Mrs. Moon?"

The woman lifted her head an inch. "Yeah?"

"Can we ask you a few questions about your son, Thomas?" Ray asked.

Silence from the shape behind the door.

"Mrs. Moon, is that a weapon in your right hand?" Sunny asked. She retreated a step, keeping her Sig Sauer holstered.

Ray stepped closer to the door. "Mrs. Moon, what's in your hand?"

Tommy Moon's mother presented her hidden right hand suddenly, thrusting her hand at him with blurring speed. The quick, possibly threatening move startled Ray, drove him back, making him reach but not pull. Sunny drew and stepped back into a shooting stance.

Mrs. Moon's speedy hand held a clear-glass, pint bottle of vodka. She used the near-empty container to push open the screen door and wave them inside. "You cops want to visit, chat about my boy Tommy, fine with me. Come on in."

Ray climbed inside, checked out Hicks as she followed him inside. An artery in her neck throbbed like she'd been running.

"Hope you special agents don't mind me having a drink while we're talking?" Caron Moon said.

Ray shook his head. "No problem."

**

While sipping the palest screwdriver Ray had ever seen, Caron Moon told them her son Tommy had come home early from work the other day, loaded two backpacks and a suitcase with clothes. He'd also filled his old, banged-up Navy duffle bag with automotive and welding tools and supplies.

He'd been in a hurry. Said he was taking a trip and wasn't sure when he'd be home.

Mrs. Moon leaned back in an overstuffed wing chair, pointed a forefinger at the ceiling for emphasis. "Now I know my boy, and his level of animation and parental abuse that afternoon indicates only one thing."

Ray glanced at Sunny. "What's that, Mrs. Moon?"

"A woman."

"Any particular woman?" he asked. "A name we could check out?"

"Well, sure, a particular one, but I don't know a name because he didn't say. He packed in half an hour, tricked me into leaving so he could break open my cash box, steal my money and my gold-finish, Desert Eagle."

"How did he trick you?" Sunny asked.

"Gave me a twenty to go to the liquor store, buy him a six-pack of Diet Pepsi. He said I could buy vodka with the rest."

"What a bastard," Ray said.

"He and his truck were gone when I got back. So was my Desert Eagle and six hundred dollars in cash."

"How can you be sure he left because of a woman?" Ray said. "No chance somebody offered him a great job in LA?"

"He wanted my money for a woman. He took my gun so I wouldn't shoot him with it when he comes back."

"But he didn't mention her name?" he asked.

"He didn't say the reason was a woman, but I know my boy."

Ray picked up the vodka bottle and poured a shot into the empty glass he'd earlier refused. Surprisingly, the tumbler was clean. "I've changed my mind about that drink, Mrs. Moon.

You're a smart woman, and I have a hunch we haven't asked the right question yet. You don't mind, do you?"

"Not at all," she said. "Everybody's allowed to change their minds. Mind hitting me again while you're at it?"

Pouring a tiny shot for himself, he drained what was left of the Smirnoff into Mrs. Moon's smudged glass. "Didn't Tommy belong to a motorcycle club?"

"He still wears his colors now and then," Mrs. Moon said.

"But not as much in the last year or so, right?"

"I believe that's correct. Motorcycles didn't excite him anymore."

"What I'm thinking," he said, "Tommy became less interested in motorcycles about a year ago, after he had a disagreement or maybe even a fight with another motorcycle club member, Nolan Maris."

"Maris?" Mrs. Moon frowned.

Sunny glanced at him, wanted to move in. "I expect your Tommy is the kind of young man who loves to do favors for people," she said. "Likes to help out."

Mrs. Moon's forehead wrinkles smoothed. "That's my Tommy."

"Someone like Jessie, Nolan Maris's wife, maybe?"

Mrs. Moon's eyes opened wider. Her jaw slipped. What it looked like to Ray, pieces of an old puzzle meshed. "Tommy always had a thing for Jessie. When her name was Jessie Costello and she was still in high school, they ran off. Last year, Nolan and my Tommy got into a bad a fight about her. Tommy gave him a nasty beatdown after Nolan pulled a weapon."

"Maybe it was Jessie he ran off with this time," Ray said.

"Maybe, but I never thought until this minute Jessie was still in the picture. Figured Tommy had enough of her and her husband. Would of a been a good choice, too, as I saw Jessie's picture on the TV last night. Threatening to kill a bunch of people this weekend."

"One more question," Ray said.

"Oh, Lord," Mrs. Moon said. "You think my boy is part of the gang who stole the Gatling gun thing I saw on the news?"

"No, not at all," Ray said. "Jessie might have tricked him into helping her afterward, though. Does your son still own his pickup?

Mrs. Moon shook her head. "Tommy bought himself a used Peterbilt this spring, started his own trucking company. He ain't doing good just yet, but he will."

"You have a license number?" Ray said.

"Sure. He formed an LLC, too. The papers are in that drawer behind you."

21

Ray used a heavy foot on the gas pedal, but their air-conditioned drive north to Phoenix seemed twice as long as the last time. The big SUV felt sluggish. Made of lead. He was antsy and not sure why.

Minutes after they'd left Caron Moon, US District Court Judge Oliver McHenry had signed an order granting Homeland Security inspection of any and all Pinacosta County records concerning Jessie Maris. By the time they reached Phoenix, the Department of Justice should have arranged a peek at that old sealed transcript of Jessie Costello's juvenile hearing.

They planned to pick up the subpoena, and viewing order personally, walk the papers over two blocks from the Sandra Day O'Connor US Courthouse on Washington Street to Adrian Fontes County Recorder's office on Jefferson.

He wasn't convinced the information would identify Maris's ambitions, but Sunny was, and that meant more to him every passing day. She might be inexperienced, but she was smart as a fox. He was hopeful the updated BOLO on Tommy Moon's big truck could eventually lead to the missing cannon, but his gut said trust Sunny.

Maybe he'd make her run through her ideas.

A patch of lighter traffic on State Highway 85 north encouraged him to talk. Maybe it would get his mind off Alissa.

"What makes you so sure we'll be smarter after reading this decades-old juvie report?"

"What she said to me. The way she said it."

"That's not much. That autocannon is worth a million or more on the black market. Her notes could be a bigger diversion than we think. Our internet people picked up chatter about a dark-web demonstration and auction. They're trying to get a ticket to the show."

"She told me she wanted to leave home with daddy, so it's another man in her life after that. A boyfriend of the mother's maybe. An uncle. That's what I expect to find in this sealed transcript."

"Is the father listed on her birth certificate? We should check him out, anyway."

"No, the line was blank," Sunny said.

"And the mother's dead, right? Eric's staff told me Jessie might have a sister, though."

"I hope so. She could know who Jessie's target is. The FBI's in charge of looking for her, but nothing's turned up yet."

Ray shifted lanes, their turnoff coming. "Okay, but why does Jessie have to shoot this somebody with a cannon? Why not a semiautomatic like she shot her husband? Why blast this abuser with exploding shells?"

"Maybe it's not just him," she said. "Maybe she wants to make a statement for women everywhere—a dramatic, attention-getting spectacle. Maybe that's what she wants. The notes kind of back that up."

A mile from their destination, Ray resumed his general questioning. "Did you sleep with your weapon last night?"

She laughed. "I did. Every night this week."

"What's funny?"

"I was thinking about something else. Not my Sig Sauer."

"I can guess. Any target practice since Wednesday?"

"No, but maybe we can stop at that range north of Phoenix after the courthouse, shoot a box."

"Sure, I'll go with you. There's a taco joint there makes *carne asada* with prime beef."

He pulled into a municipal parking lot. He'd seen Sunny fumble her weapon in that convenience store parking lot. She'd almost gotten herself killed searching the crime scene alone. Worse, he could still hear his mentor in Afghanistan, a grizzled lifer talking about inexperience. "Nothing kills you faster."

He turned off the ignition. But other things he'd noticed, Sunny was a clever investigator and thinker. Also a quick learner who grabbed hold of good advice. Sleeping with her Sig Sauer already had changed the way she treated her weapon. He'd seen her familiarity grow.

Sunny noticed the motorcyclist as Ray first parked. But she wasn't sure, the city traffic busy, so she didn't say anything, at least not until they left the shiny glass and metal US Courthouse minutes later. Carrying Judge McHenry's paperwork, she noticed the same biker—long, curly dark hair and beard—watching their movements from a block and a half away. His bike sat tucked between sedans parked along the sidewalk.

A shadow fell across her bright day.

The biker wasn't wearing his colors, the sleeveless jean jacket, so maybe she was mistaken. Long hair and dark beards were far from uncommon among motorcycle enthusiasts. Almost a cliché. But to her, the shaggy biker perfectly resembled that loser in Hollywood's gang. The man who'd called her a bitch.

And said no one would find their sexually abused bodies.

She pointed him out to Ray. "Recognize that biker from the Maris property? I saw him behind us when we parked, too."

"Could be the guy who threatened us. Let's get closer. Press him."

Ray shifted to a semi-jog, and she fast-trotted in her rubber-soled loafers. People on the sidewalk changed direction or walking speed to avoid them. The temperature had cooled off.

Only ninety-eight degrees this afternoon. She hadn't hustled twenty yards before perspiration beaded her neck. At least the humidity was practically zero. At a ninety-eight degree temperature in Quantico, she'd already be dripping.

The biker watched them approach, leaning relaxed against his motorcycle. Like he was fine waiting and having a chat. But he sparked into fast action when the traffic light changed at Fourth Avenue, opening a path for them to quickly jaywalk across Jefferson Street.

The bike took a hike, a screeching U-turn in front of a honking taxi, then burned rubber another ten yards on Fourth. Blue vapor slowly clouded her view, but she got a good look at the biker's face when he reversed direction—that twisted mouth inside a bug-infested beard, the greasiness of his long, ropey, black hair.

"That was definitely Hollywood's righthand man," she said. "I'll never forget that sneer, the oily sheen on his hair."

By the time they reached the corner, he'd raced away with another motorcycle beside him, the second bike coming out of nowhere, two blocks distant.

"He and his buddy must have followed us all day," Ray said. "I can't believe I didn't see them."

"They could have had a car, too."

"Maybe. Tell you what," he said. "At least we know why your new love interest—Hollywood, you call him—has been so helpful, don't we?"

Sunny glanced at him, shook her head. "He's not a love interest. And seeing this creep doesn't prove Dennis Williams or his gang *committed* the theft of our autocannon."

"Really? Pretty strong evidence, I'd say."

"This proves the bearded guy hopes we'll lead him to Jessie and the autocannon now, not that he stole it."

"Maris and his men stole the weapon," he said. "You saw it in his barn. These guys are in the same gang. Your logic seems strained, and my gut says different. Screams different, in fact."

He figured emotion was her problem. Her attraction to Williams. Better logic should be employed. A critical use of intelligence, the life and experiences collected to make better decisions.

They crossed Jefferson and entered the Pinacosta County Recorder's Office on Third Street beneath an enclosed walkway. The air bridge between buildings saved taxpayers on air-conditioning costs, no doubt, all those doors otherwise opening and closing all day. Attorney comfort probably had nothing to do with it.

After showing identification at the security window, explaining their official purpose, they were allowed to keep their weapons.

When Ray arrived at the front of the line, showed the man his paperwork, the clerk ran away and brought back an overseer. The middle-aged woman wore her hair short and dyed, flame red, solid red glasses, and a SUPERVISOR nametag. She wore a firm expression suggesting she was in charge of the western hemisphere.

Ray noted her name beneath the SUPERVISOR title. *Vivian Pearl.*

She smiled at him. "You're from Homeland Security—General Ray Hauser?"

"Yes I am, Miss Pearl. You have my juvie hearing transcript?"

She smiled. "Not me, no. But my boss said they set up a special reading room for you to view the sealed documents. You and your part—"

"Who's *they*?" he asked.

"The Juvenile Court. Whichever judge is in charge today."

"Okay, where is the Juvenile Court?"

"The court itself is in Mesa, about fifteen miles away."

"What?"

"No, no, you're good," Pearl said. "The documents are here. Most of the old records are. Judge McHenry's clerk called earlier to make arrangements."

Pearl stuck her hand and arm outside the sliding glass window, pointed to the main hallway. "Turn right there, follow that corridor to the end. There's a man waiting to show you to a reading room. His name's Axel Braun."

Ray frowned. "Axel? How will I—?"

"Believe me, General, you can't miss him. Axel is bigger than you. We call him Brawny, but only behind his back."

Ray didn't miss Axel. No one would *ever* miss Axel.

A human male of extra king-size proportions, Ray himself being king-size, Axel read from his cell phone. He tapped buttons every few seconds as they approached. Three-hundred pounds, plus, and nearly seven-feet tall, maybe seven and a half if you included his spiked purple hair. Six or seven sharp points rose from his scalp like stalagmites.

He posed in a wide stance before three ten-foot flagpoles at the end of the hall, Axel a highly conspicuous part of the official welcome from Pinacosta County, Arizona, and the United States of America. Staring at his phone.

Axel only looked up when Ray's shoes pushed close enough to occupy a strategic patch of marble floor behind Axel's phone screen. No smile on his glance. More of a thousand-mile prison stare, that hard, distant gaze of indifference Ray saw mostly on cops and criminals.

Different sides, but the same business.

After three beats, Axel's lips moved. "You Hauser?"

22

Ray and Axel stared at each other like schoolyard bullies trying to establish hierarchy. Axel wore the two-toned brown uniform of the Pinacosta County Sheriff's Posse. Same as Angel Alcides, the pistol-packing cowboy who'd called himself Garcia at the train tracks, tied up Sunny and kidnapped her. Not a look she held in high regard.

But Ray's hard-ass approach wasn't making progress. Maybe being allowed to see Jessie Maris's juvenile hearing transcript required honey, not hostility. Sunny shifted closer and grinned. "Hi, Axel. I'm Special Agent Hicks. The clerk said you'd show us the way to a special reading room."

Axel returned his dark gaze to Ray. For public-dealing volunteers, the Pinacosta County Sheriff's Posse appeared to lack basic skills in community relations. Not to mention a complete absence of goodwill toward man.

"The reading room," Sunny said. *"Please?"*

Axel grunted and headed for another hallway, a perpendicular offshoot of the main, flag bearing aisle. He crossed into the narrower passage like a thoroughbred, a model of coordinated movement, even grace. He didn't care if they followed or not.

Ray touched her shoulder. "Something's not right. This feels hinky. Let me walk closest to him. You keep an eye on our back."

Her forehead wrinkled. "Whatever you say, but we're in the Pinacosta County Recorder's Office. How hinky could things get inside a building filled with lawyers, cops, and cameras?"

"Your logic is always worth noting. But as you well know, past and current members of the Pinacosta County Sheriff's Posse were involved in your kidnapping and probably the theft of the Air Force's weapon."

"We're armed," she said. "Nobody's going to start a gunfight in a—"

Like a skilled dancer, Axel spun on the ball of one foot. He stopped with half a turn, his gaze pinned on Ray. "You two won't be packing long. No weapons allowed in the reading room today. Judge's orders."

Ray's thick, tanned face turned a shade darker. His forehead creased, his nostrils flared, and his neck muscles defined themselves. Axel didn't intimidate him, and Sunny figured that was maybe their biggest problem. No Recorder's Office, no Jessie Costello hearing transcript. Ray's refusal to take crap could get them tossed.

"Tell the judge I'm keeping my weapon," Ray said.

She touched Ray's arm and showed Axel a pleasant smile. "I think what Agent Hauser means to say, sir, is that our official business was established by the Recorder's main security. They said as Federal officers we are entitled to carry any—"

"You are entitled to dick," Axel said. He pointed a thick forefinger at the closed door directly on her left. "That's your reading room today. If you want to use it, you'll have to surrender your weapons to the guards inside."

Sunny hesitated.

"It closes at four-thirty," Axel said. "You don't have much time."

"We'll take all the time we need," Ray said. "And I'm keeping my weapon."

Sunny twisted the handle and pushed into a classroom-size space with two walls of bookshelves, including shelves above the door. Every inch was stuffed with red or purple-bound legal volumes. The library faced two walls of framed, stuffy photographs. Black suited, past and present Pinacosta County Recorders who glared down at the reading tables.

Less imposing despite their large size, two Pinacosta County Sheriff's Posse members sat facing the doorway behind a centrally placed rectangular table. Both men had been chosen for their physical magnitude, though neither matched up to Axel. The two posse members were at two hundred-fifty pounds, six feet or more in height. Sitting made their exact size hard to judge, their knees and legs stuffed beneath the table.

One said, "Come on in, little honey. We got what you're looking for."

The speaker's blond, butch-cut crown of hair failed to hide his balding top. As he'd spoken, he slid down in his chair and extended his legs toward Sunny and the door. Man, did those black cowboy boots stick out. And then, obscenely, the loser spread his feet wide apart. Forcing on everyone a close-up view of his bulging crotch. What a creep.

Sunny's molars pressed together. After she'd gagged.

Ray brushed quickly past Axel and Sunny to position himself between the butch blond's stretched, spread-out feet. But Hauser kept going, bumping the desk with his huge thighs. Stood between the guy's knees.

She cheered inside when Butch Blond's smile faded. He sat up and dragged his boots back, Sunny imagining his feet weren't the only body parts retreating. She touched Ray's arm again, both in congratulations and also trying to say, easy boss. Don't kick Butch between the legs or you'll get us thrown out before we see the transcript. Quite a long message for a touch, but she thought they clicked pretty well as investigative partners.

"Either one of you have my hearing transcript?" Ray said.

The two posse men pushed their chairs back and stood menacingly. Jaws and chests poked forward. Had to show her and Hauser how big they were.

Each posse man wore a semiautomatic pistol on his belt.
Behind Sunny, Axel blocked the open doorway.
Butch tucked his thumbs inside his belt, one pale sausage-thick finger touching his holster. "Let's have your weapons, agents."
Ray glared at him. "No."
Her pulse ticked higher. If she ever teamed regularly with this man, she might have to see a doctor about meds. Some kind of anti-anxiety pills.
"If you want to see those transcripts, place your weapons on the table," Butch said. "The Recorder's Office closes in twenty minutes."
Ray shook his head. "We're not disarming while you two are carrying. The last guy we saw in that puke brown uniform kidnapped my partner."
Butch's lip twitched. "We're part of Juvenile Court security. You're not."
"Juvenile Court is in Mesa," Ray said.
Butch sneered. "Listen and I will explain. Except for security officers—that's us—today's presiding judge ruled no weapons in Juvenile Court. Since this temporary reading room is an extension of that court, you *will* surrender your weapons to examine the transcript."
"No," Ray said.
She admired the direct way he talked, the nonchalance of his challenge. Axel did not. Quietly easing past Sunny, Axel sucker punched Ray in the back with two hands. More of a body smash, really, an exaggerated shove, Axel timing his open-handed punches with a transfer of his massive weight. Stepping into the slam.
Sunny shouted. "Ray!"
Axel hitting Ray like a tsunami.
"You need to stop being such a bitch, bitch," Axel said.
Sunny gasped. Axel's two-handed crash folded Ray at the waist and slapped his face on the table directly in front of

Butch. Ray softened the blow—barely—with a last-second hand catch. When he lifted his face off the desk, his nose bled.

To Sunny, the posse members' moves seemed to have been staged, Ray distracted by the discussion with one guard when Axel attacked. Plus, the current smirk on all three posse members said they'd pulled the gag before. A routine for the uninitiated.

What made her worry, they'd do this to a federal officer. An agent for the Department of Homeland Security, a Marine Corps general. Her teeth ground as she considered their disrespect for a law enforcement officer. She wanted to pull her weapon and place them all under arrest. But it wasn't her call.

Risky, too. She wasn't Wyatt Earp.

She'd wait for Ray to show her the play.

Ray's jaw flexed and relaxed involuntarily, the cycle repeating until he pressed his molars together. He wiped his bloody nose on the sleeve of his shirt, stared at the crimson smear. Maybe later he'd need the forensic evidence. There was a fight coming.

A swelling of his energy. Slowed breathing.

These uniformed men were supposed to be assistants to law enforcement, helping Ray and Sunny with their search for a deadly missing weapon. Instead, the opposite. All three of these turkeys stood directly and forcefully in the path of justice. Maybe Sunny was right in her assessment of the document's importance. The words printed on them, the names. Maybe they would help bring justice for Alissa, too.

For Ray, their hindrance made these men Evil.

He breathed deeply through his nose. Three men, one behind and two in front.

Once Ray recognized Evil, the warrior in him had been trained and conditioned to fight and never give in. The corruption could rub off if you weren't victorious, if you battled and lost.

He glanced at Sunny to warn her with his stare—be ready for anything. Agent Hicks probably couldn't believe there might be a fight or shootout in the county recorder's office. He could only hope since a man wearing this same brown posse uniform had tied her up and kidnapped her, she'd follow Ray into whatever kind of fight they encountered.

These were depraved, immoral people.

Anything could happen.

Sunny stepped back and touched her holster. She'd understood his glance, sensed whatever he planned next could start a war.

"Not so tough now, huh?" Butch said.

Facing the desk and the two standing posse members, he eased away from the desktop, pumped his right knee up waist high, then stomped back down at kicking speed. To extend the leg motion, he bent forward at the waist, snapping his right foot out behind him with all of his weight and power.

Nothing more powerful than a well-executed back kick.

His foot hammered Axel's stomach. Looking over his shoulder and back, Ray watched Axel's flesh surround Ray's boot, the foot all but disappearing into the giant's muscled but massive gut.

Air hissed from Axel's lungs, the high-pitched whistle cutting off abruptly when he crashed against the edge of the book frame. His broad back and purple-tipped head made the most direct contact. The shelves squawked. Books tumbled, including one red, leather-bound volume that bounced off Axel's shoulder, hit the floor and rolled.

Kicks, punches, and snaky moves were daily exercise. He breathed easily, ready for additional action if required, though his muscles were relaxed. The Evil which protected Alissa's killers wasn't finished with him today. Ray knew he was surrounded.

The two posse members drew weapons.

He lurched across the table and seized both men by their

gun-holding wrists. He squeezed hard, twisted, and yanked them off their feet and belly-down across the tabletop.

He pounded both men's forearms against the edge of the table.

Both pistols rattled on the hardwood floor.

Sunny scooped them up. "Guess we're not going to see that juvie trial transcript today."

TWO DAYS BEFORE THE RAIN

23

Jessie Maris cracked another egg on the rim of a stainless steel bowl, let loose the orange yolk and clear junk from twelve inches high, Tommy liking them scrambled best. He sat hunched over the table, near enough for Jessie to smell him, sipping his coffee, nervously eyeing her, working up the balls, no doubt, to ask her about what he'd seen on television. She'd been getting him to bed early for days, but last night she'd blown the news blackout, Jessie forgetting about him while she worked on her third and final note to Sunny Hicks.

"So has anybody called you from the Sheriff's office or the FBI?" Tommy said.

Here he comes, faster than she thought, Jessie figuring Tommy would wait until she was seated, not standing at the counter and stove, her hands so close to the sharp kitchen knives. She had him worried about blades. She'd seen the look in his eyes.

"Nobody's called me," she said. "Why?"

Tommy smelled like garlic, maybe too much seasoning in the spaghetti sauce she'd made last night.

"Maybe they don't have your cell or something," Tommy said. "The cops claim they identified a body they found as Nolan's. Why wouldn't they call Nolan's wife?"

Jessie poured a shot of light cream into the egg and grated-cheese mixture. "Are you sure they said Nolan *Maris*? Really?"

"Yeah. It was on the news. Sammy and Angel are dead, too. All three of them. It happened earlier this week. Just about the time you called me and said Nolan left."

She glanced at him. "Oh my God, that's terrible. Sammy and Angel."

She watched him swallow more coffee, Tommy keeping his gaze focused on the rock wall, maybe counting boulders. Each one weighed hundreds of pounds and attracted dust like a magnet.

"Come on, Jessie," he said. "What happened? The TV reporter said the cops are looking for you. Local, state and federal. The FBI, for crying out loud. A person of interest. Did Nolan and his friends shoot it out over that cannon?"

She finished hand-mixing the eggs, set aside the whisk. "They were buttheads, so I killed them all. Chopped up the bodies, fed them to the critters out back."

He didn't believe her. "Come on, Jessie. Tell me what happened. I'm in this stolen weapon thing with you, so I'm also part of whatever you did to get it. You can trust me."

She turned from the eggs to stare at him, deadpan, trying to seem like she was reading him, when in fact Jessie no longer gave a cockroach's ass about Tommy Moon. Her automatic cannon was ready to go, fully attached to the trailer by way of a long, steel-railed pedestal which shifted a total of fifteen degrees, a range of seven and a half degrees off center in each direction. Left and right. If Jessie wanted to shift the aim up or down—longer or shorter distances—she'd jack up either the rear or front of the trailer.

She was ready to change the world, help abused women everywhere by making her wasted life finally mean something. Tommy had finished installing the trigger mechanism yesterday.

They'd take her cannon out for a test firing tomorrow, get measurements on distance and arc, and check everything worked. The cannon was electronically controlled and hydraulically driven, so there were cords and tubes running everywhere on the trailer—in, on, and around two separate hydraulic motors.

Jessie would pretend to livestream the test from her laptop, telling Tommy potential customers were watching. She might record something, but not what Tommy expected. If she did, she'd send the video as an email attachment to Sunny Hicks and the media. She'd have to think more about that.

"The guys got in a fight and Nolan shot them?" Tommy said. "Is that it? You figured what a great opportunity to shoot your bastard husband? Come on, Jessie. Tell me what happened."

Keeping Tommy around for the autocannon's test would be a good idea, and always part of her plan, because anything needing adjustment afterward might require Tommy's mechanical and welding skills. But those plans were under reconsideration because of Tommy's bad habits, like no showers, offering too many opinions, and asking too many questions.

Thinking about her ultimate goal, she'd try harder to tolerate him.

"I mean, I think it would be great if you *did* kill him," Tommy said. "Nolan was a total asshole for hitting you all the time. I should have killed the son-of-a-bitch myself when he pulled the meat hook on me."

"The TV knew Nolan had been shot?" Jessie said.

"Yeah. All three of them."

"Really? It's amazing what they can find in a pile of bones," she said.

Jessie grabbed a potato from the fruit and vegetable bowl she kept on the counter. Maybe Tommy would like fried potatoes with his scrambled eggs.

"So, how about it, babe?" he said. "Nolan killed Sammy and

Angel. You just did Nolan?"

She spilled the eggs into a hot buttered frying pan, picked up the potato and a nine-inch butcher knife. She showed the blade to Tommy, sliced the vegetable in four long pieces, then chopped those into quarter-inch, pie-shaped chunks, her hands working quickly to dismember the white plant flesh. Like a French chef on television, in a hurry to show off her fancy slicing skills, her chops maybe a little loud on the chopping board.

"I told you already," she said. "I killed all three and hacked them into pieces. I'm surprised the cops found *any*thing."

That must have satisfied Tommy's curiosity because he didn't ask any more about Nolan and her dead husband's two friends. He finished his coffee, left the table, and started preparing the cannon for the next day's test.

At the DHS office in Phoenix, Ray and Sunny grabbed seats at one end of the long, conference-room table. The meeting filled only three of the table's ten faux-leather chairs, Ray and Sunny facing their commander, Eric Johannsen.

Sunny might have been surprised by the grumpy look on Eric's face. Ray, not so much. They'd already spent most of the day answering questions, writing reports, and giving verbal recorded depositions. The trouble he'd caused in that Recorders Office wasn't finished yet.

Unless Eric wanted it to be.

One wall of the room was glass. People worked or walked by on the other side in a steady parade, one or two strangers waving at Sunny like they knew her. The price of fame. For days now, Sunny's Air Force ID photo had been broadcast on local and national television stations, especially last night. There had been widespread news coverage of the Pinacosta County Courthouse confrontation, but since an attractive woman fighting was a better story, especially if she was already in the news anyway for Jessie's letters.

Ray's picture had hardly been used, although the two of them were still in the national news that morning, NBC and Fox running stories several minutes in length, both including a phone-captured video of Agent Hicks standing over Axel's unconscious and bleeding body. Phone video from the hallway as Sunny had opened the door.

The video had gone semi-viral on Twitter. Hashtag #COP-FIGHT.

Eric noticed the unwanted attention on Ray and Sunny from outside the room. He leaned behind the conference curtains and worked a white cord. Pulleys squeaked as the brightly lit office and half a dozen people disappeared behind the floor-to-ceiling, sand-colored drapes.

Unlike the media, Eric's hawkish eyes skipped over Sunny and focused on Ray. "What the hell happened yesterday?"

"They're bad guys. They started the conversation by slamming my face into the table." Ray showed him the stain on his shirt. "Gave me a bloody nose."

Eric frowned. "How could they do that?"

"The guy named Axel was bigger than me. Caught me from behind."

Eric shook his head. "You're slipping."

"I don't think so," Sunny said. "They looked like they'd worked the gag before, the guy at the table holding Ray's attention while Axel snuck up behind him. After, Ray took out Axel with a kick, then immediately disarmed the other two. Like a martial arts demonstration."

Eric's flaxen complexion turned blotchy, not a bad match for the desert camo uniform he wore that morning. "There was no disagreement about your weapons?"

"The men were carrying, but asked us for our guns," Ray said. "I said 'no.'"

"So there *was* a problem."

"There was a discussion," Ray said. "Security had approved

us to carry."

Eric checked his notes. "All three posse members separately told sheriff's investigators you and Hicks refused legal orders, were rude, violent and attacked them without cause. I have a doctor's reports on a broken bone."

"They're lying except for the broken bone," Ray said. "I fought after being attacked."

"And the broken bone?"

"I told you. They aimed weapons at me."

Eric nodded wisely. "I'm sure. But it's not like you've never been aggressively combative *before*."

Ray washed the idea away with his hand. "Their story is totally ass-backwards, Eric. Those posse members attacked us then spent time rehearsing their story."

"Yeah, I figured, but this crap requires tons of paperwork. I have to ask the questions."

"So why are we really here?" Ray asked.

"News. The FBI now believes, like Sunny suggested, that Jessie Maris' sealed juvenile transcript might be the key to uncovering her abuser."

"I knew it," Sunny said.

"They think it contains damaging information on their target," he said.

"What target?" Ray asked. "Damaging to whom?"

"I don't understand," Sunny said. "I thought the FBI was working this case with us?"

"They are," Eric said. "The missing cannon case. But they have *another* investigation going on as well. Separate, but overlapping, and the second one involves national security."

"Our missing weapon should be classified as national security," Ray said.

"A lost Avenger autocannon should be, I agree," Eric said, "but technically, it isn't. I can tell you a little bit more about the FBI's other case, but…"

"But what?" Ray said.

"The information absolutely must stay with us."

"Of course."

Eric's gaze shifted to Sunny. "If any of what I'm about to say turns up under the byline of Jordan Scott, you lose your job, Special Agent Hicks. I will call the Director of the Air Force myself."

Sunny's jaw fell. "I told that reporter nothing when he called me before, general. He already had his story. He wanted me to con—"

"Ray gave me your explanation," he said. "He also said he believes you. And if Ray believes you, I believe you. That's why you're still here. But this warning comes from a higher pay grade than mine. Your relationship with this reporter, Scott, makes you suspect. Some want you off the case, especially since Jordan Scott arrived in Phoenix last night."

Eric and Ray both studied her reaction. Ray could tell Sunny didn't fake her surprise. She hadn't heard a word.

"You swear I won't see what I tell you in the media?" Eric said.

"How can I promise that?" Sunny said. "Anybody can talk to a reporter. But I'm very happy to promise you this—and Ray will vouch for me—I will *never* talk about this case with Jordan Scott or any other reporter. With anyone, period. It's a federal investigation. I know what that means."

Ray slid to the edge of his seat. "She'll be fine. Tell us about the other investigation. How could there be others interested in the same old juvie case?"

"Looks like three cases," Eric said. "Remember the missing lawyer whose DNA turned up in Maris Canyon? Dawson? He was Jessie's attorney in the old juvie case. The guy's been missing for two decades."

Sunny's lips made a soft whistle.

"What's the third case?" Ray said.

"The FBI is vetting someone involved in that juvie case," Eric said.

Ray and Sunny said "Who?" at the same time.

"The FBI won't say. They won't even tell *me*."

"I know how to find out," Ray said. "Give me five minutes?"

Eric shrugged, and Ray withdrew the cell from his coat pocket. Information gave him a number for Vivian Pearl. Ray dialed it, put the phone on speaker.

"Hi Miss Pearl. This is Ray Hauser, one of the two Homeland agents made locally famous by visiting your courthouse."

Pearl laughed. "I remember. What can I do for you?"

"I'm still interested in Jessie Costello's juvenile matter, and I was wondering if the judge and the attorneys on her case might be listed somewhere—say on an old court schedule which was at some point scanned into the system computer."

"Probably," she said.

"Also wondering if a particular outstanding citizen, Vivian Pearl, might help me solve the puzzle."

"Sure," she said. "It's public record. I've got the password, too, so I can look it up on my home computer. Hang on."

Ray glanced up, saw he had the total attention of Sunny and Eric. Be fun if his idea worked.

"Okay, Costello, Jessie," Pearl said. "Entered in 2006 when all the old paperwork was scanned into the digital system."

"Can you see the names?" Ray asked.

"Only one attorney, which is a little odd. The petitioner, Jessie, was represented by James Dawson," Pearl said. "But her mother was not represented. Guess she trusted the judge. Oh, wow. The judge was our current congressman and gubernatorial candidate, Randall King."

Eric smiled. "Confirmation."

"Thank you, Ms. Pearl," Ray said. He looked to Johannsen. "You were thinking Randall King?"

"Since yesterday when an old friend called me about the cannon being missing."

Eric pushed intercom buttons, and the room soon filled with

the sound of his own ringing telephone. Whomever he'd called would answer on speaker. "Pearl put all three cases in perspective for me," Eric said. "This man will do it for you."

"Hey, Eric," a voice said. "What's up?"

"Hi, Tom. I wanted to introduce you to two of my agents, Ray Hauser and Sunny Hicks. They're in the conference room with me right now. Just the three of us."

"Okay," Tom said.

"So Hauser and Hicks—sounds like a shady law firm—are investigating the Air Force's missing weapon we talked about," Eric said.

"How about Sunny and Ray?" Ray said. "Sounds like a tanning salon."

"Shut up," Eric said. "Tom, tell these two what you told me last night."

"You mean about the railroad gang?"

"That's it," Eric said.

Ray's pulse leaped. "Who do you work for, Tom?"

"I'm Vice President of Security for Southern Pacific Railroad. I called Eric to tell him the railroad has been losing cargo between Tucson and Gila Bend—off and on—for more than half a century. We've had a dozen open investigations at various times."

"Is it one gang?" Ray asked.

"The thefts are so well planned, so well carried out, we think, yes. It's one group. Stuff simply disappears, half the time from open flat cars, half the time not."

"So, you think this gang might have taken our cannon?" Ray said.

"That's why I called Eric, yes. And he told me about your theory and discovery, Ms. Hicks. Congratulations. Nobody in my shop ever figured it out. You ever want a job in private industry—"

"Hey," Eric said.

"Sorry. Anyway, we were never able to prove anything or

catch anyone because this gang has some kind of connection with Arizona law enforcement."

"Or maybe law enforcement *volunteers*?" Ray said.

"Could be," Tom said. "The vast majority of those posse members are good, honest men and women, people helping out for nothing, but there are, or were, a few dirty as hell. Generations of Arizona families have worked the border, alcohol during Prohibition, drugs and human smuggling now. Maybe police officers and judges might be mixed up in it, too."

"Like who?" Ray said.

"If I'd ever turned up proof, I would have gone after them for the railroad's cargo," Tom said. "And when the FBI asked me the same question yesterday, I could only offer a hunch."

"Yeah?" Ray said. "A name?"

"The FBI said I could not talk about it to anyone, under a contempt of court threat."

"Thanks, Tom," Johannsen said. "I think we can guess the focus of their interest."

Leaving the conference room minutes later, Ray and Sunny agreed to celebrate the end of a long day by eating a multi-course Mexican dinner at Juanita's on the way back to Gila Bend. But while a cheery time had sounded like fun, neither one ordered a drink or finished their meal. In less than an hour, he paid the check and drove them back to Sunny's motel.

"Here we are," he said. "Tomorrow we'll start tracking Congressman King, figure out the best spots where Jessie might attack this weekend."

"I want to find that long-haired, bearded creep from the motorcycle gang, too," Sunny said.

"Deal. Same time tomorrow morning?"

Sunny had spotted someone and didn't answer. Her breathing changed.

Ray saw him, too. "Is that who I think it is?"

"Yup."

Jordan Scott waited inside Sunny's motel lobby. He posed at the window, tall and trim in shorts and a camp shirt. He leaned his head close to the window, his hand wedged between his brow and the glass, shading the slick surface. Trying to see inside Ray's black SUV, maybe. The reporter waiting for Sunny, wondering if this was her.

He should have made her change motels after he'd called her last week.

"Come inside with me," Sunny said. "I don't want to talk to him alone."

"You sure? You don't have feelings for him anymore?"

Sunny exhaled. "Well...I didn't think so until I just saw him."

He laughed.

24

Her quickened heart offered a warning, but Sunny decided to talk to Jordan, anyway. From her shotgun seat in Ray's mean black SUV, she highlighted reporter Jordan Scott's private number on her cell, poked *Call*.

Not like she'd ever removed him from her contacts.

While she waited, watching Jordan pull a phone from the pocket of his shorts, she hoped Ray couldn't hear her heart beating. Was the boss watching her pulse?

"Sunny?" Jordan said. "Is that you in the black SUV?"

"That's me, Ace."

She switched him to *Speaker* while assessing the impact of his deep, pleasantly sonorous voice. Hard to say, exactly, although a few old and agreeable memories returned. A few delightful sensations blossomed inside. She decided to ponder her reactions later. She liked this SOB, and there was not much she could do about it.

Or *wanted* to do about it, maybe.

"I have information about your case," Jordan said. "A solid lead, anyway. Background the FBI may not be sharing with other agencies yet. I know that sounds crazy, but I've found a source who tells me she's been sharing with the FBI, too."

She rested the phone on the console. "Why tell us?"

"I want to make up for my previous bad behavior."

When she glanced over, Ray was grinning. The guy had the nicest smile.

"What do you have for us?" she said. "And don't get cute about your body parts or start in with that alleged southern charm. You Duke University boys are all the same. My partner is sitting beside me, listening to every word."

"I don't want to talk on the phone," Jordan said. "How about I jump in the back seat? We can talk while you drive me around the block."

Ray nodded, mouthed the words, "Let's hear what he has."

"Okay, Jordan," she said. "But if you act like a loser, we'll drive you deep into the desert and gut you over a nest of tarantulas."

"Do tarantulas make nests?"

That was better. More like the Jordan she knew. "Want to find out?"

"I'll behave."

They watched him leave the lobby and hurry across the sidewalk, the six-footer in well-made, tan dress shorts, gray Sketchers, no socks, and an embroidered, white camp shirt which was probably a Tommy Bahama. Nice-looking buttons. Most of the time, Jordan dressed like an undercover Fed, but she had to admit the man looked good in shorts. Athletic legs.

The door latch popped, Jordan crawled in and sat straight away in the floor-mounted restraint chair. His weight stirred the truck chassis.

He shook the sides. "Never seen one of these before."

His presence poked at her calm. Like radar, her whole body sensed him sitting there, smelling like fresh corn tortillas.

Jordan nestled himself into the steel cage as if he were used to the threat of imprisonment. Or he wanted to impress the Feds with his manly courage.

Men were so serious about their masculinity. He made her smile.

"Hi, Sunny," he said. "Who's this big soldier?"

Silence. She eyed Ray, who twisted toward Jordan.

"I'm US Marine Corps Brigadier General Ray Hauser, currently on assignment with the Department of Homeland Security. Neither Sunny nor I can speak in any official capacity. If you *ever* use either of our names in a story, the entire Marine Corps will hunt you down and shoot you. Do we understand each other?"

Jordan nodded. "So we're off the record?"

"Ha," Ray said. "Deep background."

Jordan grimaced. "How about you, Sunny? You want to threaten me, too?"

"I already did. The tarantulas, remember?"

He shrugged. "Okay. I guess you Homeland hot-shots don't want to know the fascinating story I heard this week about Randall King, Congressman and recently named gubernatorial candidate. It's the same story, incidentally, that's caused a doubling of the FBI staff vetting him."

She and Ray glanced at each other. Sunny wondered who Jordan's sources were. The man seemed to know a lot about her case.

"Baloney," Ray said. "Other than the normal vetting process, there's no FBI investigation of Randall King."

"Yes there is," Jordan said. "And if you two don't know about it, you will soon. Those three murders last week and the missing cannon are all connected to the same FBI investigation of King. Jessie Maris is wanted for more than murder. They need to talk to her about her dead, murdered attorney. As a possible witness."

Taking Ray's lead, Sunny decided to lie. "That case is long closed. I checked. He's been missing and presumed dead for two decades."

"Well, the case has been re-opened since they found his remains."

She faced Jordan over her shoulder. "Tell us what you heard—without leaving anything out. Who's your source?"

"You still want to gut me?"

"Tell us your story," Ray said, "or get out, go eat more tacos. You smell like that joint across the street."

"That's where I had dinner."

"No kidding," Sunny said. "The story!"

Jordan sighed. "I don't know anything about Jessie's missing attorney, but here's what I know about Randall King. Before he was a judge, more than twenty years ago, King was a member of the Pinacosta County Sheriff's Posse. Back in those days, it was widely believed a few posse members ran a private army, ripping off drug dealers and illegal immigrants crossing the Mexican border."

"And Randall King was involved?" Sunny said.

Jordan nodded. "My source believes he was the big boss for more than a decade. No proof or living witnesses I've heard about. Only hearsay."

"How does this help me find Jessie Maris and our missing weapon?" Sunny said. "That's my case, not some gubernatorial vetting."

Ray poked her knee in a way she took to mean shut up.

"If the hearsay is true," Jordan said, "and King was a crook, maybe he took bribes to decide old cases. If he did in Jessie's case, she could still be mad at him, thinks he ruined her life or something."

"Mad and crazy enough to kill him with an automatic cannon?" she said. "That's a stretch. Children don't hold grudges about court decisions. A boyfriend of the mother's is a more likely abuser."

"Did you know Nolan Maris and his two friends were killed the same evening Randall King was publicly named a candidate for governor?" Jordan said.

"So what?" she said.

"Put yourself in Jessie's shoes. A judge sends you back home to be tortured and abused by your parent."

"How do you know all this?" Ray asked.

"Let me finish, I'll explain. So Jessie's been angry at this judge all these years for the denial of her petition, then one day she sees King announce he's a candidate for governor. She freaks, whatever you want to call it, fights with her husband, ends up killing everybody, and stealing their weapon."

"*Our* weapon," Ray said.

"Denial of what petition?" Sunny asked.

"The juvenile hearing was about Jessie's petition to be removed from her mother's care," Jordan said. "An aunt in California paid for Jessie's lawyer, Dawson, wanted to get Jessie out West with her, but the motion was denied. Judge King sent Jessie home to an abusive mother."

Ray shook his head. "The petition came from Jessie—a child asking to be removed from the parent. How do you know all this?"

Jordan removed a folded sheet of paper from his pants pocket. "I have an ex-reporter friend—now flacking for the US Treasury Deptartment in Washington. He covered King's first run for Congressman, wrote two stories about King's past and noting certain business connections. But his sources quit talking. One even disappeared, and serious advertisers threatened his Phoenix newspaper. Eventually, my friend got fired."

Sunny watched a motorcycle disappear around a well-lit intersection corner. The rider wore club colors, but not The Sacred Bones'. "Do you have those old newspaper stories?"

"The FBI does. And they're on film at the newspaper. You can't Google it."

"Okay, but what did the stories say?" Ray said.

"My friend admits his stories never proved anything. But they disclosed his relationship to an old smuggler named King Polanco, who was not only connected to a New York crime family many decades ago, but state and local judges. One or two police chiefs."

Sunny scowled. "But what does—"

Jordan held up his hand. "Here's the important part. Years

later, after my friend moved to D.C. but before he changed professions, someone sent him this."

Jordan passed the sheet of paper forward between the bucket-seats. His hand was large, but the long fingers struck Sunny as narrow and delicate.

"This is a copy of what he showed me," Jordan said. "My friend thought this ultimate source had to be a member of Jessie's family."

Ray hit the overhead light and Sunny leaned in. The sheet showed a case title, case number, and room assignment for three court hearings from 1998. The first listing was *Costello (minor) vs. Costello (parent)*. Across the top of the paper, written in ballpoint pen, someone had scripted, "The full and true story behind any one of these cases would put Randall King in jail."

Sunny decided to keep lying. "I don't see how this gets us closer to what we're looking for. Was there testimony about—"

"I'm not finished," Jordan said. "I've been working the phones from LA, but the paper hired help, and a private detective turned up my reporter friend's source. Jessie's older sister, the former Angie Costello, now Angie...well, I'm not giving you that yet."

"You found Jessie's sister?" Sunny said.

"Two days ago in Scottsdale," Jordan said. "I've already talked to her. Called her from Los Angeles yesterday."

"How'd the private eye find her?"

"Same way the FBI did, I'm sure. He walked Jessie Costello's old neighborhood, house by house. Took a few days but our guy found an elderly neighbor still alive and talkative. She'd spoken to the FBI days earlier, said she knew the Costellos well, gave him Angie's new name."

Ray's face turned darker.

"When I called her, Angie acknowledged sending the letter to my friend years ago. Now she's *my* source."

"Does Angie know where Jessie is?" Ray asked.

Jordan rocked his head. "She said no, but why not ask her yourself? Come with me to interview her. Maybe we all find out what happened inside that old juvie court. Get a lead on Jessie."

Big news. She glanced at Ray. Jessie could be hiding on her sister's property no matter what Angie told Jordan.

Ray's forehead wrinkled. "What's Angie's new name?"

"Not until you give me your word I can go along."

Ray sneered. "You admitted having material information about a federal investigation. You know a witness who could be harboring our suspect, or at least provide information on her whereabouts. You *will* give me that woman's name, her phone number, address, and any other information you have. Or your next stop will be a Federal Detention Facility."

"The FBI already has her name," Jordan said. "I bet they've already talked to her. Why don't you call them and ask?"

"I'm not asking you," Ray said. "Give me the name or go to jail."

"Wow, general, you're such an F-ing hard-ass."

Ray turned and grabbed Jordan's shoulder. "I eat reporters for lunch."

"I guess Federal jail in Phoenix it is then," Jordan whispered. Was Ray squeezing him?

General Johannsen didn't answer Sunny's call, so she sent a text to call Ray when he had time. They had important new information. Her fingertips left moisture on the iPhone. She was heating up from excitement.

She glanced at Jordan in the restraint chair. "I have a better idea than Federal jail. Get out your phone, Ace, and call Angie right now. Sweet talk her. Tell her you have to meet tonight. Lives depend on it. You're bringing two federal agents to her house, agents who want to arrest Congressman King and imprison him."

Releasing Jordan's shoulder, Ray's head moved like a bobble doll. "I love it!"

She pointed at Jordan. "Tell her what she wants to hear."

"And we all walk inside Angie's place together?" Jordan said.

"We don't know what we're going to find at her house," Ray said. "Jessie could be waiting there, ready to shoot it out."

Jordan wagged his face. "Angie wouldn't invite us over if her sister were there."

"Maybe, maybe not. But there's no way we take a civilian with us when we question a subject. Any civilian, let alone a newspaper reporter."

"We could leave him in the car," Sunny said.

Jordan groaned. "No way."

"The whole thing's crazy," Ray said. "We need permission from Eric *and* the FBI, and a bunch of back-up guns. Not a reporter."

"Angie's not dangerous, I promise," Jordan said.

Sunny looked to Ray. "You decide."

He sucked air. Watching his face, she knew he would rather meet with Angie, not take Jordan to a Phoenix jail. And if what Jordan said was true, especially about his newspaper's previous contact with her, Angie might not talk without him. Even to the FBI.

"Go ahead and call her," Ray said. "Find out if she's willing to see us, then I'll ask Eric's permission."

"Who's Eric?"

"Our boss," Ray said. "We'll make the decisions on who goes where, with what, when we get there. We have to see what the FBI thinks. They might not let us go in there without them, even if we have the sister's okay."

Jordan grunted. "Who goes where with what when we get there?"

"Too complicated for an English major?" Ray said.

"I was a History—"

"Oh, call her," Ray said. "Now."

25

On the way over, Ray waiting to hear from Eric, the reporter told them Angie Costello Chiarella lived with her construction-executive husband and two teenage daughters in the northern part of Scottsdale. More of a miniature horse farm, the eight-bedroom home featured a barn, a tack room, a riding trail connected to the public horse path, a swimming pool, a tennis court, and shade parking for a dozen vehicles.

Sunny grunted. "I know a couple of Beverly Hills hotels that get by with less."

Ray's thoughts bubbled inside a Congressman King stew, the politician, maybe a former chief, and apparently a part of the gang who killed Alissa. This on his mind while he drove past the Chiarella house slowly, noticed the security gate. Press a button and speak.

The neighborhood was quiet at night. Big eucalyptus trees lined the road. He parked one block over to wait while Eric spoke privately with the Federal Bureau of Investigation. See if Jordan's crazy plan had legs.

He answered Eric's call. It took a while, but the engine hadn't cooled. He put the boss on *Speaker*. "We're all listening, Eric. Are we going in?"

"First, a quick speech for the reporter. Jordan, you listening?"

"I'm all ears, general."

"I'm Eric Johannsen, the Department of Homeland Security's Principal Deputy Under Secretary for Intelligence and Analysis. I mention the full hairy title because I need you to understand how important this witness Chiarella could be to America's national security."

"We're approved?" Ray asked. He couldn't wait to get in there, find out if Jessie's sister knew anything about Alissa.

"Shut up, Ray. Jordan, you need to understand how much trust your country is placing in you."

Jordan leaned forward in the SUV's restraining chair. Earlier, a sturdy, balding FBI agent named Morelli had worked from a briefcase of electronic listening gear, tape, and other equipment to body-wire Scott with a miniature recording device.

"I'm after a story, General, that's all," Jordan said.

"Understood, son. But you've agreed to help by not publishing what you hear tonight, at least for a while. Is that right?"

"Yes. The deadline Jessie Maris gave in her note would be Sunday," Jordan said. "I'll wait until Jessie shoots someone, the Sunday deadline passes, or you say go ahead."

"And," Eric said, "if the FBI thinks something Chiarella says for your story would ruin a DOJ legal case, you'll at least talk to them about changes?"

"I agree to be sensitive to their concerns, not about my *story*. Two things are important to me, General. One, nobody knows I wore a wire for the FBI, and nobody sees a copy of my story before publication. Nobody but my editor."

"How's that going to work?" Eric said.

"The FBI will have everything Angie says on tape, right?" Jordan said.

"Yeah."

"So anything she says that worries them, tell me about it. I'll listen. I don't want to blow a legal case against a criminal. Especially an abuser who wants to be governor."

"Fair enough," Eric said. "Especially considering the FBI has been told Chiarella won't talk to the FBI except through an attorney. What I just heard, the attorney needs two days to wrap another big case. Then he wants to talk with his client. This Chiarella woman—or her husband—came up with some New York hotshot, thinks he's Alan Dershowitz and David Boies wrapped in one."

"Still," Ray said. "A reporter going on an interview?"

"Hey, a reporter that's willing to wear a wire and make promises about holding off on the story? Big shots realized we all have more to gain than lose."

"Plus," Sunny said. "If Jessie's notes are accurate, the FBI knows we have only hours to find our cannon."

"Exactly," Eric said. "So, get going."

"We're ready," Ray said. "The wire's on Jordan. We're almost there."

"Oh—one more thing," Eric said.

The atmosphere thickened inside the SUV.

"Jessie's sister asked about you," Eric said. "She wanted to know if you were related to the insurance investigator who went missing in Arizona two years ago."

Ray's stomach flipped. "That's weird."

"No kidding. Her explanation was newspapers and television. She said the case was widely covered here."

In the telephone silence, Ray heard a fuse burning, a buzz from his abdomen, something in Eric's voice.

"Maybe you should take me off speaker, Ray. Let's you and I speak privately."

"No. Go ahead. My partner needs to know this, and Jordan knows personal things are out of bounds. They're already curious."

"Angie Chiarella not only remembered Alissa's name," Eric said, "She knew Alissa's old case involved railroad theft. Even if some of those facts were on TV, they are long-remembered details. Seems odd, don't you think?"

Ray pulled into the Chiarella's driveway. "Very."

"Call me when you're finished," Eric said.

***

He kept the vehicle in Park, flipped on the interior light, and faced them both. He wanted Sunny and Jordan to see his face. Clearing his throat, he said, "You agreed personal stuff is off the record, right, Jordan?"

"I did, yes. Unfortunately."

"My wife, Alissa, worked as an investigator for a New York insurance company. About two years ago, she was kidnapped and murdered while investigating a similar crime to what we're working on."

"Theft from a moving train?" Sunny asked.

"Yes. A big generator."

"She figured out the centrifugal force angle?" Jordan asked.

He shrugged. "Maybe, but there's no evidence she did. She was searching the tracks between Tucson and Gila Bend, but I don't believe she knew what exactly what she was looking for."

He gazed straight ahead, his fingers gripping the gear shift. The light in his vision wiggled and blurred. He blinked away moisture. His guts were ripping in two different directions. He wanted to choke Congressman Randall King. And he wanted to cry like a newborn baby for missing his wife.

"I'm surprised they let you on this investigation," Jordan said. "I mean...your *wife*?"

"There's no proven connection yet," Ray said.

Jordan made a face. "But Alissa Hauser's remains showed up at the Maris property."

"Don't worry about it," Ray said.

Angie Costello Chiarella answered the door chimes herself, escorting Ray and her other guests into a *Better Homes & Gardens* living room-den-breakfast nook the size of a professional hockey rink. Three fireplaces, including a brick pit in the room's center. An exposed, wood-beam ceiling rose twenty-five feet above oak plank flooring. Five couches and a department-store inventory of chairs, lamps, tables, flower baskets, living trees, and brightly colored cushions filled the oblong space with desert shades—gold, tan, and bleached-bone white.

The room reminded him of the home furnishings department in an old-fashioned department store, an entire floor of living room chairs and couches, all the accessories. Like a dozen or more individual homes. He'd been to Macy's a few times with Etta's high school friend and her friend's mother.

"I'm so worried about Jessie," Angie said. She was still guiding the group across a landscape of furniture. "Maybe I helped her too much after our mother died, paying her rent and schooling, giving her spending money. My husband and I arranged several good jobs, too. She'd do well on the interview, work hard for a few months. But she'd always get bored and move on. Always involved with terrible men."

"Nolan wasn't the worst?" Ray said.

"Hardly. Just the most persistent."

Angie sat down in a wingback chair and waved her guests to a long sofa facing her. Angie, the beautiful and powerful, like faded pictures of Elizabeth Taylor he'd seen in old magazines his mother kept. A woman who had made her own way and arranged for all the comforts she'd wanted, he assumed.

Her living spaces were the largest he'd ever been inside. As much luxury, extravagance, and opulence as a minor Middle Eastern oil sheik. He wondered if Sunny and Jordan were, like himself, slightly uncomfortable.

Jordan introduced him and Sunny, but Angie kept her stare on the reporter. "Are you sure they want to help my sister, Jordan? I honestly don't know if she shot that husband of hers, but I'd cheer Jessie if she did. That bastard deserved to be boiled alive."

"I bet these detectives agree with you," Jordan said.

Ray leaned forward. "I've seen your sister's medical records, Ms. Chiarella. I felt dirty and angry reading them. A gruesome human, that man Nolan Maris. Wounds like a broken eye socket and a dislocated shoulder come from the cruelest kind of domestic violence. We understand your anger."

Repeating the information about Jessie he'd picked up days ago, Ray wondered again why any living creature would stay in such a self-destructive situation. A dog or cat would run, take their chances with the street. But he'd heard abuse worked like brainwashing, so he probably didn't understand. It was hard for him to think about, frankly. A grown man punching and seriously injuring a woman.

"Are you one hundred percent sure you weren't followed," Angie asked. "I know how *you* and the FBI found me, Jordan. But no one else did in eighteen years."

"Who are you frightened of?" Ray asked.

"Nolan had a goon squad of crazy biker friends, every single one a convicted criminal or a perp the cops hadn't caught yet. They could be looking for me, hoping I'll lead them to Jessie and that terrible cannon."

"There was no one behind us," Ray said. "I assure you."

He glanced at Sunny, nodded for her to take the lead. They'd discussed the move earlier.

"Why don't we start with you telling us a bit about yourself," Sunny said. "Not a three-page biography—a thumbnail sketch."

Angie shrugged. "I grew up in a house of yelling and screaming, Mom and Dad always fighting, so I wanted out as quickly as I could. Got married before I graduated high school. We kept it a secret, but there was a baby coming by the time I got my diploma."

"No college?" Sunny asked.

"Nope, just three kids, one left in high school now herself. My husband did well in the construction business. Started contracting and moved to development."

"What was Jessie like growing up?" Sunny said.

"Played victim a lot, never doing what Mom asked, always

in trouble. Dad leaving us made everything worse, but Jessie and I both understood why he had to go. Our mother was obsessed with herself, her good looks and her figure. The crazier Mom got—"

"When did your father leave?" Sunny asked.

"Jessie and I were both in grammar school. Like six and nine."

"Is that when your mother started her abuse?"

"Oh, no, but she got worse after Dad left, especially with Jessie. Even staying all those years, I felt bad moving out. But I had to save myself."

"Was that before or after Jessie's juvie court case?" Sunny said.

"Maybe that year or a year after. Why?"

"We believe Nolan and his friends stole the Air Force's weapon," Sunny said. "And then your sister stole it from them. What we need is background on your sister so we can find that autocannon. You've read the notes she published in the paper?"

"Sure. They were scary to read. My sister sounds desperate. A little crazy."

"She needs help," Sunny said. "We know that. We want that cannon, not to hurt your sister. We'll protect her and the public."

"Even if I *totally* believed you, I have no idea where she is," Angie said.

"Okay. But can you tell us about that court hearing years ago? Your sister was petitioning to separate from your mother?"

"Now there's *another* monster," Angie said. "Much worse than Nolan."

"Your mother?" Sunny said.

Angie smiled. "She was a monster like Nolan, yes, maybe worse, but I'm talking about the judge—a current congressman now running for governor. That's the guy Jessie wants to kill."

Ray's jaw tightened. "You were in court that day?"

"Only the day Jessie's attorney called me as a witness. Nothing happened in court that day, except maybe the way the judge stared at Jessie."

Sunny and Ray traded glances.

"Could you start at the beginning, please?" Sunny said.

Angie lifted a decanter from the table beside her and poured a dark drink. Whisky or tea. "Would any of you care to join me? This is very old bourbon."

Sunny said, "No, thank you." Jordan and Ray shook their heads.

"Everything I am about to say is public knowledge," Angie said. "All the neighbors knew my mother abused me and Jessie, although Jessie got the worst. Punches. Kicks. Hot irons. Locked in the closet. The afternoon she came home from the court hearing, our mother tied Jessie to our maple tree."

Ray's throat tightened. *What kind of a parent?*

"Jessie's attorney called six eyewitnesses that day," Angie said, "including two police officers. There were hospital reports and pictures. Recordings of 9-1-1 calls. And a sworn affidavit from Jessie's school nurse on the frequency of bruises, cuts, and scrapes, the lack of sleep. But Judge King didn't care about any of that. Evidence didn't matter. He sent Jessie back for more."

"Why would he do that?" Sunny asked.

"Bribery. And sexual favors."

Sunny made a face. *"What?"*

"Let me finish," Angie said. "Our aunt paid for Jessie's attorney and showed up in court to offer her a place to come live in California. She testified her sister—our mother—was insane and had been so diagnosed as a teenager."

"She had evidence?" Ray asked.

"Letters from doctors. But Judge King still said no, said children always belonged with their mother. He spoke the words as if he were quoting the Bible."

"No wonder you called him a monster," Jordan said.

"That's *not* the reason," Angie said. "Sending Jessie home

was a good deed compared to what happened at our house that night...*his payment* for sending Jessie home."

Sunny gasped.

"Congressman Randall King was, and probably still is—" Angie's voice broke. Her eyes teared. "—a violent pedophile."

ONE DAY BEFORE THE RAIN

26

Tommy Moon hopped down from the eighteen-wheel, tractor-trailer rig he'd driven into the remote box canyon, his boots raising a puff of dust which merged with the brown cloud following him, Tommy like that character in the comic strip *Peanuts*, Pigpen, a ball of dirt always floating behind him.

He wasn't a bad guy. Handy with tools. And his tongue. But Jessie wouldn't be sorry to see him disappear.

He'd driven into the tiny canyon at dawn, ten minutes early, finding Jessie on top of the flatbed, the tarp, and the collection of cardboard-squares camouflage removed from the autocannon. She'd been inspecting the weapon, imagining what the exploding ammunition would do to Congressman King. Getting the autocannon's feel.

But Tommy had probably seen her touching something she shouldn't, the big fuzzy shark watching her from inside his private dust cloud. Seen her dare to place her hands on his metallic work of art. She didn't like the look on his face as he approached.

"What are you doing? I asked you not to touch anything before I got here. Gum and duct tape are holding everything together."

"I wasn't touching anything. I was *looking*."

"I saw your hands on the cables and the trigger. You were getting ready to hook-up the ammunition drum, weren't you? See if you could fire it, probably. Why else would the truck's engine be running, the hydraulic motors ready?"

She grinned. A passion had risen inside her, a violent seed planted long ago that had been getting stronger, forging toward release and flower. Must have been there most of her life, but she'd never known it existed until she'd killed Nolan. In this newer stare down with Tommy, she felt like a tiger.

"Isn't that why we're here?" she said. "See if we can fire it?"

Tommy put his hand on the trailer, a dirty boot on the first rung of the step-up. "Yeah, but you needed to wait for me. Let me hook it up, make sure it's right when we fire it."

Killing her abusive husband had triggered the upcoming climax of the seed which grew inside, not finished it. Was the swelling just hatred? "Oh, Tommy, relax," she said. "There's no one around for ten miles, and we need to test our machine and livestream the action for our buyers."

His face hardened. "You were supposed to set up the cameras, get the generator running. I was going to attach the ammunition feeds and set up the trigger."

Jessie shrugged. Tommy was acting more and more like a loser. If she had her Beretta, she'd consider shooting him, getting it over with, but no, she needed to test the cannon, and she might still need Tommy in case of mechanical trouble. Also, he and his big rig provided a moving and most suitable target.

"Sorry," she said.

"So why make plans together if you're going to do whatever you want?"

She kneeled to touch his face. Halfway up the trailer rungs, Tommy stayed there frozen to let Jessie caress him. The extra color in his cheeks slowly faded.

"I'm sorry, babe," she said. "I was nervous and drove too

fast. When I got here early, I couldn't help imagining what it would feel like. I'm anxious to see this thing work, aren't you?"

"I'm excited to make our score," he said. "We don't want to break something I can't fix. Those hydraulic motor cables, for instance."

She nodded. No reason to fight. This messed up relationship was almost over. "I'm sorry."

"Not like we can call an electrician," Tommy said.

Minutes later, Jessie donned her new camo earmuffs and flipped the toggle switch Tommy showed her. Instantly, the deadliest automatic cannon ever built hummed like an electric turbine, the electrically powered, hydraulically operated firing system ready to toss sticks of dynamite like a firehose spits water.

Thirty-five miles outside of Gila Bend, in the super-heated isolation of the Sonora Desert in August, she glowed inside and out. Besides explosives, many of the cannon shells were tipped with super-hard, spent-uranium to penetrate tank armor. She'd compared the pictures on Google, couldn't wait to find out what they did, especially to Congressman King and his friends.

Her heart wore angel's wings. She let out a *whoop*.

Just a girl and her new gun.

Tommy ripped the horn on his Peterbilt, two blasts as loud as a train whistle. On small-town streets, the sinister, atonal notes made cars pull over, policemen duck, and children cry, but her distance and ear protection allowed her to feign ignorance. They were on opposite sides of the narrow, isolated canyon by this time, surrounded by thousand-foot peaks. One narrow break in the rocky hills provided the canyon's only entrance, half a mile from the nearest public road.

Jessie and her cannon, Tommy with his red truck-trailer rig and the old Mercedes he'd stolen for target practice, the two of them maybe two-hundred yards apart, facing off in the middle of nowhere.

Her phone rang. Tommy. He hadn't needed ten minutes to unload the stolen car from his hollow trailer. The plan, as he understood it, was to livestream the autocannon blowing up the Mercedes—fire, smoke, steel, and glass flying. She wanted to ignore his phone summons, but answered. Why not? The autocannon was whirring, ready to fire.

She squinted to see Tommy, standing on his truck's running board, waving his phone like a tiny flag. She slid the earmuffs off, let them hang on her neck while she answered his call. "Yeah, Tommy."

"What are you waiting for?"

"Think I'm going to change targets."

"Huh?"

She set her phone on *Speaker*, set it down on the trailer bed, and slipped on her ear muffs again. Snugged and ready, she unlocked Tommy's new floor mount and shifted the autocannon's direction.

She shivered a little, Jessie sensing and relishing the machine's power. She'd seen enough You-Tube videos to know what was coming. What this machine would do to Tommy's fancy red truck.

Maybe the cannon had always been what made her keep going, the monster she'd wanted to set free since Nolan hid it from her in his new barn. She'd read so much about the weapon since then, watched films, and best of all, imagined what one-and-a-half-pound shells would do to the body and soul of US Representative Randall King.

In her mind, the abuse she suffered had created the drug addict and victim she'd become. King had ruined her life. A simple bullet in the head from a hand-held pistol wasn't grand enough revenge. The fully loaded autocannon weighed two tons and stretched twenty feet long. The statement she and her cannon would make for abused women might rattle the whole country, even promote the beginning of real change.

Her phone squawked near her feet. "Jessie! What's wrong?

Talk to me."

Relocking the cannon mount with the cannon pointed directly at Tommy's big rig, she needed to swallow, maybe lose a tinge of sadness. Nolan and his friends had tried to kill her. Tommy had been mostly nice and helped her build her weapon to assassinate King, but she'd made up her mind about Tommy long ago. Probably, before she'd called him, honestly. He'd never allow her to complete her murderous plan.

"Jessie. Talk to me."

She yanked the trigger.

Nothing happened. The deafening whirring noise hadn't changed, meaning the engines and motors and feeds were all running. But no shells fired. The ammunition drum wasn't feeding the loading racks. Something was wrong.

Her chest squeezed tight, choking her breath. Her gut flipped over, sick, like when Nolan made her stand near that cliff for a photo. Her thoughts bordered on panic, imagining herself in a mirror, her mother screaming with that horrible face, then seeing herself at home after the court hearing decades earlier.

The memories flashed, not only her mother's contorted face, shouting what to do, but the judge's horrible sneer, first in his courtroom, and then later, in her house.

In a flash, like a dream, she remembered everything.

Mother did terrible things to me all my life. I don't know why, except she complained as far back as I can remember how average and ordinary I was, how unglamorous. "Girls should be beautiful, not plain," she used to say. Over and over, for years and years. By the time I became a teenager, I believed that about myself, too, and Mother had given up talking about my shortcomings, no longer said much to or about me. She never offered any reason for locking me in the closet overnight, or kicking me, pouring water on me while I slept, or not setting a plate for me at the dinner table. Punishing my sister for feeding me scraps.

When Mother tied me to the maple tree outside after my court hearing, she'd not spoken a word, but instead whistled a song to me about being alone again, naturally, a showtune maybe. This while she tightened the rope, pressing my spine against the warped, uneven bark. If she was happy enough to whistle a song, I guessed Mother expected something special that night.

I had no clue what until the judge arrived.

Mother came running outside to untie me. "The judge is here to collect his fee."

I guessed right away what was about to happen. Mother didn't have money for cigarettes, let alone to bribe a judge. And looking in that old man's glassy eyes, even a virgin like me knew what he'd come for.

From the cell by her feet, Tommy's voice snapped her out of the reverie. "I knew you'd try to kill me. I *knew* it."

She tried the autocannon's trigger again, using two hands to push the handle forward for a reset, then pulling back to make the weapon fire. She willed the cannon to work. Begged in the name of women everywhere.

The muscles in her forearms bulged. Nothing. What was wrong? She had to figure the weapon's problem quickly, stop thinking about her miserable past. She had to forget about Judge King, her insane mother, and the night her soul died. Women the world over counted on her.

"The trigger doesn't work anymore, Jessie. I couldn't trust you after I heard Nolan, Sam, and Angel were murdered, so I installed a secret kill switch."

"Lying bastard."

"*Me?* Girl, I don't know what happened to you, but something sure did. You've gone nuts or something. And lying to me ain't the half of it."

Kill switch? Combine that with what Tommy said earlier about calling an electrician, the importance of the cables, she bet he'd fixed up another toggle or button switch on the cannon's wiring from the truck's generator.

She left the phone ON, lowered herself to her hands and knees, and checked the cannon's under-assembly, all the time considering a vocal comeback for Tommy. She pulled the cell closer, needing to distract him from coming there and shooting her. "Why would you think I was trying to kill you, Tommy?"

He laughed. Or barked. He was scared. She could hear it.

"I watched you pull the trigger on me ten seconds ago," Tommy said.

"I did not."

"I saw you, bitch."

She couldn't see anything underneath the drum or the seven gun barrels wrapped as one, or switches connected to the hydraulic motor cables. "I didn't touch the trigger," she said. "You don't mean that handle thing which looks like a parking brake?"

"I'm coming for you, Jessie. You tried to kill me."

Above the humming of the autocannon, the Peterbilt diesel raced, Tommy maybe cleaning his pipes for a run across the canyon. Jessie's heartrate ticked higher when the truck spurted forward, picking up speed, pointing its grill directly at her and the autocannon, the truck's giant diesel engine racing through the early gear changes.

Her Beretta was in the Ford 350 behind her. She could jump, run, and scramble for the weapon, hope there was time to shoot him, hope she could hit him through the windshield. Or find his backup kill switch and blow Tommy to kingdom come.

But a tinge of panic pushed her back to that terrible night.

It took both the judge and my mother to hold me down. Mother kneeled behind my head, her hands gripping my wrists, leaning so her weight pinned my shoulders to the carpet. Judge Randy sitting on my legs, unzipping and tugging at my pants. I was helpless. I cried. I screamed. I was so mad I shook.

There was a boy in school I liked, a soccer player named Cruz, the star of our grammar school team. After a graphic, girls-only health class one day, I'd wondered in bed alone that night what Cruz's penis might look like, both when he was soft, and again during an erection. When I thought about having sex someday, I imagined coaxing that change—watching his penis grow bigger and become hard enough to push inside me.

There was nothing sexy about Judge Randy's little red penis. His thing looked like a German Shepherd I'd seen, a dog my girlfriend petted until what she called "his lipstick" poked out.

When the judge pulled his pants to his ankles, his bright red dick forced my eyes up and away, and the front of his white shirt was wet with drool. I gagged and tried to vomit on him, but he scrambled on top and poked at me between the legs. I screamed as loud as I could. The whole neighborhood must have heard.

When his lipstick pushed into me, and the horror and helplessness reached a point I couldn't stand, there was still nothing I could do.

Nothing. And the helplessness destroyed my soul. I swear it. Nothing was ever good after that. At least that's what I've always believed.

Jessie didn't see the kill switch anywhere.

The roar of his Peterbilt diesel grew close, lifting her gaze to see if she had time to keep searching for the switch, or was this the point to jump from the trailer, run for the gun to save herself with a last-minute shootout. Tommy's red colossus was halfway across the narrow canyon, she and the autocannon still his bullseye.

She wished she could focus better. Rage and fear kept forcing the ugliest of memories.

To shut me up, stop my screaming, Judge Randy—what Mother called him, or sometimes Randy Judge Randy and they'd laugh—slapped his hand over my mouth, scaring me, making it hard to breathe. The terror of being held down and suffocated pumped my blood with fight juice. My jaw clenched, the front teeth biting him on the underside of his forefinger, reaching bone, blood squirting into my mouth.
 Salty and hot, his wound tasted like victory.
 He screamed, the judge's wrinkled old face scrunching up worse. Like dried leather. I recognized anger and pain, so I knew what came next. I'd seen that look a thousand times on Mother. And, as the judge's fist cracked my skull, I felt more numbness than pain. I remember hoping maybe I was tougher than I thought.

Tommy honked his truck's thunderous horn again, snagging back Jessie's focus.

His ten-ton sleeper rig roared and bounced, eighty or ninety yards away, as sturdy as a Boeing 747 and moving about as fast. She could see Tommy's wide shoulders behind the steering wheel, head back, tall and confidant, bearing down on her, no doubt certain his under-educated piece of tail could never locate a second kill switch.

Tommy was a dope.

Common sense dictated that somewhere along the black tube connected to the black ammunition-drum cable, probably wrapped tightly against, and hidden by, black electrical tape, there would be the second toggle switch.

There it was. Ten feet from the first. Her heart skipped as she flipped that final connection and jumped up behind the trigger, hesitating, worried if there was time, concerned about the shrinking space between her and the big explosions she was about to unleash.

She tossed her anxiety like a used tissue. Screw it. She'd die behind this cannon one way or another. Jessie yanked back the makeshift trigger.

Everything in front of her—the gun barrel, the trailer, the sky, the whole canyon—burst into fire, smoke, and a disturbing crush of hissing noise. In her hands, under her feet, in the air around her body, the autocannon roared, whistled, and poured out hot gray exhaust. Jessie rode a fantastic dragon, the flatbed trailer undulating and twisting like a fantastical beast's body, the cannon spitting fire.

On bent knees, her weight in her feet, she rode that dragon like a cowboy, clutching the trigger mechanism and delivering her promised rain of fire. The most joyous and thrilling moment of her life was watching the first shells strike Tommy's two-hundred-thousand-dollar rig. The bright red eighteen-wheeler exploded into thousands of pieces in the first instant, and then kept disintegrating. Like a digital game of war. Fire, shrapnel of all sizes, flames, and dark smoke soared into the sky.

The cannon hissed like a two-ton mechanical goose. The stream of explosions became a steady roar and an earthquake, and she had to force herself to pause. She'd read how hot the barrels got, how the cannon should only be fired in one to three second bursts. And she didn't need to pour it on. What was left of Tommy's truck wasn't moving anymore. Flames climbed four or five stories above the cab and the gas tank had exploded.

Red-glowing streaks burned the air, and pieces of metal or glass whizzed past Jessie.

A loose truck wheel, the attached tire shredded, rolled to a stop below the cannon, then toppled on its side. Like a burning cigarette, twisted rivers of smoke rose from the rubber.

The cannon had changed Tommy and his truck into burning scrap.

She prayed to God she could do the same to Congressman King.

As she left the canyon, a coded email arrived announcing a message for HAPPYWIDOW had been posted on the dark website she'd been using. She pulled over to use her app, Jessie still glowing inside and out from firing that dragon-like cannon and watching the destruction of Tommy's truck. The sights and sounds, the explosions, the sense of riding a living animal—these were things she would never forget.

She read the message from DESERTFLYER, answered him, and he turned it into a chat.

DESERTFLYER: *man changed plans. your best shot is appearance tomorrow morning @ saguaro concert theater. park residential hills quarter mile east. specific address to follow*

HAPPYWIDOW: *wtf?*

DESERTFLYER: *cannot be helped. will be good shot. did you learn how to calculate arc of fire?*

HAPPYWIDOW: *yes*

DESERTFLYER: *purchase equipment?*

HAPPYWIDOW: *protractor and plum and engineers level*

DESERTFLYER: *checking map. head toward fountain hills, east of Scottsdale. address and more to come*

27

Sunny lay in bed half-asleep when the cell phone rang, her head nestled inside the pillow, eyes still closed and leaden. The half of her trying to wake up listened to Jordan Scott in the shower, the man humming rhythm and blues bass lines while washing that lean, athletic body. Maybe her own flesh hummed a little, too, remembering last night.

Emotionally, she was with Jordan again—reclaimed, as it were. But a second later, when next the cell ring chimed, a vision of herself married and pregnant pushed her out of bed.

The call was from Ray. "Hey," she said.

"Where are you?"

"Phoenix or Gila Bend, pretty sure. You woke me up. I'm still groggy."

"Hey, that's great news," Ray said. "Just what a boss wants to hear."

"Sorry."

"Any idea what time it is?"

"Later than I think?"

"Always. It's nine-fifteen. I've been outside your motel since nine. Like we agreed?"

"Sorry. I'll be right down. Let me finish throwing on some clothes."

"I don't think that's possible."

"What do you mean? I'm already half dressed."

He laughed. "I think you're in Phoenix, agent. Did you ever come home last night? The desk clerk is shaking her head."

She checked her surroundings. The motel room appeared familiar, but all motels and cheap hotel space usually did, at least to her. She'd stayed in a million. Mild colors, fake wood, stain resistant carpeting, manufactured art.

Some beds were softer, though, and this king-size qualified as luxurious, also stirring a nice memory from the night before. But a warning flag as well. Tequila had been involved.

"You with Jordan?" Ray said.

"Yeah, and you're right. I'm in Phoenix."

"Be careful what you say around him. Don't let your guard down."

"For sure."

She wondered if Ray could even *guess* how far she'd let her guard down.

"You going to wait for me in Gila Bend?" she said. "Or were you coming to Phoenix, anyway, talk to Johannsen about our night with Angie Chiarella?"

"Johannsen heard everything live last night. If we have time this afternoon, he said come see him. But we need to eyeball something else first."

"Can you believe that story Angie told us about her sister?" Sunny said. "I mean, I totally believe her, but what a despicable man that guy Randall King is."

"No kidding," Ray said. "I can't get the *red lipstick* out of my mind. I'm half rooting for Jessie to blow that bastard into a jigsaw puzzle."

"I'll bet."

"So listen to this," he said. "A traffic helicopter spotted strange smoke this morning. He couldn't investigate then, but when he flew back, he found the wreckage of an eighteen-wheeler reduced to smoldering junk, called the FBI. The agency has people there now, confirmed it's likely the work of our cannon. And belonged to Tommy Moon. We need to check it out."

"Where?"

"A remote box canyon south of Gila Bend. I'll email you directions and meet you."

"You got it."

"And it's okay to bring Jordan," Ray said, "or get him to drive you. We owe him for Angie, plus this secret's out. The traffic reporter brought in media even before the FBI arrived. Three TV crews now, I hear, and more on their way."

"Jordan will be *thrilled*."

The route dictated by the GPS in Jordan's rental pointed them toward Gila Bend anyway, so Sunny easily persuaded the reporter to stop and let her change clothes. She'd showered at his hotel in Phoenix that morning, but fresh clothes sounded better than soap and hot water. Before things had gotten clothes-off serious the night before, she and Jordan had wrestled quite a while on the couch.

She turned away from him in the car, grinning ear-to-ear. Remembering.

"I'll drop you off," Jordan said, "then go find us coffee and food. For some odd reason, I'm extra *hungry* this morning."

She ignored the bait. "There's a decent coffee shop down the street."

Jordan curbed the car at her motel. "I saw a bagel place two blocks from here I want to try. How about you? You *extra* hungry this morning?"

She opened the door. "Maybe a little."

They talked of this and that on their drive to meet Ray, she and Jordan good friends again, like before. They had always viewed life in much the same way. The important things were family, friends, and having a job which contributed. But then the nosey reporter—and he was nosey—brought up her weakness, a professional shortcoming he wasn't qualified to discuss.

"Why don't you want to talk about it?" Jordan said. "Last night, the issue worried you plenty. Your first field case. Lots of potential bad guys. And you still with piss-poor, personal weapons skills."

"Hey."

"Those are your words," he said.

"I said piss-poor?"

"I am professionally skilled at remembering quotes."

"If I did say that, it was the tequila talking. And I'd say your real skill is making simple facts sound dramatic. I bet I said lousy."

"I bet you don't remember."

She groaned. "All you need know, I'm working on the problem, getting better about handling the weapon. I was open about it, okay, but that's all there is to discuss. Thank you for caring."

"I probably wouldn't ever mention it in a story."

His face said he was kidding, but that didn't stop her from softly punching his shoulder. "Ray would rip you into pieces and feed you to the dogs."

"General Hauser is your champion?"

She ignored him as they pulled to a stop. They'd driven forty minutes before hitting a waiting line of four cars. On both sides of the highway, rocks jutted toward a bright blue sky. A clear August day south of Gila Bend. Already one-hundred and five degrees and headed for one-eighteen or one-twenty, according to her weather app. They waited, unable to complete the last of Ray's directions.

A left turn into the unnamed box canyon.

Jordan shifted his gaze. "So you mean by working on the problem, you're hitting the shooting range regularly—like your Glynco instructor suggested?"

She nodded. "Three times a week."

"Did you sleep with your gun last night like Hauser suggested?"

She grinned. "No, of course not. I was too busy with yours."

He liked she joked about his penis. Give the thing a life of its own, and guys are prouder than peacocks.

"How's the new job?" she asked.

"The pay is great, although renting a decent place in Los Angeles eats up most of the difference. I have more freedom over what stories I work on and write. That's fun. I broke a story two weeks ago about gunmakers the bosses loved. Got some national play. Did you see it?"

"No. What did it say?"

Jordan had reported on graft and corruption in the Army's regular purchases of replacement parts for various small weapons. Two gun manufacturers apparently had been overcharging, according to an unreleased investigation by the US Army's Criminal Investigation Command. The national media loved his story, most news outlets printing or broadcasting their own versions.

"I was interviewed by five different TV and radio stations," he said.

"Must have been a slow news day. What kind of stuff did they want to know?"

She let him talk and talk while they waited to turn into the box canyon. The different types of reporters who'd called, the strange questions some asked. Jordan obviously had enjoyed the brief bit of semi-fame, and enjoyed telling her about his journalistic adventures. So much so, the man's voice eventually became a drone, and her attention slipped to the guards up ahead. She lost track of his monologue.

"I love you, Sunny Hicks. Will you marry me?"

What? She burst out a laugh. Jordan had been giving her a speech about the lousy interrogation skills of local TV reporters, and suddenly her mind comes up with true love and a proposal?

Did she enjoy being with him so much she'd started wishing for marriage? Wonder what he'd really said.

Jordan's jaw went slack. "What are you laughing at? That's insulting."

She gasped. She made the left turn to stand third in line at another police roadblock off the highway. "I'm sorry," she said. "I couldn't believe I heard you right. I laughed at myself for hearing what I thought I heard."

Jordan's cheeks wore a new rouge. "I *proposed*, Sunny. *Marry me* was the phrase that sent you into spasms of laughter. I don't believe taking offense is entirely unreasonable on my part."

"I didn't think you...your words honestly did not compute. You totally surprised me." Sunny pinched the armrest. At the roadblock, the police cars belonged to the Pinacosta County Sheriff, but the guards checking the incoming cars wore those now-ominous, two-tone brown uniforms of the sheriff's posse.

Were they armed?

She leaned across the driver's seat to show her badge and identification to the posse member. She watched his hands, not his eyes, and let her breast rest on Jordan's arm, a physical way of saying she was his girl, apologizing for her laughter.

A quick scowl and the sentry waved them through. No questions, no words, a quick dismissal which suggested Ray must have warned them of her impending arrival. She was grateful for his thoughtfulness. These posse uniforms gave her the chills.

In another fifty yards, the road swung hard left into the box canyon. When Jordan glanced her way, he still looked pissed.

"I apologized," she said. "But I'm happy to say it again. I'm really sorry. I didn't mean to laugh at your proposal. I'm very flattered."

Jordan grunted.

"I think, however, we might discuss the idea another time."

He placed his hand on her forearm. "I love you, Sunny. I can't explain how much I've missed you. I didn't know myself until I saw you yesterday. The whole world turned glossy and bright when I saw you. I don't want to lose you again."

She laughed. "Did you just say the 'world turned glossy and bright?'"

"I did. That's really corny, huh?"

"Especially to a woman named Sunny."

"You're right. That's awful. I meant it, though. You're a sunny, happy person. You make people around you feel better."

"Thanks, but you know this is not a good time, right?"

"Yeah, but I can't help it. I'm in love."

"But you didn't expect I'd answer on the spot, did you? Look where we are."

"Yes, actually," Jordan said. "I was hoping you'd break into song, do your happy dance and scream *yes, yes, yes* to the entire canyon of cops."

She cocked her head. "Well, maybe you should have gotten on your knees. Or at least stopped the car."

That shut him up.

At the slim entrance to the rock-walled canyon, two more posse members blocked Jordan's path. One held a leashed German Shepherd, the other brown-uniformed volunteer gripped a delicate stick with high-tech gear at the bottom. He waved the business end beneath Jordan's car.

She wondered why they worried about bombs. Only local cops, the Feds, and hired technicians were inside the crime scene. Had they received a threat? Jordan showed indifference, maybe still thinking about himself. Pouting.

The search took thirty seconds and ended with a bark from the dog.

"So, what do you think?" Jordan asked. "Yes or no? Which way are you leaning?"

Sunny let out her breath. "Where do we live, Quantico or Los Angeles? Who gives up their job? What about kids? When do we have them? I don't have that many good years left. Let's wait for another time and have a real conversation, Jordan.

These are important questions."

"What's your biggest hesitation?"

She smiled. "Nothing. I know how I feel. I want to say yes. But I need time. I can't just listen to my heart. I need to hear you say some things about our life together, what you expect. And I need to be certain marriage is the best way for us to share the...attraction we feel."

His eyebrows went up. "That's sounds complicated."

"Okay, how about this—*later* on the marriage proposal?"

He feigned surprise.

"And next time," Sunny said. "Bring a ring."

Ray watched the red-haired woman in a dark blue FBI baseball cap direct Sunny and her newspaper reporter to a parking spot. This particular federal agent had neatly stacked a dozen vehicles, so the crimson puffs of hair poking from under her cap like Mickey Mouse ears did not indicate a lack of skill.

She had a thickly freckled face like Alissa's, and the resemblance put a fire under him. He had to be careful. Inside, that loud-mouth gut talking again, Ray sensed his proximity to the cannon and his wife's killers. They had to be the same people. Maybe not this Jessie person, but her dead husband and his pals. Most likely including Sunny's pal Williams.

His chance at balancing an old score drew closer.

By the time Sunny clambered out of the reporter's car, he waited to greet her. He pointed to the smoky debris field. "That red and black pile of junk used to be a Peterbilt 579. Figure the burned remains inside are Tommy Moon."

All three of them walked toward the wreckage. He stayed closer to Sunny.

"Could be a set-up, though, right?" Sunny said. "Maybe they talked a stranger into driving the truck."

He didn't think so. "To destroy Moon's new, two-hundred-thousand-dollar rig he and his mother were so proud of? Don't you think it's more likely Jessie was through with him? Wanted Tommy out of the picture?"

The reporter pushed himself between them. "Hey, could you stop whispering, please? I need to know what's going on. You promised. That was a gigantic scoop I gave away last night."

Ray grinned. "Gigantic? Tell me, Sunny, exactly how big *is* Jordan's scoop?"

She blinked only once. "Let's say when you've been scooped by Jordan Scott, you *know* you've been scooped."

"Okay, okay. Knock it off," the reporter said. "You both know what I'm talking about, so don't pretend I'm joking. I expect information today, not jokes about my incredible manhood."

Ray and Sunny laughed. He had to admit, the reporter was pretty funny. Clever. A better match for Sunny than the long-haired biker.

"You promised, general," Jordan said. "Payback for me introducing you to the former Angie Costello, prize witness against a current candidate for governor."

"You did that to impress Sunny," Ray said.

"Maybe a side benefit. So what?"

"And what do you want, mister ace reporter?" Ray said. "You're standing inside the tape at a federal crime scene. Why don't you use your intense powers of observation and take notes?"

"Me and three television crews."

Ray strode toward the wreckage, waving at Sunny and the reporter to follow. "Come on, then. Let me show you what our missing cannon does to ten-ton truck rigs, rolled steel, and human flesh."

Jordan hurried to Ray's side. "So you confirm the Air Force's lost cannon was used to kill the driver—"

"Oh, shut up," Ray said.

28

Ray estimated Tommy Moon's red tractor-trailer was seventy-five percent gone. Rearranged around the valley anyway. The big rig had erupted, flamed, and collapsed front to back, with hundreds of separate blasts shredding the truck and over half the trailer. The remaining steel qualified as scrap, including blackened, twisted sections of door frames, grill, chassis, and bumper. Its hollow, still-burning back of the trailer remained standing.

Cannon blasts had distributed fragments of engine, cab, red siding, and the presumed Mr. Moon himself across an area bigger than a football field. A few scattered pieces still smoked.

Chunks of Moon were currently being collected.

"Forensics will need months to go over all this," he said, "but we already know what happened, right, Sunny?"

She had her eyes on the canyon entrance, interested in something other than Moon's exploded rig. She finally gazed at Ray. "Jessie tested the autocannon on Moon."

"Exactly," he said. "So if she no longer needs Moon, she must be ready to go."

"Go where?" Jordan asked.

Ray nodded to Sunny, giving her the okay to tell him.

"We think her best shot at King would be his public chicken dinner and a round of golf at his club tomorrow," she said.

"But security will be super heavy at both. I don't see how Jessie can drive up with a cannon."

He nodded toward what was left of Moon's truck. "That autocannon doesn't need to get close."

Sunny's gaze drifted back to the canyon entrance. What was she looking at?

"The cannon has an effective firing range of three-quarters of a mile," Ray said. "And hearing that story her sister Angie told us, I can't imagine anybody more likely to take risks for revenge than Jessie Costello Maris."

The reporter nodded. "Agreed. The woman has serious motivation."

Sunny raised her arm, pointed to the canyon entrance. "What happened to those two posse members and their dog?"

Five minutes later, her chest and belly flat on the dusty canyon floor, Sunny spat dirt to prepare for speech. "I don't see anything under this side."

Opposite her, Ray pushed to his feet. "Nothing here either."

Jordan shouted from his exile. "Let *me* take a look."

She aimed a horizontal forefinger at him. "Stay where you are. Civilians are not allowed to search."

"It's my car."

Leaning against Ray's black SUV, Jordan had watched them hunt for what Ray worried might be a bomb, but Jordan hadn't been happy about it. In fact, Ray had required physical and mental restraint techniques to keep Jordan away, procedures including, but not limited to, gentle pushes, a raised voice, a powerful finger-jab, and several submission holds.

Ray knew cool stuff.

"We should call the bomb squad," he said.

"I don't think the gang wants to kill us," she said. "I bet it's the same as the courthouse. The gang wants to follow us, hope we deliver Jessie and the cannon. It's a tracking device we're looking for."

Jordan waved his arms to get their attention. He'd crept halfway back. "Look closer to the rear tire," he said. "That's where the guard might have bumped his stick against the frame. Pretty sure I felt something."

She bent over the right rear tire, stuck her hands beneath the fender. Her fingers probed the dirt and grime. Nothing hard or foreign, although her nail polish might not agree. "How big is it? What am I looking for?"

"Careful," Ray said.

Jordan consulted his cell phone, circled for a better connection. "Amazon's bestselling GPS auto tracker is three inches long, one and a half inches wide. A magnetic box. And...wait a second...Google says check the steel frame behind the wheels. But we know—"

"Got it!" Sunny said.

"I don't care what it is," Ray said. "It *could* have been a bomb."

"But it wasn't," she said. "The men who planted the GPS tracker are gone. But maybe the lab can find out who they were."

When he checked, Ray found nothing sinister under his Homeland Security SUV, but when she and Jordan moved closer, he waved the reporter away, out of earshot, asking her to walk closer for a chat.

His jaw looked funny.

"We know these ass-brown posse members are *all* bad," Ray said. "Part of a gang, a criminal conspiracy run by the former judge and current congressman, Randall King. We need to call for back-up, arrest everybody in posse pants."

"You're the boss. But just so you know, you're exaggerating. The gang apparently includes *some* posse members. Not all. It wasn't the posse itself. Even that guy from the railroad said so."

"Semantics."

"Call Johannsen with your plan," she said. "If he says yes, fine, arrest everybody here. We're covered. But I think we need to spend our time finding Jessie and that autocannon, not arresting and doing paperwork on volunteers."

Ray put his cell away and strolled back to where she and Jordan waited for him, the disappointment smearing his mouth like badly applied lip gloss. "Eric says you're right. No arrests. He wants us back in Phoenix pronto."

Jordan studied his cell. "Can I come?"

Ray growled. "No."

"We've convinced everyone Congressman King is Jessie's target?" she said.

"Pretty much. Angie's tales, the old court case, Dawson's body, plus the fact King plans to attend the pro football game Sunday. The meeting could involve nothing but security for that."

"What time's the meeting?" she asked.

"Five."

Staring at his cell, Jordan's gaze turned into a frown. "Before that, Sunny, you might want to read Jessie's third note. Like the others, it's addressed to you."

Sunny found an email on her own cell.

To Special Agent S. Hicks,

When he wanted to throttle me with his hands, I shot my husband, Nolan Maris, dead. His friends Sammy and Angel wanted to kill me in revenge, so I shot them, too. Old news, I know, but many comments on the internet tell me I haven't made things totally clear. I exterminated those rats. I'm proud of it. I should have done it years ago.

Better, I should have escaped from that marriage years ago.

But I never made plans to leave, never asked a friend if I could stay for a while, or saved the money necessary to hide out. I was always afraid, and there were always his promises he'd treat me better. His voice was like magic, making me believe he was right.

Now I'm finished, too, a fugitive killer. I plan to die Sunday in a blaze of glory, so why not kill a man, blow a bastard to kingdom come, send his family, his friends, and maybe thousands of his fans along for a ride.

I need to ensure my life of suffering and this man's world of forced sex and pedophilia will be commemorated. I want all of America to discover who he really is. All the secrets of his past will come out.

Jessie, His Rain of Hell

Inside Eric's Homeland Security conference room later, curtains closed, Ray hovered with other federal investigators over a street map. The Greater Phoenix area had been shrunk to the size of a stovetop. Transformed into colored lines on paper.

He wished he'd had time for a shower.

Besides himself, there was Sunny, Eric, and two agents he hadn't met before, one from the Department of Defense, another from the National Security Agency.

Eric touched his forefinger to the map's printed version of Glendale, Arizona's State Farm Stadium. "The facility is surrounded by open areas currently being blocked off. If Jessie plans to hit King with the autocannon at this location, she'd have to attack his caravan on the way inside the perimeter we've established."

"And you can make that impossible, right?" Ray said. "You set up secondary roadblocks. Ban large trucks from the area, *and* the approaches."

The Defense Department staffer grimaced. Nice clothes, neat hair. A bright blue, intelligent gaze. Ray figured her CO sent her to the meeting with little or no background. "Sorry," she said. "I'm confused, as usual. Aren't the FBI and Arizona State Troopers in charge of protecting Congressman King now?"

Ray smiled. "It's confusing to everybody, I think. And you're right, the FBI is in charge of safeguarding King. Homeland Security's responsibility is to get the Air Force's missing weapon back. That's our case—the theft and recovery."

"The two cases are separate," Eric said, "but obviously connected. We believe tracking Randall King will lead us to the stolen weapon."

"The FBI doesn't mind you using King as bait?" the Defense Department staffer said.

"The Congressman's been warned. He's chosen to continue campaigning," Eric said. "If we get in the FBI's way or cause a problem, I won't be coordinating with them. I'll be taking orders."

"Why are we sure Jessie Maris will strike Sunday?" Ray asked. "Do we believe what she says in the note?"

Eric's eyes got bigger. "You think she has another target?"

"No, not after hearing what her sister told us. I worry about timing, not the target. Jessie mentioned Sunday, so we're focused on the big appearance with thousands of victims. If I were serious about killing my abuser, I'd divert attention from when and where I *really* planned to assassinate him. He arrives in Phoenix tomorrow afternoon, right?"

Sunny checked her notes. "He's scheduled to land at Sky Harbor International Airport between 1 and 2 P.M."

"How many appearances does he have Saturday evening and night?" Ray asked.

"Two fundraisers scheduled. And the FBI is planning a heavy guard at both. Special forces, mobile roaming patrols half a mile in every direction, stopping and searching covered trucks."

"What about the trip from the airport?" Sunny said.

"That's his big vulnerability," Ray said. "Coming and going. Right, Eric?"

Eric's cell buzzed. He took the call and listened carefully to information which wrinkled his forehead. No one spoke until Eric pocketed his phone, Ray's pulse climbing, those familiar fingers of anticipation tickling his gut.

Sure signs a climax approached, the end of his hunt.

A final confrontation with Jessie Costello Maris was coming, and maybe with Randall King, too. As former chief of the railroad-theft gang, Congressman King had been at least a co-architect of all the gang's crimes, including Alissa's murder.

Eric tabled his phone. "Everything's changed," he said. "Congressman King's people added a new event to his schedule. He's coming in tonight for an event tomorrow. Saturday sunrise prayer, but with live music, celebrities, as many as five thousand people in a rock music amphitheater outside Scottsdale."

The hair on Ray's forearms spiked like cactus. "Why a last-minute change?"

Eric's mouth set in a tight line. "King's attorneys found out the FBI expanded their investigation into King's connection with Jessie Maris today—Jessie and the murder of her missing attorney, Dawson. That old juvie case. His attorneys have stopped cooperating."

Ray nodded. "I get it. Congressman King no longer trusts the FBI."

"Apparently," Eric said. "He's arranged his own security team here in Phoenix, a dozen men from the Pinacosta County Sheriff's Posse."

Ray and Hicks groaned together. Getting to be a real team.

"And get this," Eric said. "To join that security squad, the congressman made a personal request for Sunny and Ray—the two agents working the missing autocannon case."

Ray scowled. "What? That's crazy."

RAIN DAY

29

The grassy smell of alfalfa told Jessie she'd located the right house, and the mailbox number confirmed her nose's hunch. A half-mile street offered double-entry, circular driveways for five, multi-million-dollar mansions, each one built atop the same foothill ridge overlooking Scottsdale and most of metropolitan Phoenix. The combined city lights glowed in multi-colors, a bigger sparkle than Las Vegas.

She touched the brakes, edging past the first driveway, both entrances marked by white-blooming oleander bushes. The home grouped four, two-story, geodesic globes around a central patio and swimming pool, the private area within Jessie's view because a screen of evergreen bushes had not grown enough.

She braked the truck to a squeaky halt. She didn't care about the pool or the oddly shaped buildings. Her interest was in the property's recently delivered load of alfalfa, which she could use as different camouflage, the estate's relative isolation, and—most importantly—the wide-open backyard view of the Saguaro Concert Theater half a mile below.

She'd been to the Saguaro in high school a few times, once

for a battle of the bands, another time for the concert of an old-time rocker, John Cougar Mellencamp or Tom Petty, she couldn't remember which. Back in her parents' day, the 1960s, the Saguaro hosted the really old stars like Jerry Garcia, Frank Zappa, Joan Jett, and dozens of other big name players. The theater's bandshell was designed for fans, offering super acoustics and direct lines of sight.

Five thousand people would show up in a few hours, donate cash to hear a preacher bless the congressman's campaign, then hear a country boy band play a gospel set, including their new hit record. Grammar school girls and the handicapped from several local homes would be in heavy attendance.

On the drive over, she'd listened to news of the congressman's event with sadness. The risk of killing such people wounded her sense of logic, not that it would stop her. The former judge surrounded himself with innocents, like insurgents in a civil war, shielding himself with the flesh, blood, and future of others. Jessie was fighting a war against abuse, however, not running a charity. Collateral damage was sad, but not her fault or responsibility.

She tried to keep the engine noise down as she rolled sixty feet past the private driveway. DESERTFLYER's latest private post had included instructions on approximately how far down the driveway to position the cannon, and even provided a range of angles to measure on the cannon's seven barrels.

She hoped she was right trusting him. Or her. The source had been right so far about Congressman King, including the arrival in Phoenix late tonight and a morning speech at the amphitheater. The radio news had confirmed everything.

But the extreme detail of the texts worried her. Maybe DESERTFLYER's instructions were the set-up, a way to bring the cannon to a specific spot so someone could confiscate her weapon. Good luck with that. She was almost *expecting* a hijack attempt, her Beretta cleaned, loaded, and beside her on the seat.

Reversing direction, she backed into the driveway and down the sloped asphalt path. The congressman's schedule changes did make sense. Seeing pictures of what the cannon had done to Tommy's giant red truck on television, the congressman's security team probably demanded a rescheduling of the whole Phoenix visit.

She hummed inside. A week earlier, even getting *this* far with the cannon had seemed like a longshot—setting up with no one around, the news media confirming her target would soon arrive. But here she was, her heart thumping with a hero's purpose, her chance to rid the world of a violent pedophile.

Make a newsworthy show of it, too.

Pressured by the cannon's fully loaded, four-thousand-pound weight, the truck's reverse gears whined, Jessie fighting gravity as she backed down the slope. Through the cab's back window, the lights of Phoenix flickered, a multi-colored parade. Closer, at the bottom of the hill, she already could read one sign—*The Saguaro Concert Theater.*

She tried not to worry about DESERTFLYER's sincerity, or how his important information might be a trap. She expected to be caught or killed. DESERTFLYER could be anybody with access to that dark web account, anybody with detailed information about the congressman and his travel plans. Even a cop, if some paid hacker had located Nolan's connection.

Drawing a long breath, she braked beside a five-foot-high stack of baled alfalfa. A soft breeze brushed her face through the open window, cooling the sweat from her neck and stirring the white oleander blossoms. Could she really blame her troubled life on Randall King? Maybe not everything. If you wanted help in this world, you had to ask.

But King had done enough.

She hopped from the cab, disrobed the cannon's façade of cardboard boxes, then wrapped her arms around the closest bale of alfalfa. The dry, green taste filled her lungs as she hauled her package to the rear of the trailer, nestled the block of horse food exactly on the rear corner. A first brick in her planned wall around the cannon, a new disguise. She wouldn't pull it away until seconds before she fired.

With one line of alfalfa bricks installed, and movement on the theater property below her, Jessie lifted her night-vision binoculars to scope the amphitheater, and behind the buildings and shell, the various parking lots. The place was coming to life, men and machines arriving, getting things ready for the morning show.

The scene inside her binoculars wiggled a bit, and she realized her hands shook in a way she couldn't stop. Weird after all that had happened, all that she'd done, all the different people and things she'd faced over the last week. Why was she nervous at this moment, her dream of redemption only hours away?

Maybe it was the significance of what she planned, the assassination of a creepy pedophile, a criminal who probably murdered her attorney all those years ago. Maybe the importance of success overwhelmed her.

She didn't want to fail others as she had failed herself.

She focused on her breathing, imagined herself on an air-filled mattress, racing down the front of an ocean wave. Maybe her happiest time as a child, the week her aunt in California had taken the two sisters to the beach. Jessie used the memory of that old excitement, those sandy days of pure, true joy to wash away her distress.

The gun range boys had taught her. How to calm the mind beforehand, so you could stay focused on gripping the weapon, breathing out to relax, and squeezing the trigger.

And she had to focus. Assassinating Congressman King would be a world-changing event for hundreds of women, maybe thousands, wives and lovers who would read the headlines and in-depth stories and finally perceive their abusing partners for the monsters they were. See them with clear eyes.

And ask a friend for help.

She shifted the binoculars above the amphitheater, found a VIP parking lot and, leading to it, a back road onto the property. She clicked on the binocular's range finder. She did the same with the front of the stage, a distance of fifty yards shorter. The shaking in her hands had stopped.

She smiled. Nerves were not a problem for her. Eight football fields were no problem for the cannon. And who cared if she had to fire over a dozen ranch homes and the terraced theater audience. The people down there were supporters of King. Every sacrifice, including Jessie's own expectation of death, would be for women everywhere.

When she'd completed her measurements and the trailer's alfalfa camouflage, Jessie hopped in the truck cab, unleashed the emergency brake, backed farther down the hill. She needed to lower the aim of the autocannon barrel. There was time. King wasn't expected for an hour.

Truck and trailer repositioned, the angle had changed but not enough. Jessie hauled a heavy-duty floor jack from behind the driver's seat, dragged the steel-wheeled equipment beneath the trailer axle farthest from the target. What Jessie figured, and what DESERTFLYER had suggested, Jessie would aim a little high at first, then zero in by lowering the cannon's trajectory— if needed—by raising the axle farthest from the target. But the current angle was way too high.

The massive cannon had minor, side-to-side motion, thanks to Tommy, but she might not have enough wiggle room when the shooting started and Congressman King became a cowardly rabbit. The shot would be difficult. Too bad she couldn't fire a few practice shells.

A light popped on in the house behind her. One of the back porch lamps, a circle of illumination above an entrance to the largest white dome. The house was supposed to be empty,

DESERTFLYER said, and Jessie's heart raced again like yesterday when she'd yanked the cannon's trigger and nothing happened.

A human silhouette appeared and walked toward her and the cannon. Her pulse buzzed faster, and ramped up again when her night-vision binoculars showed her the intruder's face.

In the back seat of Congressman King's Cadillac Escalade, Ray and Sunny scowled at each other in mutual disbelief. Not an easy trick, both forced to peer around the congressman's gray Stetson, his basset hound belly, and those loose, hanging jowls.

Ray broke the non-verbal communication to stare at the congressman and point at the politician's chief of security, Claude Dunn. "What the hell did your man just say?"

Claude rode shotgun and seemed proud of his shaved head, thick neck, and permanent sneer. Sure acted tough for a guy over sixty and half the size of Ray. He'd tried to explain why he'd been "forced to include a broad" on the night's security team.

King had no answer, so Ray repeated his question. "Broads? Is that what he said?"

On rare occasions, he had stared at someone with hatred, maybe his father, that cruel assistant high school basketball coach. But the burning inside at Congressman Randall King singed his nerves. A desire to choke the silent congressman tickled his hands and curled his fingers. The wrenching of his internal organs was no doubt the result of King's unknown role in Alissa's death, not Dunn's ignorant comments.

But he couldn't help himself. Or he wouldn't. The anger seemed fair.

"I do not understand why you'd hire a man like that," he said. "Why you would ask *us* here tonight if that's the way you and your people think?"

"I am sorry Claude talks so poorly," King said. "He's definitely not my best public relations guy. But see, I trust him. He's good at what he does, which is taking care of me—an old man who finds himself in trouble now and then."

Ray forced himself to breathe. Slowly. This hadn't been a great idea to put himself in the back seat of a car with King. That night in the Hyatt bar, he and Eric had discussed King's likely guilt. Eric said the FBI had gathered "seriously damaging" testimony. What if Ray actually strangled this man?

Breathe, Ray. Just breathe.

King sipped from the same glass of bourbon he'd carried off his private jet. He and Sunny had been at the airport at King's request, a night without rest, because Eric insisted they shouldn't miss the chance. Like the proverbial lost sheep, wherever Randall King went, their cannon would likely follow. Eric had trusted Ray could keep cool.

He wished he did.

The congressman licked his lips. "What Claude was trying to say, but using terms of poor taste, is we can't trust the FBI anymore. Claude and I are worried the FBI is part of a political conspiracy to take me out of the gubernatorial race."

Ray shook his head.

"Perhaps even get me killed," King said. "I know that sounds crazy, but…"

"Nothing about you sounds farfetched, congressman. Nothing."

"Thank you," King said. "But you two are protecting me now, because, like Claude, I can trust your motives. You want that automatic cannon back."

Ray nodded. "That's right, congressman. You can definitely trust our motives."

The familiar guy kept coming down the slope toward the trailer, Jessie moving again to stay hidden. One hand held her night-vision binoculars, the other her Beretta.

"Jessie? Where are you?"

Standing behind her cannon, she let the binoculars hang on her chest. She'd been hiding behind bales of alfalfa, ducking whenever the flashlight beam passed her way. Could this be DESERTFLYER? It was definitely the handsome guy from the party last year, the Sacred Blood biker with connections.

"Hey, Jessie. Come on out. It's DESERTFLYER. Dennis. Remember me from the river party?"

Dennis Williams. Sure, she remembered. He kept calling her name as he walked down the hill, searching for her with his flashlight, momentarily showcasing the thick, mid-summer bug life. Film them with close-ups, you could make a horror movie.

"Jessie?"

If Dennis wanted to help, why did he have a gun stuffed in his belt?

She let her body and mind talk before walking out of the shadows. Dennis had always been the best-looking man in the motorcycle club, maybe the whole Sonora Desert with that long, blond hair, those arms and shoulders. She loved the way he knew everybody, too, got politicians to participate in the club's fund-raising drives. Mr. Charming. Mr. Horse Crap.

The whole truth hit her like one of Nolan's punches.

Dennis worked for Congressman King and the Polanco gang. Nolan told her the two were the same. It all made sense, the congressman tied to the biker gang. How else would a guy like Dennis even know the governor, or get his last-minute schedule?

Dennis had directed her to the perfect place for a shot at Congressman King, but he had to know he'd never collect the commission she had promised. He was here to kill her, or at least prevent her from killing King, maybe keep the cannon from being reclaimed by the Air Force.

The gang wanted their cannon back.

"Come on, Jessie," he said. "I know you're here."

The sky wouldn't be dark long. She had the Beretta in her hand, the noise-suppressor screwed onto the barrel.

"Jessie?" Dennis said. "You behind that alfalfa?"

Or could Dennis be on his own? Double-crossing King and his motorcycle pals to take and sell the autocannon for himself? So greedy and so sure of himself, he actually believed he could fool her, take her down all by his lonesome.

Either way, the sky was bluer than thirty seconds ago. Indirect sunlight warmed the foothills above. She had seconds to use her night-vision advantage, and only one thing seemed certain. Her priority was to kill Randall King. Dennis was there to stop her.

30

Shading the window with his hand, Ray peered outside Congressman King's Escalade. The blackness was impenetrable on his side, thanks to the SUV's special dark glass, a parking-lights only edict from security chief Dunn, and the current time of day. The Phoenix sun had yet to make her grand and eternal appearance.

Like the goddess she was.

He and Sunny were part of a three-car caravan which snuck inside the *Saguaro Concert Theater* the same way burglars might. Low lights on the event site's rear access road for entertainers and work crews. Red-flowered bottle-brush trees grew close to the path. Between ten and twelve feet in height. Unevenly spaced.

Congressman King sat between them in the back seat. So far, he'd behaved like a prince, although Ray had to block out Alissa's murder and Angie Chiarella's red lipstick story. He spent a lot of time looking out the window because every time he saw the creepy pedophile, he wanted to choke him.

One way or another, King was responsible for Alissa's death.

"There are lights on that ridge above the theater," Ray said. He used his hand against the glass to peer outside. "Maybe half a dozen estates overlooking smaller homes at the bottom of the hill."

"Those ridges are eight-hundred yards off," Dunn said. "Maybe eight-fifty."

"That distance is within the autocannon's effective range," Sunny said.

Dunn groaned. "Effective for what? The best military expert in America couldn't target an individual from the back of a flatbed at that distance. How could a mentally incompetent trailer park housewife? You're a joke."

Ray watched Sunny buzz down her window like she was ready to puke. He decided on more aggressive action. He reached between the head rests to seize Dunn's shoulder. Maybe only a number five grip on his scale of ten because the security chief was old. He didn't want to give the loser a heart attack.

Dunn gasped loudly.

"Seventy shells a second," Ray said. "Each one explodes like a stick of dynamite. That cannon doesn't need to get close."

He upped the squeeze to a six. Dunn cried out.

"And you should probably read that mental incompetent's file," Ray said. "So far, Jessie Maris has killed at least four men who underestimated her."

He let go of Dunn and fell back against his seat, rolled down his window, let the fresh air rid his nose of the old man's aftershave. Outside, the entertainment center stirred with life. Teams of ticket-takers unlocked the gates, letting inside early arrivals. Lots of men and women in T-shirts and shorts, the air already hot. Other workers rolled up steel shutters, opening food counters to sell the customers hot coffee, breakfast rolls and wraps.

The trio of Escalades parked near the theater's main three-story office building behind the amphitheater's stage and bandshell structure. Men appeared in golf carts to meet the congressman's limos. Dunn pointed to a steel door marked as Security. "In there."

Everybody piled out.

Ray gulped more fresh air. Like a watercolor, the eastern sky washed pale at the jagged horizon, dawn less than ten minutes away. For obvious reasons, a climax to Alissa's case seemed imminent. Congressman King was the right guy, the mastermind of the gang who had murdered his wife, if not the actual murderer. The FBI told Eric last night they believe he never gave up control, just moved all communications to the dark web after his first election.

He walked, then jogged back along the access road to where he could examine the hillside lights he'd spotted earlier. Another morning gust of soft wind touched his cheeks.

On the ridge he'd noted earlier, two estates had been painted a pale shade which visually popped in the pre-dawn sky. Both homes topped the same hill within half a mile of the Saguaro Theater, and both offered barns or other structures capable of hiding a cannon.

A voice from behind made him twist.

Sunny had followed him, a phone against her ear. Now she stood beside him.

"You stay with the congressman," he said. "I'm going to check out those homes." He pointed to the ridge. "That's where I'd put the cannon, wait for King to get on stage. Or maybe wait until the convoy heads out later."

"The sunrise service is supposed to start in fourteen minutes," Sunny said, "We don't have much time, but the book says we wait for back-up. I called Eric—I mean General Johannsen. Did you call him, too?"

"No. We can't wait for back-up. We have to stop Jessie before she uses that cannon. Look at all the people already here."

Sunny nodded. "You're right, but *I* need to be the one who goes up there. The senior agent—you—has to stay with Congressman King. Imagine the worst happens, and you assigned a rookie to protect him."

Ray frowned.

"Yeah, I know," Sunny said. "You want to go shoot it out

with Jessie James Maris and her automatic cannon."

"I'm a better gunfighter," he said.

"That's why you *have* to stay with our charge, keep him safe. Let me go up there and earn my stripes. Besides, a man your size isn't sneaking up on anybody."

He made a humming sound. Staying here with King maybe fit Ray's plans, too. But so many lives could be at stake. "You're ready to shoot it out with Jessie? You're not going to fumble your weapon and get killed?"

"I'm ready."

He spread his lips. "Good. It's attitude, too, you know. Being calm and confident with someone firing at you, returning the fire. Experience really helps. I think you're ready, too, but what about getting one of Dunn's armed drivers to go with you?"

Sunny wagged her head. "We shouldn't even tell them I'm going. I don't trust King or his men. How can you?"

"You're right. Did Eric say how long before the back-up would get here?"

"Ten minutes."

"Did he mention a helicopter?" he asked.

"Soon as the sun's up. The county won't let law enforcement use spotlights this early on their biggest taxpayers' estates."

"All right. Get going. If you see her, be the one who shoots first. How are you getting up there?"

Sunny pointed to the Security door. "I'll take one of those golf carts."

She couldn't see, hear, or smell her in the fresh morning, but Sunny knew Jessie waited for her. They'd spent that time together, had a girl's moment over their troubled childhoods, and she sensed Jessie's hatred, knew the angry woman was on this hill somewhere, her only intention to murder Randall King.

Alone in the electric three-wheeler, she traveled a residential street still dark and quiet. A few kitchen lights. She unbuttoned her holster and accidentally touched the Sig Sauer. A vivid picture of her father tried to flash into her head, but she blocked them out. The feeling of its steel wasn't the horror it used to be, plus there wasn't time for that crap. Not now. Her life and many other's depended on her focus.

She didn't believe she'd ever use a pistol without remembering him.

But she could block the bad feelings. The gun was just a tool.

The Beretta snuggled into Jessie's grip like a friendly puppy, but when she aimed and squeezed the trigger twice—always a double-tap—Dennis Williams shifted position. Her firing action came off jerky and imprecise.

Ten yards away, on a horizontal line across the hillside, Dennis must have heard or felt Jessie come out from behind the alfalfa. He'd spun and ducked as she fired, his long hair trailing.

Her initial bullet missed, but by yanking the barrel lower in mid-double tap, she'd earned a lucky shot. The second bullet hit his leg.

Even wounded, Dennis refused to keep himself an easy target, rolling down the hill like a wind-driven tumbleweed. He bounced hard on the dirt slope. The pistol flew from his hand.

She fired twice more, missing, erupting only the soil near his scrambling frame. Worse, the sun was up, bright golden shafts topping the eastern peaks, warm air stirring and clearing the day of shadows.

The cannon and trailer were lit up like a movie set.

Soft music and distant murmurs of an assembling crowd carried up from the Saguaro. Jessie knew she had only minutes before Congressman King spoke. She had to focus, get that Avenger cannon ready to fire.

* * *

Sunny parked the battery-powered golf cart on a residential street one-hundred yards below the first of the two estates Ray located from the theater. The house sitting closest to the Saguaro stage was the logical place to start. Her breathing had quickened. She sucked in harder and blew out slower. Closed her eyes. Nothing slowed her tick-tock pulse.

The desert dawn stirred with buzzing insects and gusts of gentle wind. The sun's rim burned all the way above the McDowell Mountains, and behind them, the Tonto National Forest. Bright golden rays struck the hillside beneath Sunny's feet, and light switched on everywhere.

A text from Ray said Congressman King would walk on stage in seven minutes.

She had to hurry.

Sunny pushed through a six-foot-tall forest of tamarisk and fountain grass in a ditch beside the paved street. Scaly stalks pulled at her hair and scratched her bare arms. Her sneakers crunched on dry grass.

A hard-packed slope, dotted with tall saguaro, greeted her on the other side of the roadside hedge. She stopped to survey ahead. A few low-spreading patches of weed-grass or cactus grew on the slope, most groupings in shallow depressions. At the top, a single-family home resembled a futuristic castle of geodesic domes. On one side of the property, a parked truck and trailer carried a green block of fresh hay.

But something looked strange, out of place.

She hopped from the tall grass to the sloped hillside, Sunny heading for two thick saguaros she could hide behind. Her plan was to advance steadily toward that truck and trailer, investigate, but stay behind cover. Moving cactus to cactus until…what was that?

Something stirred the bushes behind her.

"Hey, Sunny."

Heart thumping, she found the male voice. Hollywood. Wearing his motorcycle club vest jacket and jeans. He crouched on one knee beside a thick clump of tamarisk grass, his bloody hands wrapping a tourniquet on the opposite leg. His fingers slipped tying the knot. Dark red liquid soaked his jeans.

"I've been shot," he said.

No kidding. His voice was thin and weak. Hollywood was seriously wounded. His new tourniquet already had changed color and begun to drip blood. On the other hand, there could not be a good reason for Hollywood to be on this particular hill with a gunshot wound. He was definitely a bad guy.

"Help me stand, please?"

She declined the hand he offered. "So you can punch me and take my weapon?"

He scowled and whined. "Aw, come on, Sunny. I'm hurt."

She shook her head and leaned in. "I wouldn't trust you to—"

His hand blurred and a shotgun blast of sand and grainy dirt splashed against her face, getting in her eyes and mouth, forcing Sunny backward and away from Hollywood. She stumbled wiping the grit from her eyes.

She saw his shape coming but couldn't get out of the way in time, ducking the wrong way and catching Hollywood's closed fist in the side of her head. Her ear screamed with pain, and she toppled all the way over on her back. The shock was as immobilizing as the pain.

Comets and asteroids spun in her vision. Hollywood must have heard her crunching the grass, so he'd waited on the other side, hiding like a snake. And to think she'd once dreamed of those shoulders holding her. How could she have been dumb enough to even talk to the rotten, woman-hitting, thieving rattlesnake?

He snatched the weapon from her holster. "I lost my Glock when Jessie shot me," he said. "I had to roll down here and hide. But then, what's that I hear? Looks like Special Agent S. Hicks with an Air Force-issue, Sig Sauer. Christmas in August."

He sounded manic. Maybe losing too much blood. He aimed

her primary weapon in her face while he searched and found her ankle-strap, back-up, a Smith & Wesson .38 revolver. "Stick out your hands," he said.

Bright sunlight warmed her face. She stayed on her back, arms reaching up toward Hollywood while he wrapped her wrists in a self-locking plastic strip. In special agent training, they called them zip ties. And by binding her hands in front of her, Hollywood made a mistake.

"You taking the cannon for yourself?" she said.

"Who else? Think I care about the Congressman's war chest? Or a fat addition to the Sacred Bones pension fund? But no more chatting, Sunny. I have to run. Jessie's going to fire up that monster any second, and then nobody wins the lottery."

"Maybe those people down below," she said.

Her cell chimed with a text, and Hollywood came back to yank the phone from her pocket. His hands were rough, poking her thigh. They both saw Ray's name on the screen, and the reminder she had a partner bolstered her spirits. That punch had also delivered a nasty dose of reality. She was no trained killer.

But she'd fight. She'd fight like Ray would. Hard.

Hollywood tossed her phone deep inside the strip of tall grass along the road. "Sorry I had to rough you up. You're not a bad person."

"Oh, thanks, Dennis. Another time, another place, right?"

"For sure."

She got a better view of his leg injury. The torn strip of thin cloth—his T-shirt—was saturated and steadily dripped blood. Not really working as a tourniquet. "That's a bad wound, Dennis. The bullet might have nicked your femoral artery. You'd better get to a hospital, let *me* rescue that cannon."

"I'm fine. And don't come after me because I *will* shoot you. I don't want to. Take me days to get over it."

He flipped his back to her and forced limping steps up the hill. He gripped her Sig Sauer in his right hand, arm hanging against his good thigh, her revolver in his back pocket. "But I will get over it. Promise."

She sat up. "You're doing this for the money?"

"Half a million is more than money," he said. "It's a new life."

31

Sunny fought a jackhammer inside her skull to watch Hollywood lurch up the hillside, his blond hair damp and stringy against his neck. Her senses still jangled from the big man's punch. She needed to free herself and stop Jessie Maris from raining dynamite onto a crowd full of boy band music fans.

Families with children. Bubbly gangs of pre-teens.

She focused on the pain of the plastic strip biting her wrists. Limiting the circulation to her fingers. Pinching nerves.

Two things worried her about her assignment to stop Jessie. Call them handicaps. First, there were *two* perps she'd have to battle, what with Hollywood showing up, threatening to kill her. Second, the golden-haired SOB had appropriated both of her weapons.

She rolled into a sitting position. Screw the impediments. Ray and those people below were counting on her to prevent a disaster. Also, her lace-up sneakers provided an opportunity.

Adrenaline helped her concentrate. Her butt flat on the ground, knees up, she reached low between her legs, used her numb fingertips to untie her shoelaces. Took her a while. But next she knotted a left shoelace to a right shoe-lace, positioned the doubled-length ribbon of tough fabric over the plastic strip between her wrists. Then she sawed her feet up and down, knees sticking out and pumping like she rode a child's tricycle.

In less than half a minute, the back-and-forth rubbing created enough heat to melt the plastic zip tie. Thank you, special agent school. Also, the physical activity and success in freeing herself bumped her confidence.

She rose to her feet. Attitude counted.

She'd asked Ray for the chance to handle Jessie. The chance to risk her life to protect others. And she would. Happy to do what was expected of a law enforcement officer. Scared, too, maybe, but that was part of courage, Uncle Sal taught her. Doing your job despite the fear.

She headed up the hill after Hollywood.

Not that she was tough like Ray. Slightly gangly, a little clumsy, Special Agent S. Hicks considered herself but one of hundreds of thousands of police officers and law enforcement personnel sworn to do the same. In America, carrying a gun and a badge meant personal risk. You weren't supposed to let fear hold you back.

Hollywood hadn't gotten far. He wasn't twenty yards away, not even halfway to the trailer. His back was to her. A tall, well-armed man. But bleeding out, in most likelihood. Already less strength than when he'd hit her so hard in the head.

As quietly as she could, she fast-walked to a group of cactus in Hollywood's blind spot, forty yards short of the flatbed trailer. Movement by the flatbed twisted her head, and she recognized Jessie Maris and the cannon. Camouflaged behind alfalfa bales edging the trailer. Seven long black barrels, banded as one, protruded from a seam of haystacks.

This was it. Jessie's position. Ray had picked the spot from the SUV. Too bad she couldn't call him. All she had to stop this was her wits and her determination.

Hollywood stumbled higher up the hill, angling toward the trailer. His limp had grown more exaggerated in the last minute. The left foot dragged, and bright red blood trickled down his boot. Sunny didn't think he'd last much longer. A pang of sadness for him appeared in her throat, although she couldn't understand why.

She was lucky he hadn't killed her.

She ran to the next saguaro. Hot brassy sunlight colored the air like a transparent film. Flying bugs and winged, airborne seeds danced in a hot, mildly stirring draft. A quiet August morning. Felt like ninety degrees minutes after dawn.

A helicopter buzzed far away. Her heart tapped louder. The adrenaline had bumped her pulse into a steady roar. Sweat formed around her eyes and neck.

She wondered if Hollywood could get to Jessie before his blood supply gave out. Or Jessie shot him. She figured Jessie hadn't seen him yet, her binoculars searching the amphitheater from the bed of the trailer, but she would soon. This was the first moment Sunny had gotten a good look at Jessie since their meeting in the barn. All Jessie's notes made the connection and the case seem personal.

Her adversary. An abuse victim.

Hollywood sidestepped to avoid a boulder and his gaze caught Sunny staring at him from behind the saguaro. Without hesitation, he lifted the Sig Sauer, leveling her own pistol at her from thirty-five or forty feet away, Hollywood higher on the slope. Even from that distance, though, she saw the pain on his face, the fear of dying.

He probably understood he'd been losing too much blood.

Another flash of regret zapped through her, sorry Hollywood would never enjoy his fortune. He risked everything for it. But why? The guy had lied, tricked, and punched her. Now he aimed a weapon at her. What a softie she was for feeling anything for him.

In the six-foot fountain grass by the street, her cell phone faintly sang a familiar tune in the quiet morning. A new text had arrived. She guessed the message came from Ray, a signal worked out earlier. King and his family prepared to walk on stage. If busy, she wasn't expected to answer.

Good thing, because she judged herself extremely busy, hiding behind a cactus, waiting for Hollywood to shoot her.

The buzz of the helicopter became a *chop-chop*, louder by the second, but still not quite matching the throb of Sunny's pulse. She breathed now through her mouth. Full fight or flight. She could hope for reinforcements, Johannsen's promised backup, but she figured the chopper more likely carried news reporters. Men with microphones instead of guns.

The task of stopping this catastrophe was hers. And she had to do it without a weapon.

A bus or truck engine strained at the bottom of the hill somewhere. The amphitheater crowd broke into applause, a distant hum. And up ahead on the slope, Hollywood collapsed to one knee, the impact loosening his grip on the Sig Sauer. His chin dropped to his chest. If he keeled over, Sunny had to make a charge, get her hands on...

Movement higher and to the left snapped Sunny's gaze. Jessie had dropped the binoculars to her chest and was removing an extended-length pistol from her waist. She must have noticed Hollywood, or maybe even Sunny. The agent ducked for cover beside a Saguaro.

She realized Jessie's pistol seemed too long because it had a noise suppressor attached to the muzzle. Jessie lowered herself flat on the trailer, then snuggled against the cannon in a standard prone shooting position. Maybe she expected Hollywood and Sunny to attack in unison. From Jessie's position, Sunny and Hollywood existed on the same line of sight.

Hollywood staggered back to his feet. He looked wobbly, but lifted the Sig Sauer toward Sunny on a pretty good line. His two-handed grip wavered, though, and he was wide open to a shot from Jessie, his back to the trailer.

"Get out of here," Hollywood said. "Not another step or I'll—"

Jessie fired twice—two muzzle flashes and two noisy *pops*.

Two things happened. Hollywood collapsed again and the saguaro beside Sunny's ear lost a fist-sized chunk of ribbed flesh.

She caught her breath, staring at the wounded cactus. That sizeable hunk of living vegetation had disappeared like trick photography, and the bullet traveled only ten or twelve inches off line with Sunny's head.

She flattened herself in the dirt and crawled behind the saguaro. Her heart could not beat any faster. She checked for Hollywood's prone body. She knew where he was, but couldn't tell how badly he was injured.

"Throw down your weapon," Jessie said.

Sunny remembered how many men Jessie had killed at the barn. Then Tommy Moon. And now Hollywood, who most likely was number five. This woman was an excellent marksman.

"Dennis has my weapons," Sunny said. "I'm unarmed."

Jessie thought about it, and Sunny's truth must have made sense. After all, Hollywood had showed up with a different weapon.

"Stand up, raise your hands, and walk toward me," Jessie said.

Her throat felt frail. Sunny coughed to change the pitch. "I'm thinking you've missed your chance to get the congressman. My partner signaled King was headed for the stage a minute ago. He won't be up there long."

Jessie lifted her binoculars toward the amphitheater.

Sunny scooted closer to Hollywood.

The helicopter came around again.

"I haven't missed anything," Jessie said. "King is still waiting. Even after, I could get his Escalades when he leaves."

Jessie rose to her feet and let the binoculars rest again on her chest. She aimed her semiautomatic carefully at Sunny. "But you're right. Time is short. Get up and walk over here."

Sunny tried to make herself smaller. "That helicopter is the cavalry, Jessie. You should give yourself up."

Jessie shook her head. "I can't believe you want to die. Walk over here and get on your knees."

Sunny gauged the distance between herself and Hollywood at fifteen feet. Three for four bounding steps to her Sig Sauer.

"You have three seconds to start walking," Jessie said. "Come toward *me*."

She ignored Jessie's semiautomatic to glance one more time at Hollywood and make her choice. Her bloodstream buzzed with adrenaline. Her throat had dried from breathing through her mouth. Fight or flight? Run and dive for the gun, or surrender, get closer to Jessie and the cannon, see what happens next.

She raised her hands higher and walked toward Jessie and the deadly black eye of that noise suppressor. Slowly, on purpose. Shuffling her retied sneakers. Her pulse and juices had been on high so long, being unhurried, keeping a leisurely pace required every atom of her will.

"Stop stalling," Jessie said. "Or I'll shoot you."

"I'm not exactly one-hundred percent."

She shuffled to a spot five yards from Jessie, her gaze level with the first row of pale green alfalfa stacked along the truck trailer. A glance to her left confirmed the amphitheater was filling with people, and that one man on stage wore a Stetson and a big belly waiting to be introduced. Looked like Ray directly behind him.

"Get on your knees," Jessie said. "I'm going to kill a slimeball, and I'm going to let you watch."

Sunny kneeled, balancing herself on the uneven ground. She kept her hands raised above her shoulders, and for some crazy reason, worried again about Hollywood. The bastard had kicked and punched her, lied to her, threatened to kill her, yet she now found him sad, such a handsome, potentially likeable guy, driven to extremes by...greed?

Jessie stared at her. Sunny stared back, wondering if she was about to die.

The one great thing she'd learned from her father's suicide, an idea she needed to think about more, maybe every day,

Sunny believed happiness came from loving and being loved, plus having a job which contributed. You helped somebody with your work. Made a difference somewhere with someone.

Jessie walked near a lever mounted to the trailer, a homemade lever rising waist high beside the cannon's ammunition drum. The drum not only held unspent shells ready to fire, Sunny knew, but also collected the spent cartridges, a necessary design to keep the expired shell casings from flying into aircraft engines.

Jessie placed an aluminum carpenter's level on the black barrels of the cannon. Measuring the angle. She nodded her approval.

No more time, Sunny figured. Jessie was about to fire her rain of hell on an unsuspecting crowd, half of them children.

Sunny scrambled to her feet and ran at the trailer. She had to stop Jessie. And she had to crash the party without a weapon.

Her terrible past did not excuse Jessie's violence against innocent people. An unfortunate woman, a soul perhaps crafted by betrayal, rape, and torture. An adult bent early by a gruesome childhood without love and affection. But her commitment to death, the way she planned or risked children's lives...

She'd lost her humanity.

Sunny reached the trailer at full speed and tried to use her momentum, throwing her knee up high onto the flatbed, jumping with the other leg, tossing herself onto the platform. Her plan was simple—rip off any one of the cannon's wires and cables. Of course, to do that, she'd have to avoid Jessie's bullets.

She successfully landed on the trailer and raised her head to find the threat.

Jessie fired twice.

32

The first gunshot buzzed Sunny's head and ricocheted low off the truck cab's rear bumper guard. The second bullet struck her right leg, the limb she'd first kicked up onto the flatbed. High on the outside of her thigh, the blow knocking Sunny off the trailer, tumbling backward.

She crashed hard on the slope. Dazed. Her ears hummed like electrical transformers. The top of her head was hot. Stars, planets, and a maze of tiny white lights zoomed across her blurred vision. But her leg burned as if she sat in a campfire. She explored her leg and the wound with her fingers. A missing chunk on the outside. Like the saguaro minutes ago.

Sunny stayed flat on her back. Breathe. Just breathe.

As predicted by firing range instructors, classroom lecturers, and anyone else who'd ever been shot, the bullet trauma converted her leg into a roaring, crackling fireplace. The worst burning sensation she'd ever experienced, including spilled boiling water. Her eyes teared from the angry, searing heat which refused to fade.

The breathing worked a little. Extra oxygen kicked in basic instincts, including survival. Another shot or two from Jessie's semiautomatic could explode any second in her direction. If she wanted to live, if she wanted to do her job, protect those innocent people down below, live up to the promise she'd made

Ray, she better recover and fight back.

She checked the trailer. No Jessie.

Now, honey. Move.

She tried to stand but couldn't. The bullet hadn't broken any bones, maybe, but her leg burned so badly, the pain lingered with such intensity, her large thigh muscles didn't respond to her brain signals. They were getting their orders from somewhere else.

Unnerving. She'd never experienced such helplessness.

She had to find a way to change position. But how?

Pushing with her good leg, she slid her butt against the nearest trailer wheel. She huddled against the steel and rubber, a tiny bit of cover. Still no sight or sound of Jessie. Why wasn't Jessie coming after her to finish the job?

She checked her wound again. A chunk of her outer thigh was missing, about the size of an unshelled walnut. More blood this time, but the bullet wasn't inside her. She covered the wound with her hand and pressed, then kicked herself up to sit higher against the rubber tire, focused on her breathing and locating Jessie. She had to before moving again. But Jessie was nowhere.

Blood oozed steadily from her wounded leg, but the flow didn't pump in rhythm with her pulse. She'd been luckier than Hollywood. No arteries had been hit. She sucked air as deeply as her lungs allowed, letting the exhale slide out slowly through pursed lips. The sky glowed deep and rich blue, nearly cobalt.

"Sunny."

Had Hollywood returned to life?

"Sunny," he said. "Over *here.*"

There he was, Hollywood on his back and trying to be heard above the swishing blades of a non-military, white-painted helicopter. Glare off the bright morning sun made identification of the chopper impossible from Sunny's angle. She needed help, and surely those ten minutes had elapsed. Maybe the 'copter was General Johannsen's back-up team.

Hollywood waved at her. "Sunny."

In her peripheral view, Jessie's feet appeared underneath the trailer, on the opposite side, then all of Jessie's legs. She was about to jump to the ground.

Sunny jerked her head behind the truck's rear wheel and held her breath, hoping she wouldn't give herself away. Jessie must be looking for her. This was it.

She heard Jessie crawl beneath the flatbed, then a metallic squeaking. Equipment working. She peeked, saw Jessie pumping a long handle, lifting the rear of the trailer with a heavy-duty floor jack. Jessie totally focused on the floorjack. She paid no attention to the wheel shielding Sunny. Jessie must have realized she was running out of time. The governor wouldn't be on stage long.

The helicopter twisted, and she saw they would be no help. The call letters WPZO were painted in gold. It belonged to a Phoenix TV station. If Jessie fired the cannon again, those people would be thrilled to make digital recordings of the death and destruction.

Broadcast the violence for their viewers live.

What went through her head again, there was no one there but her to stop the potential mass murder. Unless she personally prevented the attack, Jessie Maris could unleash hundreds of explosive shells on a crowd of five-thousand humans, half of them children. Not to mention the target she'd sworn to protect, Congressman King.

"Sunny," Hollywood said.

How many lives were at risk? Thousands of voices sang along now the speeches and long prayer had finished. She could see the top curve of the amphitheater, the image of a saguaro cactus imprinted in the top seal. The congressman's voice rasped on the microphone, missing all the notes.

Bringing in the sheaves, bringing in the sheaves,
  We shall come rejoicing, bringing in the sheaves

***

Another two minutes, King would be off premises, out the back road in his three Escalades. She'd seen the SUVs turn around while she followed Hollywood up the hill.

Beneath the trailer, Jessie gave up on the floor jack and headed topside. By pumping the long handle up and down, she'd raised the trailer's rear end at least six inches, maybe more. Up in back meant down in front. The aim of the cannon had lowered considerably.

Sowing in the morning, sowing seeds of kindness,
  Sowing in the noontide and the dewy eve;
  Waiting for the harvest, and the time of reaping,
  We shall come rejoicing, bringing in the sheaves.

"Sunny."

Her leg still burned like glowing charcoal against her flesh. The top of her head itched and hurt at the same time. Jessie's first bullet might have barely missed her.

She hoped her luck held.

If Jessie had seen or heard Hollywood, she didn't care. Her priority was firing that automatic cannon at Congressman King, and she only had seconds to pull the trigger before King left the stage.

Bringing in the sheaves, bringing in the sheaves,
  We shall come rejoicing, bringing in the sheaves.

"Sunny! Catch."

She glanced at Hollywood, saw whatever he'd thrown at her

sailing up high into that cobalt heaven. She followed the black, irregular shape across the blue canvas, no clue at first what the arriving missile could be.

Her focus sharpened when she recognized her Smith & Wesson.

She had to catch it. She couldn't imagine how her internal glands had any supply left, but a distinct surge of new adrenaline hit her bloodstream. The pain in her leg eased a little.

As heard Jessie above her on the trailer, she eyed her target's direction and distance. Would the weapon arrive before Jessie started shooting? No numbers existed for Sunny to calculate, no maps to hunt locations, no pieces to assemble, no related information she could analyze. All she had to compute and solve the puzzle of catching that weapon was instinct and a mental image of the twisting, spinning shape.

Hollywood's toss appeared long, as in over her head.

Maybe if she reached up higher on one side, with one hand, her longest fingers could touch or even snag the two-pound semiautomatic. Drop that odd-shaped, high-flying steel object within her catching range.

Maybe. Sunny's outstretched hand fanned the air like a parading queen, her gaze focused on the weapon. The grip hit two of her fingers, but she missed holding on, the weapon landing behind her in the dirt beneath the trailer.

And down below, on the microphone, the congressman's voice was saying goodbye, thanking the crowd. She realized she didn't have time. Even if she'd snagged that semiautomatic in midair, she couldn't shoot Jessie from here, flat on the ground, and she couldn't stand up. She'd waste precious time looking for her back-up weapon now.

Only one thing to do. A sudden idea that had to work.

Jessie raised her binoculars.

She wished she could aim the powerful cannon while firing, but she'd have to see where the first burst of shells landed, then stop to shift left or right, maybe raise or lower the cannon's reach again by adjusting the floor jack. Her skin glowed with exhilaration, a sign of emotion she fought to control. Hurry. The governor was walking offstage.

Too bad she'd had to kill that Air Force agent, Sunny Hicks. Jessie had liked her.

She let the binoculars slip to her chest and reached for the cannon's improvised trigger. She'd killed four men and one woman to get this far. Hollywood's death would make it six in all, but each killing had been necessary to the cause, each helping position her for this chance to murder the son-of-a-bitch pedophile, Randall King. To make those deaths count, she had to fire and blow up King's ass.

She flicked a switch and tugged back on the trigger.

At the same instant, as roaring sound and smoke covered the platform with instant pandemonium, the floor sank beneath her—the trailer's rear end sitting down fast and hard. Her five-ton floor jack must have failed or slipped, and the smoking, hissing cannon's burning shells overshot the stadium. A handful landed behind the stadium, where King's SUVs took a hit or two. But many more explosions blossomed on the back road.

Jessie stopped firing.

Sunny had twisted the floor jack's release valve, dropping the autocannon's rear end closer to the ground and within inches of her own head. The sudden collapse would have scared her if she weren't already juiced to the max.

The shade beneath the trailer had filled instantly with smoke. The ground shook as the trailer above her twisted and torqued to one side. A sound like a screaming dragon rattled her brains.

But then the autocannon stopped. Maybe her idea worked, although she could hear hundreds of people howling in the distance.

The autocannon's sound and fury rubbed acid on her already

challenged nerves. Though she'd cutoff the autocannon's fire, in reality she'd failed. For a second, the terrible weapon had been unleashed. The question of how many casualties needed to be forced from her thoughts.

So did the fire in her leg.

No matter what happened, she had the same job as before—prevent another burst. She rolled out from underneath the trailer on the same side she'd entered, away from the bales of alfalfa and toward Hollywood. The hay could be great cover if she wanted to hide, but first, she needed her weapon.

More crowd noise reached her ears, now thousands of frightened concert-goers as the explosion had continued.

Block them out, Sunny. Do your job. The intense pressure, maybe desperation, felt like a hand inside her ribcage, squeezing her heart and lungs, telling her how urgent her actions had become. The bleeding in her thigh had slowed, but the pain and muscle revolt kept her from standing up or walking.

Lives depended on her breaking Jessie's attack. She scrambled on her belly, searching the sand and dirt for the Smith & Weapon she hadn't caught. It had to be close—and there it was, just underneath the trailer bed. Half hidden by the trailer's tire. She had a chance.

She checked her weapon, then dragged herself higher on the slope where she could see some of the frantic scene below. Smoke streaked the sky above the shell-shaped stage of the emptying amphitheater. Fires burned near the theater's back road and the bottle bushes she'd driven past with Congressman King. Another blaze burned nearer the amphitheater. A vehicle.

Maybe part of the King's SUV caravan.

She had to change positions, drag her wounded body somewhere. She'd kept fighting longer and harder than she'd expected, doing okay for a rookie. But she had to do better than okay.

She glanced at the bales of alfalfa, made up her mind, and crawled toward the closest stack.

33

Though a klick away, the autocannon's one-of-a-kind, hissing dragon imitation had filled the morning air with a buzz of incoming rounds, and for Ray, the world stopped. Frozen to acknowledge Sunny's failure and her odds-on death. Then the earth rotated again, jerking forward, the new moments trembling with a dozen nearby detonations and hundreds more fiery explosions on the exit road.

The smell of exploding shells and burning gasoline filled his nose, became a taste and coated his throat. Old, locked-up memories flooded his head. Even as the shells stopped erupting, his senses staggered with detailed information about this new combat setting. The brigadier general had been launched back into war, back to a place where sudden death loitered openly or snaked behind cover. His blood surged with adrenaline, his fight-or-flight fuel.

But there was no choice for Ray.

Marines don't run.

Two of the congressman's three lined-up black SUVs had been hit, and before he could formulate action, the first of those struck exploded in flames. The searing blast knocked Ray and others off their feet. On his butt, he watched the driver of the flaming second car tumble onto the ground and smack at the back of his burning coat.

The guy not winning against the flames. Gasoline.

Ray reached the younger man in three long strides to peel back the flaming coat. His palms ignored the heat as he ripped the material straight down and off the guy's arms. The man looked as if he'd been too shocked or frightened to do the obvious. Probably a security guard soon to consider new occupations.

Ray checked his surroundings.

Two of the congressman's three cars were out of commission, with King inside the undamaged third SUV. Dunn and his men climbed back on their feet after being knocked down by the blast. The burning man whom had Ray de-coated now jogged toward the theater office, leaving his clothes smoldering on the asphalt.

Maybe it was the adrenaline, but he sensed opportunity in the chaos.

If he wanted to risk his career, not to mention his brother-in-law's, he knew there was a chance to avenge the murder of Alissa. No guarantees. But maybe. He'd might have known it all along. Maybe that instinct was the reason he'd let Sunny go after Jessie Maris, a proven gunfighter.

The abused child Jessie had grown into a woman as deadly as Lucrezia Borgia.

But he sent the rookie nervous with guns.

Clouds of black and gray smoke soared two stories over the tennis-court-size rear parking area and the black caravan of Escalades, two of them burning. One wrecked. Bushes, cars, and sidewalks covered in fuel flamed high. Three house-size blazes burned fifty yards away, along the rear and unoccupied exit road—where most of the cannon's shells landed.

Running people screamed or shouted in a thousand voices, the crowd noise uniting in his ears as one panicked cry of humanity. The theater behind him, the air overhead, and the men with Dunn all buzzed with fear.

His gaze on Ray, King's security chief, Dunn, waved two

arms at his men, gathering them close. "Let's get the congressman back inside the theater. Now."

Ray pulled in a breath. Time was up.

Make up your mind. Commit.

When the smoke cleared, Jessie used her binoculars.

She'd cut a long swath, but missed everything but the far road gate at one extreme, and two of Randall King's three Escalades at the other, lined up behind the amphitheater. One had been blown to pieces, another set afire. Everything landed past her target of King on stage. Her first few shells must have fired before the cannon's platform dropped in back.

She ground her teeth when Randall King let himself be helped from the third SUV's shotgun seat, the cowboy hat easy to spot. He looked frightened maybe, unstable on his feet, but King found balance and support inside a tight circle of his men. The quarterback in a football huddle. Such a lucky SOB, sitting in the only Escalade she'd missed.

Looked like his men were walking him toward the theater.

Out of her kill-zone.

Ray wasn't going to murder the guy, but he had choices.

Sitting this close to Congressman King was tough. When Ray looked at his stupid hat and the jowly face, what he mentally pictured was everything the monster had done. The loser's characteristic features turned Angie's stories into related images. The red lipstick. A family court judge holding down a child for sex.

A lightning bolt of anger flashed and went.

But the loser was flesh and blood. Another human. An evil guy, sure. But who was Ray to judge. That's why America had courts and juries. The law. Even Ray's personal laws got in the way of judgement. Treat others like you'd want to be treated. Arrest and a trial would be what he'd want.

In his gut, he knew *everybody* should get back inside the building. Out of the line of fire. Yet the books on VIP security he'd seen suggested the client should always be herded off premises. Away from the gunfire or otherwise violent scene.

He had a choice with his recommendation.

His heartbeat at a firm, steady pace. Ready for action, but not racing. He'd been through worse, and he was thinking how he might let King's personal higher power do the judging. He kept coming back to his gut. Like instinct. Nature. Genetics. What evolutionary purpose was the male of a species if not to protect, defend, and fight for his female? Yeah, maybe you could name creatures which didn't work that way. Some spiders. A Praying Mantis. But they were exceptions, not the rule.

On average, males were bigger, stronger, and less sociable for a reason.

Strength for battle and to kill for food. Drive off the beasts and rogue men who wanted your family as sustenance. Stand in the enemy's path to die protecting the family's retreat.

That's what men were designed for.

Most of the world had changed. Women fought most of their own battles now because that's the way they wanted it. Independence. Courage. His wife Alissa had been a victim. Someone in a gang of railroad thieves had killed her. The muscle in his heart ripped again, and he remembered the pain he'd been through. His temper, his drinking, his lost sense of being human. Alissa had meant everything, and he hadn't been there to protect.

But maybe he could force Mr. Lipstick to stand before his higher power.

Ray went after three of Claude Dunn's men at the same time, side-kicking the first guy into a second. Their heads hitting and knocking them down was pure luck.

Catching the third man's punch in mid-air was something he practiced, as was using that same man's momentum to crash his arm against the open SUV door. His bone cracked loudly, and his scream sent a current of doubt through Ray.

But the shadow passed.

Dunn stuck a large revolver in Ray's face. Figured the little man would carry a .357 magnum. The weapon was close enough for his nose to smell the gun oil.

"Get out of our way, Hauser," Dunn said. "I'm taking the congressman inside. I warned King about you."

He snatched Dunn's wrist to the side, slamming the revolver and Dunn's hand against the Escalade. Again, all in a single motion. His quick, strong action the result of two decades instruction, training, practice and repetition. Same way anybody got proficient at anything.

The .357 dropped to the ground.

He kicked the gun beneath the SUV, then picked up Dunn by his coat and slammed his head and shoulders against the door frame. Dunn's eyes rolled back to the whites. Extra pain for using the word *broad* to describe his partner Sunny.

Special Agent Hicks was likely dead. Although there'd been no more cannon fire. Maybe...

The two guys who butted heads from his first kick scrambled to their hands and knees, but all they could do was rub their heads. He disarmed them without protest, picked up the semi-conscious Dunn, and lifted him into the third SUV.

He buckled him into the passenger seat, then chased the dazed congressman a few steps and seized his flabby arm. "Looks like you're driving, Representative."

Ray felt committed now.

Jessie grinned. What a break. Maybe she didn't need to hop down again and reset the floor jack. Looked like the big man kicked ass on the congressman's entire security staff. He was forcing King to drive out.

She could leave the cannon right where that dragon aimed now, nail the bastard pedophile with a repeat.

She wrapped her fingers around the trigger mechanism.

Watching and waiting, her coolness evaporated. Her breathing was fast and shallow. Worlds and lives hung in the balance, dancing on her skin. This was her one chance for serious cosmic revenge, her golden opportunity to reach and teach millions of abused women everywhere. They would read her notes and ask for help.

This was her last prospect for a meaningful life.

Ray leaned through the open driver's door open to buckle up Congressman Randall King. The turkey still had on his cowboy hat. He wanted to make him eat it.

"Start the engine," Ray said.

King's eyes lifted from the dashboard. Like little frozen pizzas. "Hauser? Claude thinks you might be related to that insurance investigator who went missing a couple of years ago. That what this is all about? The woman was your sister or your wife?"

Thank the Lord, King hadn't mentioned Alissa by name. As it was, his hands instinctively shot out for King's neck, but stopped before contact. He made himself breathe as trained. In the nose. Out the mouth. Block the smell of war and the license to kill. The screaming of people. The chaos. His violence needed containment.

Besides, he'd already made his choice. "Start the engine."

King stared, frozen, his hands in his lap. One held the SUV's key fob.

Ray grabbed his shoulder, applied the slightest of pressure. "Start the engine."

King fired up the SUV. His face flushed red. Sweat beads formed and rolled off his forehead. Ray almost experienced sympathy, but the emptiness which had been Alissa sucked up the congressman's fear like a black hole.

"Leave as quickly as you can," Ray said. "Floor it, straight out the back."

King stared straight ahead. "Claude said we should go back inside the theater."

Ray considered pulling his weapon, shooting this murderer and the raper of children. But he couldn't. Best he could do, force the gods to say yay or nay.

"The theater is under attack, Congressman. You need to leave."

The Escalade burned rubber, heading out the back. Jessie figured when to fire, fought the urge not to hurry. At the third red tree, she tugged back the trigger, then held on for her life as the autocannon and the floor of the trailer merged, the two separate bulks melding into a spitting, screaming, flame-breathing, mechanical monster, a bigger-than-life steel beast filling the world with hot gray smoke and burning metal.

The dragon warped and writhed with effort, the cannon shrieking, hissing, and twisting the flatbed beneath her feet. Knees bent, riding the incredible energy, she held on as fire and smoke erupted fifteen yards in front of the congressman's fast-moving Escalade. Two nearby red flowered trees toppled in flames.

Flames and black clouds billowed across the pavement. The SUV tried to stop, blue smoke coming from the wheels. But the congressman's steel coach skidded straight into a burning rain of hell.

The fire expanded as the congressman's vehicle disappeared inside, the flames popping and billowing into a three-story inferno a full second before the sound of the secondary explosion reached her ears. Maybe the gas tank.

Jessie released the trigger, but shells landed on the fire for seconds more. Maybe fifty. The fire soared as high as the theater grandstands.

A perfect and fearsome rain of hell.

Her spirits soaring like the black smoke behind the amphitheater. Tears flooded her eyes. She fist-pumped the air. She was as happy as she'd ever been about anything. Maybe even proud. She'd never been proud before.

That bastard Randall King was dead. And she'd done—

A bullet slammed the trailer near her feet.

She jumped back, her pulse skipping and racing. She looked up to the source, a helicopter painted like a TV traffic chopper. Hot splinters from another overhead shot landed against a bale of alfalfa. The vegetation browned by the cannon's smoky exhaust now burst into flames.

Bales on either side flamed as well.

The helicopter shooter had multiple straps holding him, the man not in uniform like a SWAT outfit, but wearing bright colors. Red pants. A blue shirt. Hamza? Yes, the Afghani convenience store clerk had shot at her with a long gun.

She noticed the fire spreading, but she didn't care if the cannon, Scottsdale, or even the State of Arizona burned to ashes. Mr. Lipstick had suffered a violent, terrifying, and agonizing death. Better than she'd imagined, the car skidding into her rain.

A sound beneath the trailer made her hurry to the edge. She hesitated. Was Agent Hicks alive and under the trailer? Maybe the agent had thrown a rock, like a trick. She glanced behind her, carefully, saw nothing but the stacked bales of alfalfa, one end beginning to burn. She crept again toward the other side, wanting to peer over the trailer's edge, see what made the noise. The front site of her Beretta walked point.

No sign of Sunny Hicks, only disturbed soil and two small patches of blood. Maybe that suggested the federal agent was alive, and had crawled beneath the trailer.

Hicks could have been responsible for the jack dropping.

"Drop your weapon."

34

Jessie froze, startled by the familiar voice. Agent Hicks, speaking from twenty-five or thirty feet away. Not on the trailer. Behind her, and lower, on the ground behind the alfalfa. How had she managed so much distance, wounded in the head? She'd watched Hicks' hair part and the agent's blood on the trailer.

No big deal. A brand new Air Force cop was no match for her, especially this one. Agent Hicks must have forgotten they'd met, traded stories, and if there was one thing Jessie was confident about, it was little orphan Hicks was no gunfighter.

In swift but separate motions, she twisted one-eighty degrees and fell to one knee. Her Beretta outstretched, she easily found her target, Special Agent Sunny Hicks, sitting in the dirt between two hay bales, her own weapon outstretched.

In that millisecond before she could squeeze, surprise hit Jessie like a cold glass of water. Deep inside the tiny black hole of Hicks' gun barrel, Jessie glimpsed a telltale spark.

Agent Hicks had fired first.

Her gunshot spilled Jessie near the cannon's twin hydraulic motors, Jessie prone and straddling the trailer's edge, one arm over the side, her feet near a twisted coil of black cables. A pang of grief poked Sunny's gut, her spirit unhappy about shooting another human being, especially another woman, most especially this sad victim of abuse.

But she remembered how fast Jessie had dropped to her knee, how quickly that Beretta found its target. Had Sunny been a split second slower, Jessie would have killed her. A perfect double-tap it would have been, too. She'd probably taken Jessie's life. But she'd saved her own and perhaps many others.

Sirens approached from a dozen directions. Gray smoke spread out around the trailer and gusted into a rising column above the trailer. The acrid taste varnished her throat. Flames sparked in half a dozen different bales.

Jessie looked dead, but what if she wasn't?

Another worry smacked harder. If the fire reached the cannon's ammunition drum, and the live rounds inside started firing, half of Pinacosta County might experience the fireworks. Hundreds of shells could explode randomly across the surrounding square mile.

Hundreds could be killed. Or nobody.

She had to *do* something.

Crawling on her belly was lousy transportation, but she had no choice. She tucked the Sig Sauer in her pants at the small of her back and pulled herself underneath the trailer. Tugging with her hands and pushed with her good leg, her path aimed at Jessie's hand and wrist dangling over the far edge of the trailer. She'd most likely killed Jessie, but she didn't want to find out she hadn't by listening to Jessie wake up screaming, fire eating her flesh.

White smoke drifted everywhere and kept getting thicker.

She couldn't let Jessie burn alive. Jessie deserved a trial and a jury to hear her story. It was her job to bring Jessie in. Make the arrest.

Beneath the flatbed, she noticed the truck-trailer coupling apparatus had been damaged and partially dislodged, maybe by one of the helicopter's bullets, a ricochet, or Jessie's first shot at Sunny. Jessie jacking up the trailer must have injured the connection, too. Fluid leaked from a broken hose, and jagged shards of steel poked from the truck's ball mount. There was a chance—

Metal above her groaned. The flatbed jerked forward.

She fought a surge of heart-drumming fright, her imagination generating an image of being mashed in two halves by heavy wheels. She pushed faster with her good leg, pulling dirt with her hands. Not frantic, but close, her painful, wounded leg holding her back.

She dragged herself out as the coupling snapped and the trailer rolled free.

Rolling on her back, she snatched Jessie's hanging forearm as the flatbed rolled. Her shoes and butt scuffed forward on the hard-packed slope as the trailer picked up speed, descending the slope. Gathering momentum. She didn't have long.

She tugged hard on Jessie's arm. But Jessie didn't budge. Something must be stuck.

The fire had engulfed every bale of alfalfa onboard. Flames licked the hydraulic hoses near the ammunition drum. She couldn't see how near.

The cannon's weight and the slope attracted the trailer to the bottom like powerful magnets. Jessie, Sunny, bales of fiery hay, and the deadly Air Force weapon all picked up speed together, the trailer and its cargo of spent and unspent cannon shells rolling untethered toward suburban homes below.

With one hand, she clasped her revolver. Her aim was disturbed, shaky, but she nailed the trailer's left front tire. A chunk of rubber disappeared. The trailer immediately lurched lower in the front and slowed.

But didn't stop.

She fired over her shoulder, missed once, but shot out the trailer's rear left tire. She tugged again on Jessie's arm. Something gave.

The flatbed tilted toward her, the trailer seconds from tipping over. A burning bale of alfalfa rolled off and exploded less than a yard from her head. Sparks burned her cheek, and as she wiped them away, stilling tugging with her weight, Jessie slid off.

The burning trailer traveled another forty feet before the left front dug itself into the slope. The cannon and its ammunition drum stayed attached, but the blazing bales of alfalfa and one generator did not. Fiery rectangles of hay bounced down toward the homes, families, and pets watching in the street.

But each bale fell apart to burn harmlessly. A handful of the fathers and children cheered.

She lay on her back next to the still-breathing Jessie and listened to the chopper land on the slope, maybe by the street in front of the multi-domed house. Her whole body glowed with relief. The rookie had come through.

A man shouted her name. Multiple sirens drew closer. The theater was a distant buzz, but at lower decibels than previous.

The man kneeled by her side. "Nice shooting, Special Agent."

"Hamza?"

"It's me. Is Jessie Maris alive?"

"She's breathing. But her pulse is weak."

He pointed up the slope at Hollywood. "What about him?"

"He's might be worse," she said. "Bleeding to death."

Hamza's voice made her insides warm, like coffee in the morning. Safe routine. Someone close by not trying to kill her.

"How much damage did the two bursts do?" Sunny asked.

"Only three casualties at the theater so far. Looks like Congressman King, his security chief Dunn, and one employee are dead, killed in the congressman's SUVs. No other deaths or injuries reported yet."

"Hauser's okay?" Sunny asked.

"Yeah. That's who texted me the info. You know you saved a lot of lives today by dropping that trailer's ass when you did."

"Thanks. But I couldn't stop Jessie from killing the guy she wanted."

"Think Hauser wanted him dead, too?"

***

Ray ran the sixty yards, physical exercise a welcome release. Seeing the congressman's car slide into the fire and explode, watching the steel mess burn had shocked him. His rhetorical analysis of a judgement by King's higher power had incredibly materialized, and in a most brutal and astonishing way. King's gods had spoken directly and savagely about the man's life and the kind of ending he deserved.

But what had Ray done—sending King out to die, the one man who could have given him and Sunny the name of every gang member. A list of corrupt judges and law enforcement personnel. Maybe the name of the man who'd actually murdered Alissa. Probably wasn't King himself.

As he approached the wrecked SUV, a burning memorial to corruption and the black-hearted, the heat of the flames slowed him. The smell of cooked flesh made him stop. No reason to get closer.

Nothing alive in that blazing headstone to wicked.

35

Days later, Sunny poked the mute button when General Eric Johannsen walked in. Her hospital room's television showed a Dodger-Giant afternoon game with playoff implications, but she knew the score. Homeland's Principal Deputy Under Secretary for Intelligence and Analysis didn't have time for baseball.

Johannsen nodded at the others standing around Sunny's hospital bed; Ray Hauser, Jordan Scott, and Sunny's old Commanding Officer, Air Force Colonel William Seager. But when Johannsen spoke, the words were for her.

"How are you feeling, Special Agent?"

She smiled. "Not bad, considering. The bullet wound still burns, but I'm pretty sure I'm lucky to be alive."

Johannsen walked closer. "Not too much luck detailed in the reports I read. You performed like a seasoned veteran. Courageously. You're right about the bullet wounds, though. They hurt. I have a couple myself."

"You going to show us?" Ray said.

Johannsen ignored him. He pointed at the hanging television. "Turn the channel to a news station. One of King's sons did a perp walk this morning, and they're rerunning film every ten minutes."

"What's the latest on Jessie?" Sunny asked.

"She's in a coma, not expected to make it."

She clicked to a black-bordered image of Congressman Randall King, the news anchor talking over King's photo, and next a crowd of reporters sticking microphones in the face of a balding, fiftyish man, King's son. FBI agents had him in handcuffs, hustling Junior by both arms into a four-door sedan.

The arrest had come hours before bombshell news in *The Los Angeles Times*. Jordan's above-the-fold, page one story quoted the Department of Justice indictment, which among other things, charged the candidate for governor with pedophilia (a case unrelated to Alissa), theft, extortion, tax evasion, and two dozen other Federal crimes. Also charged with racketeering crimes, including murder, were his son, several state government officials, and six members of the Pinacosta County Sheriff's Posse.

Jordan's biggest scoop. Ever.

She glanced at him while the news played. He was proud of himself. And why not? The exclusive story had been picked up by stations and papers all over the world, kicking serious butt on the so-called King-Polanco gang. The story's publication obviously had been coordinated with the Department of Justice. In an author's note, Jordan admitted he'd taken part in the FBI's investigation, thus earning the Fed's co-operation.

When the TV mentioned Hollywood had survived, Johannsen turned to Sunny again. "Looks like Dennis Williams earned himself a prison sentence with an early release date. At least his blond hair won't be gray. He turned informant against the whole operation. Even his mother."

Johannsen nodded toward Jordan. "And your *other* friend, this guy Scott. He has better connections at Justice than I do."

"Oh, I doubt that," Jordan said. "Most of my story came from Angie Chiarella and the court transcripts. The Feds only confirmed."

Ray gave him a look. "Like you didn't get to pre-read their indictment?"

Jordan ignored him.

"Is that Axel guy I tangled with part of the gang?" Ray asked. "I'd love to hear he's going to prison for a while."

Johannsen shook his head. "The two posse guys, maybe. The guards slipped Axel two hundred bucks to ruin your day. He was told the grudge against you was personal."

Pain poked around inside Sunny's skull like a bear going through a trash bin. Hollywood's punch, Jessie's scalp-burning first gunshot, and/or the fall from the trailer had given her a minor concussion. Both of her eyes were black.

Black, blue, and purple, actually.

She also had a cracked rib and a missing chunk of leg.

"I meant what I said on the phone last night," Johannsen said. "You and Ray could be one of our elite investigative teams. That guarantees you substantially more pay than any Air Force job."

"Eric can't believe I agreed to an occasional partner," Ray said.

She smiled. "Honestly, General Johannsen, after what's happened, the pain pills inside me now, I need a couple of days. There's a dream quality to everything."

She hadn't felt much at the time, or while she was sliding down that hill with the trailer on fire, but her cracked rib hurt as much as the bullet wound that evening. She shouldn't complain, though.

"How does Homeland's vacation and personal time compare to the Air Force's?" Jordan asked.

Everybody ignored him.

The talking head on TV called Sunny Hicks a hero, but she didn't feel like one. Letting that cannon go off twice felt like a failure. There seemed little doubt the death toll would have been much worse, though, without Sunny working the jack, then preventing the ammo from blowing up. But she'd gone up that hill to *stop* the attack, not limit it.

Johannsen shook her hand. "You had some first field assignment, Special Agent. Homeland Security could really use your brains and courage. I hope you'll give my offer serious consideration."

"Where would Sunny be stationed if she joined the Department of Homeland Security?" Jordan asked.

"How is that *your* business, son?" Johannsen said.

Jordan lifted his chin. "I've asked Sunny to marry me. I hope she's going to say yes."

"So sweet you're hopeful," Ray said.

She shook her head at Jordan. "Same speech for you, Romeo. I need to regroup. No major decisions for a few days."

Jordan frowned. "I'm giving you all the time you need, but shouldn't you know whether or not you love me?"

Johannsen touched Ray's arm. "I think it's time for us to go."

"No way," Ray said. "I want to see if Sunny's going to marry him."

"Come on, Sunny," Jordan said. "Don't you know how you *feel?*"

She wasn't ready to say yes now, but she might be next week. Postponement was the solution to this puzzle. "Let me ask you, Jordan. How come you keep proposing without a ring?"

Unlocking his Chevy Suburban in the hospital parking lot later, Ray answered a telephone call from his sister. "What's up?"

Etta slurped coffee. "How does it feel, Ray?

"How does *what* feel?"

"What do you think? Finding Alissa. Solving her murder."

He opened the driver's door and sat down. "Honestly, sis, I liked it better when I held a crazy hope she was still alive."

"Stop," Etta said. "Alissa's gone two years. We both knew she was dead. Finding her remains doesn't change anything except, oh, yeah, I almost forgot. You caught the gang who did it, Ray. The mastermind is dead."

"I can't tell you what happened."

"My God, Ray. It was all on the news. The boss of the railroad gang—that awful congressman—got blown up in his own limousine. Everybody who loved Alissa has a lighter heart today. Aren't you happy?"

"That son-of-a-bitch King did get blown up, didn't he?"

"Ha. He sure did, although the video clip is getting hard to find on the internet. Lots of censoring. But you got to see it live, didn't you?"

"Oh, yeah," Ray said. "I was there."

Ray figured the mouthwatering smell would snap her awake. He guessed right, Sunny's nose twitching, her eyes opening. He'd snuck back into her hospital room with a paper sack containing soft beef tacos with chopped cilantro and onions. Ray preferred the Southern California, crispy version. Crunchy corn shells packed with lettuce, cheese, and red taco sauce.

"What's in the bag?" Sunny asked.

He settled into the chair beside her bed. "Tacos."

The TV blinked with light, but operated without sound. Talking heads, a man and a woman, commented on the night's baseball games. On a screen below the heads, he saw Sunny's Dodgers had won.

She sat up and pointed at the tacos. "The Mexican food for me?"

He stared at the TV, kept the bag in his hands. "So when you were on that slope, did you see me and that Claude Dunn guy by the congressman's Escalade?"

"No. Can I have a taco?"

Ray handed her the food, including chips, salsa, and napkins. "I brought the bag for you."

"Oh, thanks. Gerber makes the meals around here. You could eat the stuff with a straw, except they don't allow them."

"So you didn't see me and Dunn at all? I saw the photos.

Jessie had binoculars."

"Do you need a witness or something? Why the questions?"

"I don't need witnesses. No, what happened, happened. The congressman panicked and tried to run back inside the building. Dunn, the security chief, and I discussed it, and we agreed he'd be safer getting in the Escalade and departing."

She cocked her head. "So you and Claude totally agreed?"

Ray coughed. "Eventually."

Sunny put down her taco. "Three of Dunn's men said you beat them up and forced both Dunn and the congressman to drive away."

He raised his chin. "Well, that's only partly right. Me telling Dunn how important it was for them to listen to me got a little heated, me saying how much safer it was for the congressman to leave. Dunn was adamant for a while, tried to use those three guys to get past me. I was forced to employ some martial arts training."

"One of the Dunn's men said his boss pointed a gun at you, but you disarmed him and knocked him cold. You had to lift Dunn into the vehicle."

"It might have looked like that to them. What did the other two men say?"

"They claimed to be unconscious. Couldn't remember. Didn't Eric ask you about these depositions? What some people accused you of?"

"Sure, but let me ask you, Sunny. Why would Dunn point a gun at me?"

Sunny swallowed a bite of taco, pinning him the whole way down. Her throat reminded him of a pretty snake swallowing a rat.

"Maybe because Dunn guessed the SUV—correctly, I might add—could be hit on the way out?"

"Are you saying I *wanted* that murdering pedophile to get blown up? Just because he headed the gang who killed my wife?"

Sunny reached up from her hospital bed, squeezed his forearm. Her fingers to thumb reach didn't go halfway around. "Of course not. No one in your position could have known where or even *if* other shells would land. Fast out the back is always the safest call."

"That's right," he said. "Always."

Nobody had to tell Special Agent Sunny Hicks a thing.

As usual, she'd figured everything out by herself.

JACK GETZE is the author of the award-winning, darkly comic Austin Carr Mystery Series, plus a stand-alone thriller, all from Down & Out Books. A retired former newsman, public relations consultant, and telephone-based, municipal bond salesman, Getze understands communications and works hard to make reading easy. The most recent of his Austin Carr novels, *Big Shoes*, won Deadly Ink's Best Mystery Novel of 2015.

On the following pages are a few
more great titles from the
Down & Out Books publishing family.

For a complete list of books and to
sign up for our newsletter,
go to DownAndOutBooks.com.

Operation Snow Queen
A Jim Grant Thriller
Colin Campbell

Down & Out Books
February 2024
978-1-64396-354-9

Before Jim Grant was a cop, he was a soldier in the British Army. With only two years' service, he is posted to Germany after a runaway suitcase at Waterloo Station breaks a civilian passenger's leg. He replaces a Company Clerk who lost his head in an accident, and a smuggling ring that doesn't want him.

Following an explosion at the Ammunition Depot, and a court martial in Dusseldorf, Grant is assigned to *Operation Snow Queen,* a training exercise in Bavaria. A place where landslides and falling off a mountain are the least of his worries.

An Only Child
A Novel of Suspense
Les Roberts

Down & Out Books
February 2024
978-1-64396-355-6

The highly successful mystery author who'd never been arrested for jaywalking, spitting on the sidewalk, or driving too fast for the Chicago speed limit, has to spend seven years in prison for a crime he didn't commit.

When finally released, he finds himself rich and almost famous again, though he seems to have forgotten how to write, searching for a woman who cheated on him years before and is now married to another man and has vanished. He realizes there are dozens of Chicago places in which to hide—and several people who wanted him gone for good.

Playing Dead
The De La Cruz Case Files
TG Wolff

Down & Out Books
February 2024
978-1-64396-356-3

Alexander "Rotten" Carter is dead. But when his body is dumped in Cleveland Homicide Detective Jesus De La Cruz's neighborhood, there are more questions than answers. Rotten was dressed up like the king of hearts, right down to the dagger in the suicide king's temple. The elaborate staging is perplexing at the same time seems to be sending a message.

As Cruz investigates, he discovers Rotten Carter was more complex than the simple villain he had painted him to be. So is his murder, which is related deaths of his two lieutenants months prior. Both were strangled and found, with playing cards in their mouths. Jacks.

Geisha Confidential
An August Riordan Mystery
Mark Coggins

Down & Out Books
March 2024
978-1-64396-357-0

A roiling *chankonabe* (sumo wrestler stew) of love hotels, cryptocurrency fraud, "soapland" brothels and the Japanese Adult Video industry, *Geisha Confidential* is an immersive exploration of a culture like no other and a must-read for fans of international crime fiction.

www.ingramcontent.com/pod-product-compliance
Lightning Source LLC
Chambersburg PA
CBHW020405040426
42333CB00055B/471